HISTORY OF COUNTERTRANSFERENCE

From Freud to the British Object Relations School

Alberto Stefana

Routledge
Taylor & Francis Group
LONDON AND NEW YORK

First published 2017
by Routledge
2 Park Square, Milton Park, Abingdon, Oxon OX14 4RN

and by Routledge
711 Third Avenue, New York, NY 10017

Routledge is an imprint of the Taylor & Francis Group, an informa business

Chapter 1 translated from Italian by Aldo Grassi. The remaining chapters translated from Italian by Joyce Myerson.

British Library Cataloguing-in-Publication Data
A catalogue record for this book is available from the British Library

Library of Congress Cataloging-in-Publication Data
A catalog record for this book has been requested

ISBN: 978-1-138-21458-3 (hbk)
ISBN: 978-1-138-21461-3 (pbk)
ISBN: 978-1-315-44560-1 (ebk)

Typeset in Bembo
by Apex CoVantage, LLC

HISTORY OF COUNTERTRANSFERENCE

The constant and polymorphous development of the field of psychoanalysis since its inception has led to the evolution of a wide variety of psychoanalytic 'schools'. In seeking to find common ground between them, Alberto Stefana examines the history of countertransference, a concept which has developed from its origins as an apparent obstacle, to become an essential tool for analysis, and which has undergone profound changes in definition and in clinical use.

In *History of Countertransference*, Stefana follows the development of this concept over time, exploring a very precise trend which begins with the original notion put forward by Sigmund Freud and leads to the ideas of Melanie Klein and the British object relations school. The book explores the studies of specific psychoanalytic theorists and endeavours to bring to light how the input from each one may have been influenced by previous theories, by the personal history of the analyst, and by their historical-cultural context. By shedding light on how different psychoanalytic groups work with countertransference, Stefana helps the reader to understand the divergences that exist between them.

This unique study of a key psychoanalytical concept will be essential reading for psychoanalysts in practice and in training and academics and students of psychoanalytic studies and the history of psychology.

Alberto Stefana is a psychotherapist in private practice in Brescia, Italy.

To my son, Octavio

History. – *The best way of understanding psycho-analysis is still by tracing its origin and development.*

S. Freud, Two Encyclopaedia Articles, *1922*

Referring to the necessity of checking the dates of the papers written on analysis Freud remarked, "It is just this which the critics fail to do. They seem to think that analysis was dropped from heaven or erupted from hell – that it is fixed like a block of lava and not a body of facts which have been slowly and painfully gathered by scientific research".

S. Blanton, Diary of My Analysis with Sigmund Freud, *1971*

Psychoanalysis is such an essentially historical subject and method that it really doesn't make sense to talk about it any way but historically and, of course, we have to start with Freud. However, history is like the law; the law is what the courts do, and history is what historians say; and my history is different from your history and you mustn't expect it necessarily to correspond. It's just my way of understanding psychoanalytic history.

D. Meltzer, Adhesive Identification, *1974*

CONTENTS

FOREWORD

"Concepts," Soren Kierkegaard (1841) said, "like individuals, have their histories and are just as incapable of withstanding the ravages of time as are individuals. But in and through all this they retain a kind of homesickness for the scenes of their childhood" (p. 47). And there is no doubt that countertransference is a concept that has had a rich life. Whether it looks back to its childhood – with suspicion and scandal in the early days before World War I – or not is doubtful. It is now embraced with a great deal of loyalty by many psychoanalysts, who use it to inform their practice, judging it an essential channel of communication. Freud was puzzled by what he recognised as unconscious-to-unconscious communication, and he even considered the possibilities of telepathy.

Today, the nature of countertransference is pictured in very different ways by analysts from very different theoretical backgrounds, who start from very different assumptions about the human mind and its unconscious domain. The meanings of the term have ramified in a bewildering series of directions; it is like a vine run wild across a wilderness. I know because I have tried to survey this geography from a single perspective, that of Kleinians in Britain, as if taking photographs from a geostationary satellite. But this book is close to the ground, a tourist's guide to every nook and cranny. I am impressed at such a comprehensive and yet detailed account of a complex cartography, and, as Kierkegaard said, a similarly complex biography.

That said, we have therefore to be prepared for a complex book, which takes us in an unhurried way through the thinking of various people with various conceptual orientations and across various phases in the history of psychoanalysis. It covers debate from the very beginning with scandals that overtook Freud's closest workers to the most recent splintering of psychoanalytic schools. In the long withdrawal from the mechanical thinking of the economic model and drive theory, thinking about countertransference and projective identification has been 'used' in all sorts of respects.

This book gives us a comprehensive story of how the problem of countertransference overtook the early pioneers, and as it proceeds through history, we become lost in the fragmented state of theorising where anyone can freely have an opinion, without the rigour of placing it in a context of neighboring ideas for comparison. The history of countertransference is like a river dissipating in multiple directions as it runs into its delta. The connections and interconnections between different thinkers and different groups become myriad and lost to view.

This is a source-book for anyone wanting to advance their understanding of countertransference; but it is also a warning that more than enough has been said already in our literature, until the time when we can more systematically digest our hurried originality and effectively evaluate it in practice. This book is a start.

Bob Hinshelwood
December 2016

ACKNOWLEDGEMENTS

Stefana, 'Cenni storici sul controtransfert: da Freud alla scuola inglese delle relazioni oggettuali' *Psicoterapia e Scienze Umane* 47, 3: 443–488 (2013), is reprinted here with permission of *FrancoAngeli*. Material from this work appears in Chapters 3, 5, 6, 7, 8, and 9.

Stefana, 'Lo sviluppo del concetto di identificazione proiettiva: il contributo degli analisti kleiniani di Londra' *Il Vaso di Pandora* 24, 3: 15–62 (2016), is reprinted here with permission of *La Redancia*. Material from this work appears in Chapter 8.

Stefana, 'Sigmund Freud e l'origine del concetto di controtransfert' *Medicina nei Secoli*, 26, 3: 943–960 (2014) is reprinted here with permission of *Medicina nei Secoli*. Material from this work appears in Chapter 1.

Stefana, 'The origins of the notion of countertransference' *Psychoanalytic Review*, 102, 4: 437–460 (2015), is reprinted here with permission of Guilford Press.

Quotations from Edward Glover, *The Technique of Psychoanalysis* (London: Baillière, Tindall & Cassell, 1955) are given with permission of Elsevier. All efforts have been made to contact further copyright holders of material in this book. Errors brought to the attention of the publisher will be corrected in future printings.

INTRODUCTION

Since its inception, psychoanalysis has experienced a constant and polymorphous development, creating such a multitude of theories, techniques, and models that it is reasonable to suggest that there is more than one psychoanalysis (Wallerstein, 1988). Even though each of these is an offshoot of the same tree (Fonagy and Target, 2003), only some analysts are willing, to a greater or lesser degree, to concede to this. There are others not disposed to do so at all. Such a variety of psychoanalytic 'schools' explains the diverse routes that analysts have followed, based on their particular interest in certain typologies of patients (hysterics, children, narcissists, borderline, psychotics, etc.). Within the treatment of such patients, a specific clinical material emerged, one whose theoretical reformulation – first and foremost a theory of pathology – was then presented as a general psychoanalytic theory (Sandler, 1993) with its own unique theory of technique.

Is it possible to identify a common ground in this kaleidoscopic panorama? And if so, where? It seems possible to find the answer in the role attributed to transference (Wallerstein, 1990) and countertransference (Gabbard, 1995), as well as to the psychoanalytic setting, indispensable to their emergence and evolution. These two concepts, united in a common destiny that has seen them transformed from obstacles into essential tools of analysis, have undergone profound changes both in terms of definition and clinical use. To this day, there exists a wide variety of ways in which they are understood, conceptualised, and employed by different psychoanalytic authors.

In this study, I will focus attention on a very precise trend in the development of the concept of countertransference (seeing as there exist so many psychoanalytical schools of thought), one that proceeds from the original notion put forward by Sigmund Freud and leads to those proposed by the analysts of the British object relations school (including the input on the subject from the Kleinian and Independent groups and by some American analysts heavily influenced by them). The contributions from this school were fundamental in the diffusion of the discussion regarding countertransference in all its theoretical-clinical aspects. It will become clear to the reader that the British contribution to the development of countertransference is in relation to projective identification, particularly in what I term the 'first phase'; while in the 'second phase' authors talk less of projective identification, or not at all. Despite this treatise's focus on the British input on the subject at hand, I am well-aware that there exist other major theoretical positions on countertransference that over time developed in various nations and continents. In this regard, it should be remembered that important debates, as well as a subsequent proliferation of highly relevant theoretical-clinical research, were ongoing in Latin America, beginning towards the end of the 1940s with the work of Heinrich Racker, as well as throughout the 1950s and 1960s with the work of Madeleine and Willy Baranger (cf. de Bernardi, 2000). In France, until the 1970s, the discourse surrounding this concept was strongly influenced and perhaps ultimately inhibited by the philosophy of Jacques Lacan, (who preferred to use the term 'the desire of the analyst' instead of countertransference; cf. Duparc, 2001). It was not until the mid-seventies, when the United States abandoned the classical point of view, represented by the works of Annie Reich, did we see in that country a growing number of studies on countertransference, inspired in particular by Erich Fromm and Heinz Kohut (cf. Jacobs, 1999).

The criteria upon which I have chosen to investigate certain authors are based on a personal leitmotif, in keeping with my ability to sense, in their writings on countertransference (just as any other psychoanalytical concept), an echo of a filiation relationship (as for example in the 'training analysis' or in supervision) or a relationship based on friendship or collaboration. There must also be present in their writings a familiarity with certain theories and specific linguistic terminology, as well as a connection to their own psychoanalytic and cultural milieu (in this case the British Psychoanalytical Society). These criteria, to my mind, represent a useful key to comprehension, in terms of contextualising, connecting, and personalising their individual contributions to the subject.

Lastly, I would like to point out to the reader that, from the perspective of a historical reconstruction of the development of concepts, in the cases where the year of an article's or book's publication does not coincide with the year in which it was orally presented, I will state in the text the year when each work was presented for the first time, where it has been possible to track it down. For example, I will indicate the year 1951 when referring to Donald Winnicott's essay 'Transitional objects and transitional phenomena', read at a meeting of the British Psychoanalytical Society on May 30, 1951, and published in the *International Journal of Psychoanalysis* in 1953. However, in the bibliographical references at the end of the text, I will indicate both dates. The year of the presentation of the work will immediately be mentioned after the author's name, while that of publication will be cited after the name of the journal or book publisher. Here are two examples:

Bibliography

Winnicott D.W. (1951). Transitional objects and transitional phenomena. *International Journal of Psychoanalysis*, 1953, 34: 89–97.

Winnicott D.W. (1960). Ego distortions in terms of true or false self. In *The Maturational Processes and the Facilitating Environment*. London: Hogarth Press, 1965, pp. 140–152.

1

THE ORIGINS OF THE NOTION OF COUNTERTRANSFERENCE

The notion of countertransference (*Gegenübertragung*) was introduced by Sigmund Freud, and yet we rarely encounter it in his writings. It was used the first time in a letter dated June 7, 1909, in which Freud answered a letter sent to him three days earlier by Carl G. Jung, who informed him about the difficulties he encountered in the treatment of a twenty-year-old Russian patient (Sabina Spielrein).[1] Freud wrote:

> Such experiences, though painful, are necessary and hard to avoid. Without them we cannot really know life and what we are dealing with. I myself have never been taken in quite so badly, but I have come very close to it a number of times and had *a narrow escape* [emphasis added for phrase appearing in English in original]. . . . But no lasting harm is done. They help us to develop the thick skin we need and to dominate 'countertransference', which is after all a permanent problem for us; they teach us to displace our own affects to best advantage. They are a '*blessing in disguise*' [quoted phrase is in English in original].
>
> *(Freud and Jung, 1906–13, pp. 230–231)*

Consequently, for Freud, the feelings and the countertransference temptations experienced by the analyst in his or her work with patients must not be denied; rather, the analyst should try to reach a position of uninterest towards them in this regard.

As regards Spielrein's treatment, Freud did not know the whole story; Jung had not been clear about his own degree of involvement in the erotic transference-countertransference dynamics that had been established with Spielrein. Freud got the complete picture only after receiving two letters, one from Spielrein and the other from Jung. In the first letter, dated June 11, 1909, we read: "Four and half years ago Dr. Jung was my doctor, then he became my friend and finally my 'poet' i.e. my beloved. Eventually he came to me and things went as they usually go with 'poetry'. He preached polygamy; his wife was supposed to have no objection, etc., etc." (Carotenuto, 1982, p. 93). In the second letter, written on June 21, we read: "Although not succumbing to helpless remorse, I nevertheless deplore the sins I have committed, for I am largely to blame for the high-flying hopes of my former patient . . . imagining that I was talking theoretically, but naturally Eros was lurking in the background. Thus I imputed all the other wishes and hopes entirely to my patient without seeing the same thing in myself" (Freud and Jung, 1906–13, p. 236). Learning about these facts, Freud wrote to Spielrein to apologise for having damaged her with his untrue allegations, acknowledging that it had been Jung's fault, not hers (cf. Carotenuto, 1982).

It is however necessary now to mention the influence that Otto Gross had on Jung during the (almost mutual) analysis of the former on the latter; they were the only psychoanalysts that, in Freud's opinion, were really original thinkers (Jones, 1953). Gross's name appeared in Jung's correspondence with Freud on June 28, 1907, in a letter in which the Swiss analyst described Gross as psychopathic, despite being gifted with a very brilliant mind.[2] Regarding the psychoanalytic thinking of Gross, who had been a pupil of Emil Kraepelin in Munich, it is important to remember that he saw Freudian psychoanalysis as a helpful tool both for the therapy of a suffering individual and for the establishment of a sexual revolution – *pour épater la bourgeoisie* – on a collective level, but attributed little value to sexuality as an aetiopathogenetic element in mental illnesses, envisaging psychoanalysis as closely linked to the quality of the social context and to the frustration of the 'relational will' of each individual (Heuer, 2001).

However, as mentioned earlier, Gross suffered from psychic disorders and had been addicted to cocaine and opiates for a long time; for this reason, in the early months of 1908, his father Hans Gross (a famous Austrian jurist and magistrate, professor of criminology in Prague and Graz, the father of modern criminal psychology) got in touch with Freud, asking for help. In turn, Freud contacted Jung (letter of April 19, 1908), asking him to start an analytic treatment with Gross. In the end, Jung took on the referral, with the promise on the part of Freud (letter of May 6, 1908) that it would be a short-term referral (a few months), to give Freud enough time to take on the patient himself in analysis. The promise to see the patient starting in autumn, however, was retracted only a few days later (letter of May 18, 1908). The resulting treatment, in the end, became one of the elements that damaged the relationship between Freud, Jung, and Gross (Vitolo, 1987). The deeper Jung delved into the analysis of Gross, the more he became aware of the enriching element of that experience, an analytic journey in which "whenever I got stuck, he analyzed me. In this way my own psychic health has benefited" (Freud and Jung, 1906–13, p. 153). As we know, the end of this psychoanalytic treatment was unfortunate, even if it cannot be said that it came out of the blue. It is enough to remember the distress of Jones, who knew both of them, when he learned about this analysis, at the beginning of May: "I hear that Jung is going to treat him psychically, and naturally feel a little uneasy about that for Jung does not find it easy to conceal his feelings and he has a pretty strong dislike to Gross; in addition there are some fundamental differences of opinion between them on moral questions" (Freud and Jones, 1908–39, p. 1). An example of these differences regarding moral issues is given by Jung himself in a letter written to Freud on September 25, 1907:

> Dr. Gross tells me that he puts a quick stop to the transference by turning people into sexual immoralists. He says the transference to the analyst and its persistent fixation are mere monogamy symbols and as such symptomatic of repression. The truly healthy state for the neurotic is sexual immorality. Hence he associates you with Nietzsche. It seems to me, however, that sexual repression is a very important and indispensable civilizing factor, even if pathogenic for many inferior people. Still, there must always be a few flies in the world's ointment. What else is civilization but the fruit of adversity? I feel Gross is going along too far with the vogue for the sexual short-circuit, which is neither intelligent, nor in good taste, but merely convenient, and therefore anything but a civilizing factor.
>
> *(Freud and Jung, 1906–13, p. 90)*

It is well known that Jung was never convinced of the sexual origin of neuroses, and he deeply criticised the Freudian theory of sexuality (see 'Transformations and Symbols of the Libido', written in 1911). Indeed, it seems that the incapability to acknowledge the role played by sexuality within human relationships and neuroses was already present in Jung from the very beginning of his relationship with the father of psychoanalysis; this issue eventually led to his breakup with Freud when what had initially been a personal need to deny the importance of sexuality later became a technical problem (Bettelheim, 1983). However, in the years 1907–1908 Jung was a fervent sexualist (Appignanesi and Forrester, 1992). His relationship with Spielrein was at the same time the cause and the effect of this new temporary attitude towards sexuality, a turning-point in which the almost mutual analysis with Gross was a crucial element. This can be clearly inferred from Spielrein's words, when she told Freud that Jung "arrives, beaming with pleasure, and tells me with strong emotion about Gross, about the great insight he has just received (i.e., about polygamy); he no longer wants to suppress his feeling for me, he admitted that I was his first dearest, woman friend, etc., etc. (his wife of course excepted), and that he wanted to tell me everything about himself" (Carotenuto, 1982, p. 107).

Going back to the topic of Gross's treatment: On June 19, 1908, Jung gives up; in his letter to Freud, after explaining his reasons and affirming the impossibility of a positive and stable outcome of Gross's psychic conditions, the Swiss psychiatrist confesses that "For me this experience is one of the harshest in my life, for in Gross I discovered many aspects of my own nature, so that he often seemed like my twin brother – but for the Dementia praecox. This is tragic. You can guess what powers I have summoned up in myself in order to cure him" (Freud and Jung, 1906–13, p. 156). Finally, it is interesting to point out that Jung himself compared the treatment of Gross to that of Spielrein: "Like Gross, she is a case of fight-the-father, which in the name of all that's wonderful I was trying to cure gratissime (!). . . . During the whole business Gross's notions flitted about a bit too much in my head. . . . Gross and Spielrein are bitter experiences. To none of my patients have I extended so much friendship and from none have I reaped so much sorrow" (Freud and Jung, 1906–13, p. 229).

The privileged position as an 'external observer' in which Freud found himself, not only in the Jung-Spielrein affaire but also before, first with Josef Breuer and Bertha Pappenheim (Anna O.) and then with Sándor Ferenczi and Elma Pàlos, allowed him to reflect with greater objectivity and to reach some conclusions on a phenomenon from which he was not himself immune. According to Johannes Cremerius (1986), if one follows the various stages of the 'Spielrein tragedy', one can notice certain correspondences between the dates in which he learned more about her and those in which new aspects of the transference-countertransference dynamics emerged from his thoughts.

Before moving on, it would be interesting to take a step back, to the pre-analytical origins of the so-called talking cure, that is, Breuer's treatment with Pappenheim, which took place between November 1880 and June 1882. Freud was informed about it by Breuer himself in November 1882, and he came to know all its details in the summer of the following year. What captured Freud's attention and made him think about this clinical history in depth was not its theoretical explanation as formulated by Breuer, which included hypnoid states and catharsis, but rather the sexual significance present in the clinical material and, even more so, the revelation of the transference-countertransference dynamics established between the doctor and the patient. One should remember that it is precisely in *Studies on Hysteria* (1892–95) that Freud introduced the notion of transference (*Übertragung*), that is, a phenomenon that was so frequent as to be an established fact in certain analyses, according to which "the patient is frightened at finding that she is transferring on to the figure of the physician the distressing ideas which arise from the content of the analysis" (p. 302). In this early formulation the transference was simply seen as one of many forms of resistance, an obstacle against the establishment of a necessary trusting relationship between doctor and patient, whose unconscious motives had to be discovered and interpreted.

It might be helpful to remember that the choice of the name Anna, in order to conceal that of Bertha Pappenheim, had been neither casual nor exempt from transference-countertransference connotations. One should consider, first of all, that in the same year, 1895, Freud gave the name Anna to his younger daughter. Anna was also the name of one of Freud's favourite patients, Anna Lichtheim, a young widow, the daughter of Freud's teacher of religion, a relative of Sophie's godmother, and a friend of Mathilde Breuer's (the godmother of Mathilde Freud, whom Freud had wished Ferenczi to marry). Moreover, it seems that the name of Irma, mentioned in the famous dream about the injection (Freud, 1900), concealed a combination of two patients: Anna Lichtheim and Emma Eckstein (who would later become the first woman psychoanalyst). We have already mentioned the former; the latter was the patient that Freud, preoccupied with neglecting organic causes in favour of psychogenic ones, asked Wilhelm Fliess to see. He operated on her, leaving in her nasal cavity almost half a metre of gauze. In the light of these data, it is possible to assume that the presence of Irma in Freud's dream represented at the same time an erotic countertransference, medical malpractice, disappointment in idealised colleagues, and his wife's pregnancy – all elements that were also present in the Breuer-Pappenheim treatment (Britton, 2003). In his letter dated January 9, 1908, Freud later shared with Karl Abraham his own free associations about that dream as well as his interpretation of it: "Sexual megalomania is hidden behind it, the three women, Mathilde, Sophie and Anna, are the three godmothers of my daughters, and I have them all!" (Freud and Abraham, 1907–25, p. 21). Having said this, it should be acknowledged that Freud did not allow such deep and secret awareness to become an inhibiting source of shame, which was what had happened to Breuer; instead, it became the source of his brilliant intuition and the driving force for the constant evolution of his ideas about the transference and the countertransference (Britton, 2003).

Let us now consider the notion of transference for a moment. It made its appearance on the psychoanalytic scene in *Studies on Hysteria* (Breuer and Freud, 1892–95), but it is in *Fragment of an Analysis of a Case of Hysteria* (1905) that Freud reached a veritable formulation of a theory about the transference. One should consider that such revision/elaboration of the theory of transference, which was later the object of constant development for many decades, was not an element separated from the rest; indeed, it was part of the context of the new understanding of the genesis of neurosis that Freud had reached after abandoning his theory of seduction (cf. Makari, 1997).

'Dora's Case' is the clinical history of Ida Bauer, an eighteen-year-old girl who came to Freud's study in October 1900; she was taken there by her father because of her neurotic disorders and depression. Let us briefly see what Freud tells us about the history of this young patient. Ida was holidaying in Merano with her parents, Philip and Katherina Bauer, and a couple of friends, Hans and Peppina Zellenka (Mr. and Mrs. K.). During this holiday, Hans Zellenka discovered that his wife was betraying him with Philip Bauer, a fact which led him to court his rival's daughter. One day Ida, who was secretly in love with Mr. Zellenka (who reminded her of her father), was approached by him; he suddenly embraced her and kissed her on her mouth. Upset by this, she slapped him and ran away. During her psychoanalytic treatment, Ida confessed that in that situation she had felt a certain sexual excitement, aroused by the pressure of his erect member against her body: "She declared that she could still feel upon the upper part of her body the pressure of Herr K.'s embrace" (Freud, 1905, p. 29). Such a feeling upset her and made her feel deeply ashamed. According to Freud, this was a real and present event which had brought her back to past childhood phantasies of being seduced by her father. From that moment on, the first signs of hysteria began to appear: feeling nauseated and horrified by men.

When Ida informed her father about the event a few days later, he (and Mr. Zellenka) called her a liar and accused her of having made everything up.

At that point she left the holiday resort ahead of time. Ida's psychoanalytic treatment, which was interrupted by the patient only eleven weeks after it had started, seemed to fully confirm Freud's hypotheses on the sexual origin of hysteric symptomatology and on dreams as revelations of unconscious conflicts. Preoccupied as he was about retrieving his patient's memories and reconstructing her past history, Freud did not notice in time the resistances that his explanations caused in the patient, and he was not aware of the transference which, otherwise, he might have interpreted to the patient. (Freud himself, in his afterword, suggested other interpretations that he could have made.) This, however, was not the only reason for Freud's difficulties in handling this case; there was another, less clearly visible reason, albeit cumbersome and compelling: his own countertransference.

'Dora's Case' was drafted by Freud immediately after the premature end of the treatment, within a few weeks, but it was only in 1905, when he wrote his afterword and then decided to publish his work (without his patient's authorisation, which fuelled a great argument), that the father of psychoanalysis fully realised that Ida had interrupted the treatment because of the transference of loving and erotic feelings towards him.[3] Apparently he did not realise, or at least he did not declare publicly, that his difficulties in the treatment of Ida also derived from his own countertransference. At this point we might ask ourselves, together with Freud (1905): "What are transferences?"

> They are new editions or facsimiles of the impulses and phantasies which are aroused and made conscious during the progress of the analysis; but they have this peculiarity, which is characteristic for their species, that they replace some earlier person by the person of the physician. To put it another way: a whole series of psychological experiences are revived, not as belonging to the past, but as applying to the person of the physician at the present moment. Some of these transferences have a content which differs from that of their model in no respect whatever except for the substitution. These then – to keep to the same metaphor – are merely new impressions or reprints. Others are more ingeniously constructed; their content has been subjected to a moderating influence – to sublimation, as I call it – and they may even become conscious, by cleverly taking advantage of some real peculiarity in the physician's person or circumstances and attaching themselves to that. These, then, will no longer be new impressions, but revised editions.
>
> . . . [T]ransference is an inevitable necessity . . . there is no means of avoiding it . . . [it] has to be detected almost without assistance and with only the slightest clues.
>
> *(Freud, 1905, p. 116)*

Even if this definition is the most complete that Freud ever gave of the concept of transference, it is evident that it was still not considered as the real driving force of the analytic process. However, it should be noted that for Freud the transference, or rather the transference interpretation, never became the only therapeutic instrument; in his clinical practice with patients he also established a personal, non-technical relationship (cf. Freud, 1937a; Lipton, 1977).

Another fundamental contribution on the transference is 'The Dynamics of Transference' (Freud, 1912a), the first work that the Viennese Master devoted entirely to this topic. In this essay, Freud used the term *imago* (introduced in psychoanalysis by Jung in 1911) to indicate the internal figures (mother, father, siblings, etc.) that belong to the subject's past; such figures constitute the object of transference shift on the person of the analyst. More precisely, what is transferred are some elements of the unconscious parts of infantile conflicts. Moreover, in the wake of the contribution of Ferenczi (1909), who had shown the patient's tendency to try to get the analyst to play the role of a parental figure, loved and feared at the same time, Freud examined the role of the transference affects of love and hate within the analytic process, ultimately believing that it was necessary for the analyst to take into consideration the affective qualities of the patient's transference.

Freud suggested the distinction between a 'positive' transference (friendly, affectionate feelings that can reach consciousness; it is an instrument of cooperation), originating from the loving relationship with a preoedipal mother (the tender feelings that are typical of this kind of transference are seen as originating from erotic sources; the earliest relationships are always established with sexual objects) and a 'negative' transference (hostile, erotic-aggressive, unconscious feelings; it expresses itself as a resistance against treatment), which derives from oedipal desires and conflicts. These two components of the transference, the positive and the negative, are often both present in the transference that the (psychoneurotic) patient develops towards the analyst; they must be acknowledged and treated separately. Therefore, a certain ambivalence (a term introduced by Bleuler in 1909 and again in 1911) is normal; however, it becomes a problem when it is excessive, as in the case of neurotic individuals, because the transference may become essentially negative, thus hindering the positive outcome of the therapeutic work: "Transference to the doctor is suitable for resistance to the treatment only in so far as it is a negative transference or a positive transference of repressed erotic impulses" (Freud, 1912a, p. 105). To conclude this brief discussion of the concept of transference, we can say that Freud envisaged it as a resistance, or an obstacle, letting other people investigate the notion of irreprehensible positive transference (in more recent terms, secure attachment); this legacy was particularly evident for Ferenczi, whose works were all approved by Freud, except 'Confusion of the Tongues Between the Adults and the Child' (Ferenczi, 1932), which he criticised for political, not scientific reasons.

Going back more specifically to the countertransference, we could say that Freud linked the transference-countertransference dynamics of the 'analytic' couple Breuer-Pappenheim to that of the Jung-Spielrein affaire; two stories distant in terms of time, which share surprising similarities, with the difference that the erotic involvement of the first couple took a symbolic, symptomatic form and remained at an unconscious level in both members, whereas in the second couple it reached a conscious level and was enacted with great awareness.

Going back more specifically to the countertransference, we could say that Freud linked the transference-countertransference dynamics of the 'analytic' couple Breuer-Pappenheim to that of the Jung-Spielrein affaire; two stories distant in terms of time, which share surprising similarities, with the difference that the erotic involvement of the first couple took a symbolic, symptomatic form and remained at an unconscious level in both members, whereas in the second couple it reached a conscious level and was enacted with great awareness.

It is clear that the countertransference was initially noticed as an erotic countertransference of male analysts towards young women patients, and that "Dominating the countertransference means . . . that the (male) analyst will not succumb to the (female) patient's seduction" (De Urtubey, 1995, p. 684). This fact, however, should not be seen with contempt or as the source of facile accusations, at least not before considering it within the historical-sociological context of that time. First of all, it should be remembered that most of the patients who went to the studies of psychoanalysts were women (until 1905 all clinical cases were women patients) who suffered from hysteria, that is, a disorder that belongs to the oedipal stage, which, by means of an amorous transference, reproduces and tries to fulfil instinctual (tender and sensual) desires within the analytic situation. Freud's idea of the analyst's rule of abstinence derives from the problems related to the oedipal, amorous desires of his women patients, and not from drives of any other type; this rule was based on the following principle of the psychoanalytic method, according to Freud:

> I shall state it as a fundamental principle that the patient's need and longing should be allowed to persist in her, in order that they may serve as forces impelling her to do work and to make changes, and that we must beware of appeasing those forces by means of surrogates. And what we could offer would never be anything else than a surrogate, for the patient's condition is such that, until her repressions are removed, she is incapable of getting real satisfaction.
>
> *(Freud, 1912a, p. 165)*

In addition, substitutive satisfactions, external to the analysis (e.g., repetitive or perverse sexual practices; Freud, 1918) as well as those concealed within it (e.g., unconscious masturbatory behaviour; Ferenczi, 1919) were abolished; the only possible discharge was verbalisation, since it allowed interpretative work to take place.

Going back to the link between the concept of abstinence and the instinctual needs of hysteria, one should remember that it was Freud's lifelong concern, and that it was inappropriately extended also to the treatment of other forms of psychopathology (Cremerius, 1984). But the ethical-professional preoccupation about abstinence which Freud had to deal with was also mixed with feelings of pride: "To be slandered and scorched by the love with which we operate – such are the perils of our trade, which we are certainly not going to abandon on their account" (Freud and Jung, 1906–13, p. 210). One should also keep in mind that the pioneers of psychoanalysis saw themselves, each one from his own perspective, as a new kind of scientist. Ultimately, scientists are not like philosophers who leaf through pages of books to inquire about knowledge and construct their thoughts and new structures of knowledge; rather, they are empirical explorers who find their way through human territories and unexplored materials, possibly jeopardising their objects of study and also, in some way, at their own risk (Meneguz, 2011).

The public debut of the concept of countertransference took place in the course of the Second International Conference of Psychoanalysis, which occurred in Nuremberg on March 30–31, 1910; Freud had already talked about it in the course of a meeting of the Psychoanalytic Society of Vienna on the ninth of the same month. On that occasion, it seems that Freud had decided to discuss the fundamental and delicate issue of the analyst's psychic state, following the suggestion of Ferenczi (Jones, 1953), who had published one of his works on technique the previous year. Talking about innovations in the technique, Freud said:

> We have become aware of the 'countertransference', which arises in him as a result of the patient's influence on his unconscious feelings, and we are almost inclined to insist that he shall recognize this countertransference in himself and overcome it. . . . We have noticed that no psycho-analyst goes further than his own complexes and internal resistances permit; and we consequently require that he shall begin his activity with a self-analysis[4] and continually carry it deeper while he is making his observations on his patients. Anyone who fails to produce results in a self-analysis of this kind may at once give up any idea of being able to treat patients by analysis.
>
> *(Freud, 1910a, pp. 144–145)*

Countertransference, therefore, was seen as "the whole of the analyst's unconscious reactions to the individual analysand – especially to the analysand's own transference" (Laplanche and Pontalis, 1967, p. 92), as an endopsychic response of the clinician due to a personal, unresolved resistance (that is, an unconscious which is still too extended; 'blind spots' in his or her analytic perception, according to Wilhelm Stekel's 1911 metaphor), which made working on the patient's unconscious difficult.

The fact that Freud (1910a) introduced the concept of countertransference when talking about 'The Future Prospects of Psychoanalytic Therapy', however, suggests that he did not just see the countertransference as an obstacle to get rid of (such a position is a given fact), but he also perceived, as in the case of the transference, that a better understanding of it might lead to new, important contributions to the psychoanalytic technique. A confirmation of this hypothesis can be read in the letter that Freud wrote to Ferenczi on January 4, 1928:

> For my recommendations on technique which I gave back then were essentially negative. I considered the most important thing to emphasize what one should not do, to demonstrate the temptations that work against analysis. Almost everything that is positive that one should do I left to 'tact', which has been introduced by you. But what I achieved in so doing was that the

> obedient ones didn't take notice of the elasticity of these dissuasions and subjected themselves to them as if they were taboos. That had to be revised at some time, without, of course, revoking the obligations.
>
> . . . What we undertake in reality is a weighing out, which remains mostly preconscious, of the various reactions that we expect from our interventions, in the process of which it is first and foremost a matter of the quantitative assessment of the dynamic factors in the situation. Rules for these measurements can naturally not be made; the analyst's experience and normality will have to be the decisive factors. But one should thus divest 'tact' of its mystical character for beginners.
>
> *(Freud and Ferenczi, 1920–33, p. 332)*

It is, however, necessary to contextualise Freud's intervention in what can be defined as the third level of the development of the technique: to identify and overcome resistances. The first two levels had been (a) to interpret symptoms and (b) to discover complexes.

Freud's comment on the countertransference at the Nuremberg Conference deeply affected Ferenczi, who felt he was not receiving from the Master all the affection he would have needed. The Hungarian analyst agreed with what Freud expressed, but in a letter dated April 5, 1910, it is possible to read how he found the constant repression of the countertransference extremely exhausting. At the beginning of that letter Ferenczi quotes a sentence that Freud said to him: "Man *must* love something", referring to manual work or science; however, he adds that this is not enough, because "one must also love people if one wants to be happy" (Freud and Ferenczi, 1908–14, p. 158, emphasis in original). A few lines later, the Hungarian analyst writes that

> continuing analytic practice brings with it an increase in this need for support. Already, before the establishment of your requirement of 'suppression of countertransference', we all did this instinctively, and this continual suppression has to add up to something disturbing when one such as I, after ten to twelve hours of work, is so completely isolated and does without every love object.
>
> *(Freud and Ferenczi, 1908–14, p. 159)*

Ferenczi seems to complain to Freud, stating that such repression is even more difficult for someone who, just like him, is not (or does not feel) loved enough (*in primis* by the very father of psychoanalysis).

Still in 1910, in response to a 'self-analytic' letter in which Ferenczi apologised for having 'drowned' him with excessive questions, requests, and demands during a holiday they had spent together in Syracuse, Italy, regretting that he had not been reprimanded enough so that a good relationship might be reestablished, Freud wrote: "Quite right, it was a weakness on my part; I am also not that ψα superman whom we have constructed, and I also haven't overcome the countertransference. I couldn't do it, just as I can't do it with my three sons, because I like them and I feel sorry for them in the process" (Freud and Ferenczi, 1908–14, p. 221). It is clear that such paternal and positive countertransference had prevented Freud from acting and behaving in a certain manner, the way he saw as 'correct', towards his favorite pupil, the only one with whom he entertained a true extraprofessional relationship.[5]

Four years later Freud wrote 'Observations on Transference Love' (1914a) which, quite probably, is the result of his reflections on the Jung-Spielrein affaire and on the relational dynamics between the Swiss doctor and the Russian patient. In this essay Freud follows the same line he traced in 1910, but this time he invites his colleagues to pay more attention to the transference situations in which they become the objects of erotic attraction on the part of their own patients:

> For the doctor the phenomenon signifies a valuable piece of enlightenment and a useful warning against any tendency to a counter-transference which may be present in his own mind. He must recognize that the patient's falling in love is induced by the analytic situation and is not to be attributed to the charms of his own person; so that he has no grounds whatever for being proud of such a 'conquest', as it would be called outside analysis.
>
> *(Freud, 1914a, pp. 160–161)*

> Our control over ourselves is not so complete that we may not suddenly one day go further than we had intended. In my opinion, therefore, we ought not to give up the neutrality towards the patient, which we have acquired through keeping the counter-transference in check.
>
> *(ivi, p. 164)*

The notion of countertransference remained essentially the same for the rest of Freud's life, who from the year 1915 stopped making reference to it. It is, however, possible to perceive a different view of such phenomenon when, in 1912, suggesting the use of free-floating attention, Freud described an emotional-receptive unconscious, never fully theorised, as the basis of analytic listening:

> [The analyst] must turn his own unconscious like a receptive organ towards the transmitting unconscious of the patient. He must adjust himself to the patient as a telephone receiver is adjusted to the transmitting microphone. Just as the receiver converts back into sound waves the electric oscillations in the telephone line which were set up by sound waves, so the doctor's unconscious is able, from the derivatives of the unconscious which are communicated to him, to reconstruct that unconscious, which has determined the patient's free associations.
>
> *(Freud, 1912b, pp. 115–116)*

The doubt remains whether with the choice of the telephone metaphor Freud wanted to implicitly convey that unconscious transmission in analysis is a two-way road, or if he remained faithful to the view of an objective analyst-observer. In

Freud we find two notions of countertransference. In one, the countertransference is linked to the concept of transference (endopsychic, nonhistorical, impersonal, automatic), in which the role of the analyst in the transference of the patient is not considered active.[6] In the other, the countertransference is seen as a tool for analysis: 'the unconscious as a receiving organ', 'using one's unconscious as a tool for analysis', and so forth (on the importance of the analyst's personality, cf. Freud and Pfister, 1909–39; Freud, 1913a). These two notions show two opposite conceptions of countertransference. The first refers to a monopersonal view of the analytic relationship: That is, the unconscious is a tool for analysis, but the analyst must limit himself or herself to performing a receiving function, like a telephone, because if the analyst enters into a relationship of affectionate confidence with the patient, he or she loses the possibility of analysing resistances (Freud, 1912a). The second refers to an interactive view of the analyst-patient relationship based on the premise that "the Ucs. is alive and capable of development . . . subjected to influences from the Pcs" (Freud, 1912a, p. 74), and that "the Ucs. of one human being can react upon that of another, without passing through the Cs" (p. 194). Also remarkable is the comparison of the analyst-patient interaction with the game of chess (Freud, 1913b). Freud was not able to conceptualise this interactive dimension because he was surrounded by a context of irregular conduct on the part of some colleagues, and he had to 'rule over' the phenomenon. Moreover, he was not fully aware of the role of women in society and of the shadows of men in relation to women as dangerous, instinctual creatures who threatened the spiritual, orderly world of men (something which had already been well described by Henrik Ibsen, Guy de Maupassant, Arthur Schnitzler, August Strindberg, Frank Wedekind, and others).

In a letter on December 31, 1911, Freud wrote to Jung that "an article on 'counter-transference' is sorely needed" (Freud and Jung, 1906–13, p. 476). Unfortunately, it was never written. One of the possible reasons for this may be that, as Freud wrote in a letter sent to Ludwig Binswanger, dated February 20, 1913, "The problem of counter-transference . . . is – technically – among the most intricate in psychoanalysis" (Freud, 1908–38, p. 112). In the same letter, it is also possible to discover that Freud was worried about what the analyst might need to do if the obstacle of the countertransference was encountered:

> What we give to the patient should, however, be a spontaneous affect, but measured out consciously at all times, to a greater or lesser extent according to need. In certain circumstances a great deal, but never from one's own unconscious. I would look upon that as the formula. One must, therefore, always recognize one's counter-transference and overcome it, for not till then is one free oneself.
>
> *(Freud, 1908–38, p. 112)*

Freud (1914b) also suggested being wary of the countertransference that might be developing in the analyst, and not abandoning the impassibility that has been reached by restraining it.

Let us now pause to reflect some more about the reasons that may have ultimately convinced Freud of the need for an article on the countertransference. To do this, it is necessary to step back and see what recent events (obviously, in addition to past events) might be the basis of the firm stance of the father of psychoanalysis.

The previous statement taken from the letter of December 31, 1911, to Jung was linked to the story of Mrs. C, a patient who was in treatment with Freud beginning in October 1908, whom he, at a certain point, had tried to refer to Oskar Pfister. Mrs. C, taking advantage of a break in her treatment with Freud, had gone to Zurich to talk to Jung about the condition of her sister. On this occasion she also had the opportunity to complain to him about the reserve and the scarce affective participation of Freud. According to what Freud wrote, Jung's reply to Mrs. C on that occasion was that "I myself was unable, often very much *malgré moi*, to keep my distance, because sometimes I couldn't withhold my sympathy" (Freud and Jung, 1906–13, p. 447). But let us see now what Freud thought about it:

> Frau C – has told me all sorts of things about you and Pfister, if you can call the hints she drops 'telling'; I gather that neither of you has yet acquired the necessary objectivity in your practice, that you still get involved, giving a good deal of yourselves and expecting the patient to give something in return. Permit me, speaking as the venerable old master, to say that this technique is invariably ill-advised and that it is best to remain reserved and purely receptive. We must never let our poor neurotics drive us crazy.
>
> *(Freud and Jung, 1906–13, pp. 475–476)*

Moreover, in the same period Freud was unwillingly about to begin a psychoanalytic treatment of Elma Pàlos. Elma was the daughter of Gizella Altschul-Pàlos, the woman with whom Ferenczi had had an affair since 1904. In July 1911, Ferenczi had decided to take Elma in therapy, even if she was the daughter of his own partner, because of the deep depression in which the young woman had fallen after the death of a friend who had killed himself because of her. From the very beginning (see the letter of July 14), Freud had expressed to his pupil and colleague his own doubts about the possibility that the treatment of a person belonging to one's own personal milieu might take place in a positive way (this might make us smile if we think that in the years 1919–1921 Freud himself would analyse none less than his own daughter Anna). Quite soon, the relationship between Ferenczi and Elma took a nonanalytic direction: In November, the Hungarian analyst confessed to Freud his phantasy of marrying Elma and by December he first admitted that he had not been able to maintain the "cool superiority of the analyst" (letter of December 3) and then that he wanted to marry Elma (letter of December 30). It must be said that, during the whole period in which these events took place, Ferenczi continued his relationship with Gizella; she was aware of what was happening between her lover and her daughter and she had also contacted Freud for advice.

The constant warnings and invitations to caution that Freud gave to Ferenczi, who in the meantime had become engaged to Elma, in the end gave some results:

On January 1, 1912, Ferenczi wrote that "the scales fell from my eyes, and . . . I had to recognize that the issue here should be one not of marriage but of the treatment of an illness" (Freud and Ferenczi, 1908–14, p. 324); he asked Freud to treat Elma, who had accepted this possibility. Considering the situation, Freud felt obliged to accept the referral, hoping that the analysis of the erotic transference and the oedipal complex would prevent the marriage. In the same month, Freud started the psychoanalytic treatment of Pàlos, a tranche of analysis that lasted from New Year's Day until Easter 1912. Even if at that point Ferenczi claimed that Elma's love for him was mostly a transference towards the father, after all, he thought that the analysis with Freud would allow him to marry Elma 'free from transference' because if it is true that the erotic transference was very visible to him by now, the same thing cannot be said about his erotic countertransference. Moreover, it is possible that such referral to Freud concealed Ferenczi's own unexpressed desire to be analysed by Freud. Elma remained in analysis with Freud until April, and in the same month she restarted her treatment with Ferenczi, but this time only to finish the analysis. In the end, Ferenczi married Gizella in March 1919, while Elma married another man.

It should be remembered that erotic relationships between analysts and patients were a very common thing in those years. A direct and raw account of this was given by Wilhelm Reich, a psychoanalyst (who became a member of the psychoanalytic society of Vienna in 1920) who was often accused by many of improper sexual behaviour with his patients. In the course of an interview, Reich (1967) said that during the first years that followed the birth of psychoanalysis there were cases in which psychoanalysts, with the pretext of a medical examination, inserted their fingers in their patients' vaginas. This was a rather frequent occurrence. Some psychoanalysts were hypocritical about such things; they wanted their women patients to believe that nothing was the matter and masturbated them during the sessions. Reich's denunciation is confirmed in the minutes of the psychoanalytic society of Vienna. For example, in the one dated November 3, 1909, Eduard Hitschmann saw as a prejudice (*Befangenheif*) the refusal of Isidor Sadger to perform the 'absolutely necessary' examination of the sexual organs of the women patients who requested psychoanalysis (Falzeder, 1994). In the light of what has been said, one can quite understand Freud's concerns about the public view of psychoanalysis, his passionate defence of it, and his incessant activity in order to prevent his 'creature' from going astray or from running into any judiciary problems.

As Antonio Imbasciati (2007) suggests, it seems that Freud's deontological preoccupation prevailed over the scientific question: what is the meaning of this phenomenon in terms of the analyst's unconscious? This question was dismissed by considering the countertransference (or rather, countertransference enactments) as the analyst's own responsibility, as the consequence of a limited, incomplete analysis. This gave the phenomenon an embarrassing, damaging reputation, thus making a dialogue and exchange with colleagues difficult. As we have seen, however, Freud encouraged his followers to examine the issue in depth, probably seeing it as closely linked to the future of psychoanalysis, recommending that future works related to that issue should be circulated only among experienced colleagues, and not published: "I believe an article on 'countertransference' sorely needed; of course we could not publish it, we should have to circulate copies among ourselves" (Freud and Jung, 1906–13, p. 476). One should note, however, that some authors (Strachey, 1958; Blanton, 1971) believe that the limited amount of information divulged by Freud showed not just fear of the threat that psychoanalysis might have had to face if the phenomenon of countertransference (here meant as the analyst's falling in love with a patient) had become public, but also, and mainly, reluctance to make the psychoanalytic technique known to patients in specific detail.

Freud already shows his knowledge that the analyst constantly influences the progression of the treatment in his reflections on the case of Dora (Freud, 1905), but it is in *Analysis Terminable and Interminable* (Freud, 1937a) that he not only confirms Ferenczi's (1927b) position in 'The Problem of the Termination of the Analysis', but also goes beyond it and transforms it, acknowledging that the treatment is affected not only by the weaknesses of the analyst, but also by his or her whole personality, by what makes the analyst what he or she is, for better or worse. More precisely, Ferenczi (1927b) expresses his conviction that "analysis is not an endless process, but one which can be brought to a natural end with sufficient skill and patience on the analyst's part" (p. 86), and reaches the conclusion that "when we have gradually learned to take into account the weak points in our own personality, the number of fully analyzed cases will increase" (p. 86). From this, Freud reaches the conclusion that during the analytic process it is indispensable to consider not only the ego of the patient but also the personal characteristics of the analyst as factors that influence the psychoanalytic treatment, facilitating it or making it more difficult.

Notes

1 Sabina Spielrein was admitted to the Burghölzli neurological clinic of Zurich on August 17, 1904, and the doctor who took her on and filled in her file was Carl Jung. Her discharge from the clinic took place in June 1905, but the therapeutic treatment (in which Jung used the psychoanalytic method for the first time) went on for several years, and their extra-analytical relationship lasted until 1910. The Burghölzli was the most important psychiatric clinic in Europe. Jung had been working there since December 1900 as an assistant of Professor Eugen Bleuler, who was famous for having introduced the new term 'schizophrenia', whose underlying concept rejected the merely organismic view of mental illness and distanced itself from Kraepelin's nosographic configuration, embracing the psychogenetic hypotheses of mental illness introduced by Pierre Janet and Freud. Bleuler had been interested in the work of the father of psychoanalysis since he had reviewed his book *Studies on Hysteria* (Breuer and Freud, 1892–95; cf. Bleuler, 1896).

2 Ferenczi was of the same opinion; in a letter sent to Freud on March 22, 1910, he claimed: "There is no doubt that, among those who have followed you up to now, he is the most significant. Too bad he [Gross] had to go to pot" (Freud and Ferenczi, 1908–14, p. 154).

3 In 1905, when he wrote his afterword and published his work, Freud had in mind only the heterosexual dimension of the transference developed by Ida, in which he could only play the part of Philip Bauer or Hans Zellenka; as a matter of fact, he wrote that "at the beginning it was clear that I was replacing her father in her imagination" (p. 118). Freud acknowledged Ida's homosexual link to Peppina Zellenka only many years later, in a note added in 1923: "The longer the interval of time that separates me from the end of this analysis, the more probable it seems to me that the fault in my technique lay in this omission:

I failed to discover in time and to inform the patient that her homosexual (gynaecophilic) love for Frau K. was the strongest unconscious current in her mental life. . . . Before I had learnt the importance of the homosexual current of feeling in psychoneurotics, I was often brought to a standstill in the treatment of my cases or found myself in complete perplexity" (p. 119, n.1). One should note, however, that Freud did not seem to become involved as a 'female' object of his patient's transference; apparently, he had not yet grasped the fact that an analyst, regardless of his or her actual gender, may represent both male and female figures in the transference.

4 Subsequently, under the influence of Jung and the Zurich group, Freud will ask for a personal analysis (Freud, 1912b), and he will suggest different ones for them every five years (Freud, 1937a), keeping the self-analysis (knowing that it alone would be incomplete). It is interesting to know that by 1920 that which had been known as 'didactic analysis' was called 'control analysis' (cf. Eitingon, 1923); basically it was about the discussions and the difficulties that the candidate found on the supervised cases that he or she followed on his or her training (Hinshelwood, 1999).

5 According to Judith Dupont (1989), nephew of Alice Balint (first wife of Michael Balint, a pupil and friend of Ferenczi), this holiday period spent together was disappointing for both of them. Each one wanted to make the other 'fit the mold' of their desires: Ferenczi wanted an exclusive, almost fusional relationship with a friend; Freud was looking for an efficient companion, devoted, attentive, independent, and respectful of his reserve. On the issue of the analyst's reserve, Freud (1912b) claimed that it was necessary not to reveal to one's patient any information about oneself, such as one's private life, vices, or virtues: "The doctor should be opaque to his patients and, like a mirror, should show them nothing but what is shown to him" (p. 118).

6 One should remember, however, that in 'Remembering, Repeating, and Working-Through', Freud (1914b) wrote that transference proper, that is, "transference neurosis", is caused by the psychoanalytic treatment (hence transference as an "artificial illness" that appears in the analytic situation, p. 154). It is in this work, probably, that Freud began to give shape to the idea of "the transference as the only working tool", which later became "the transference as a necessary working tool". Also, in 'Observations on Transference Love', Freud (1914a) wrote that the love of the patient for her analyst "is provoked by the analytic situation" (p. 168). Therefore, the transference became the lynchpin for the theoretical modifications that followed. This is not surprising, especially if one considers that in Freud, more than in other analysts, theory is rooted in clinical experience, and the best innovations originate from clinical failures. This process of revision also had an impact (though not explicitly) on the concept of transference itself (cf. Freud, 1937a, 1937b, 1938).

2

FREUD AND THE PSYCHOANALYTIC MOVEMENT BETWEEN THE FOUNDATION OF THE IPA, THE GREAT WAR, AND THE TURNING-POINT OF 1920

On April 27, 1908, in Salzburg, at the Congress for Freudian Psychology, today considered to be the first International Psychoanalytical Congress, the idea of establishing an International Association was discussed and approved. It became a reality at the 1910 Nuremberg Congress. The International Psychoanalytical Association (IPA) was born and its objective was to promote connections and scientific exchange between psychoanalysts from different countries through the organisation of international congresses, the publishing and distributing of an up-to-date newsletter on the activities of various Societies, and the founding of scientific journals. Despite the opposition of the Viennese group, but backed by Sigmund Freud who saw him as "the man of the future" (Freud and Ferenczi, 1908–14, p. 246), Carl Gustav Jung was elected the president of the fledgling Association, whose official headquarters was to be Zurich, where the president resided.

As we know, after a short time, during which Freud had seen Jung as the 'crown prince', the personal and scientific relations between the two men began to deteriorate. As a result of the escalation of tensions and the theoretical and clinical rupture between Freud and Jung, or rather between the father of psychoanalysis and the official representative of psychoanalysis, in the summer of 1912, an informal and secret institution came into being, one that was grafted onto the official institution of the IPA – the 'Secret Committee', whose formation had been proposed to Freud by Ernest Jones, on the basis of an idea previously put forward by Sándor Ferenczi. This Secret Committee was composed of Karl Abraham, Ferenczi, Jones, Otto Rank, and Hans Sachs, men who were obviously in close contact with Freud. In 1919, Max Eitingon joined them, and in 1925, Anna Freud substituted Rank who had distanced himself from Freud and psychoanalysis. The aim of the Committee was to preserve the Freudian creation, by discussing and devising through mutual agreement the future development of psychoanalysis and the policies of the IPA. Each member was committed to discussing with the group any and all ideas that went contrary to the fundamental principles of Freudian theory (unconscious, infantile sexuality, repression, etc.), before airing them in public. The Committee functioned satisfactorily for about a decade, or rather until the occurrence of a series of events that undermined the group's stability. These events were a) the emergence of Freud's cancer in 1923; b) Rank's publication of *The Development of Psychoanalysis* (written in collaboration with Ferenczi in 1923) and *The Trauma of Birth* (1924),[1] works which formalised the beginning of the split between Rank and Freud; and c) the death of Abraham on Christmas Eve of 1925. Ultimately the Committee ceased to exist as such in 1927, but it instead took the form of the General Directive of the IPA. At the Innsbruck Congress, Eitingon was nominated president, succeeding Abraham. Ferenczi and Jones became the vice-presidents, Anna Freud the secretary, while Sachs left the Committee for good. This new arrangement lasted until 1936, after which the activity of this small grouping permanently came to an end.

Up until this point we have talked about what strictly pertains to the psychoanalytic movement; however, it was not only influenced by the encounters and clashes that took place within it, but also by the external socio-political circumstances. We know that even though Freud had already described in 1912 what he called the 'stormy' political situation in Austria, one which he did not follow with keen interest, but from which he did expect 'bad times', the outbreak of the First World War took him by surprise. On June 28, 1914, as soon as he heard the news of the assassination of Archduke Franz Ferdinand of Hapsburg, presumptive heir to the Austro-Hungarian throne, Freud wrote a letter to Ferenczi, in which he spoke of being "under the impression of the surprising murder in Sarajevo, the consequences of which cannot be foreseen" (Freud and Ferenczi, 1908–14, p. 562). From another letter, dated the July 26 and addressed to Abraham, we know that Freud reacted to the entry into war with euphoria and a renewed sense of being Austrian (a sentiment that had been hibernating for over thirty years), convinced as he was of the legitimacy of the cause (Freud and Abraham, 1907–26, pp. 264–265). On August 23, Freud wrote to Ferenczi that the war had had the effect of mobilising within him a sudden libido for Austro-Hungary; but a few lines before, he had confessed to having noticed that he was becoming more irritable, hinting at diversions he had dreamed up to escape distress, and he asked himself whether "one won't be able to go to England for a long time after the war. Who knows whether to Italy?" (Freud and Ferenczi, 1914–19, p. 14).

This patriotic spirit proved to be more the exception than the rule and in fact Freud began to view the war more and more negatively. His initial enthusiasm did not last more than a few weeks, the Austrian army petering out, due to the difficulties, unexpected by Freud, that it encountered in its conquest of Serbia – a fact which made him shift his remaining hopes for a final victory onto Germany. The idea of war that was prevalent at the time was tied to the type of wars that had been fought up to that moment: bloody conflicts, lasting a few months at most, fought by armies without the involvement of the various populations, and whose outcome, often the result of pacts or negotiations, almost exclusively concerned the reorganisation of the political geography. But already towards the end of 1914, last-minute hopes for an easy victory were vanishing and Freud became caught up in a phase of depression and mourning for his lost libido spent in the cause of the Central Powers. However, once the 'work of mourning' came to an end, Freud was able to invest his newly available libido in his own scientific activity, which attained a pinnacle of productivity in the year 1915. The turmoil that gripped Freud in that period is revealed in his correspondence. For example he asked Abraham to come and reassure him, and he turned to Lou Andreas-Salomé in search of "a word of comfort from you" (Freud and Andreas-Salomé, 1912–36, p. 20). In more general terms, after the first two or three years of war, it was becoming apparent that a pronounced scepticism over the final outcome of the military conflict was growing within Freud.

War and the barbarity that comes with it was interpreted by Freud as a huge step backward, with respect to the conquests made by civilisation up until then: "We cannot but feel that no event has ever destroyed so much that is precious in the common possessions of humanity, confused so many of the clearest intelligences, or so thoroughly debased what is highest. Science herself has lost her passionless impartiality. . . . Anthropologists feel driven to declare him [the adversary] inferior and degenerate, psychiatrists issue a diagnosis of his disease of mind or spirit" (Freud, 1915c, p. 275). Thus, for the Viennese Master, war was a cause for disillusionment and, consequently, a source that induced him to deepen his knowledge of the psychic dynamics of both individuals and groups (cf. Freud, 1921). This entailed a revision of his drive theory, with a theorisation of a death instinct beyond that of the libido (cf. Freud, 1920). For Freud, from a psychoanalytical point of view, war arises out of the destructive and homicidal tendencies possessed by every individual, tendencies usually kept at bay by the fear of social disapproval (subjectively experienced as a 'moral conscience'). Freud saw war as a manifestation of the death drives. Moreover it sweeps away that conventional view (at least in times of peace) of considering death as something that does not pertain to either us or our loved ones, as happens in the midst of the reality of war: "Death will no longer be denied; we are forced to believe in it. People really die" (Freud, 1915c, p. 291).

The years of the First World War were also marked by other conflicts and personal losses that affected Freud: the death of his half-brother, Emmanuel, in a train accident (1914); the rupture of ties with Alfred Adler (1911), Wilhelm Stekel (1912), and especially, Carl Gustav Jung (1913); the call to war of his sons, Martin, Ernst, and Oliver (who against their father's wishes enlisted as volunteers, but while the first two were engaged on the front, the third worked in military intelligence), as well as of some friends and colleagues, such as Abraham, Ferenczi, and Eitingon (who were called up as doctors; the first into the German army, the others into the Austro-Hungarian army); his sixtieth birthday and the ensuing anxiety over death (in 1915, he believed he had no more than a few years to live); the discovery of the pre-cancerous state of his palate; the suspension of the meetings of the Vienna Psychoanalytic Society until the winter of 1915, meetings which did resume if only on a monthly basis; a fear for the uncertain future of psychoanalysis; the precarious economic circumstances (during the War the number of patients in analysis were at a minimum, and for long periods of time he had none at all); the lack of any heating in his home and the difficulties of procuring food for himself and his family.

Despite all this, the years 1914–15 were a period of intense and creative scientific accomplishment. On March 15, 1915, Freud began work on his *Papers on Metapsychology* (this is the term which he used to express the analysis of the psychic processes in their dynamic, topographical, and economic aspects), an ongoing project of a few years, and a work that would constitute the underlying structure of psychoanalytical science. Originally composed of twelve essays, the first five ('Instincts and Their Vicissitudes', 'Repression', 'The Unconscious', 'A Metapsychological Complement to the Theory of Dreams', and 'Mourning and Melancholia') were written over a period of six weeks, the following seven (on consciousness, anxiety, conversion hysteria, obsessional neurosis, sublimation, projection and paranoia, and transference neuroses) were completed by the beginning of August. Unfortunately Freud never published these last seven essays, and no one ever asked him what became of them. It is thought that he destroyed the manuscripts after the end of the war. In this same period he also produced the *Introduction to Psychoanalysis* (1915–17) and the case study of the 'Wolf Man' (1914b).

The year 1916, on the other hand, was quite uninspired. Freud's creative output was rather meagre, as was his clinical activity. Moreover, Otto Rank was transferred to the Polish front, to Krakow, where he was assigned the management of the city's most important newspaper. This left Hans Sachs as his only close collaborator in Vienna. The loss of Rank's precious help also meant that the already difficult survival of psychoanalytical journals was further jeopardised, and these periodicals represented all that was left of the psychoanalytic movement during the war years. In 1914 the *Jahrbuch für psychoanalytische und psychopathologische Forschungen*, founded in 1909, closed down, and so the only journals left were *Imago*, founded in 1912, dealing with applied psychoanalysis and edited by Sachs and Rank, and the *Internationale Zeitschrift für (ärztliche) Psychoanalyse*, founded in 1913 and edited by Ferenczi, Jones, and Rank. The latter replaced the *Zentralblatt für Psychoanalyse* as the official organ of the IPA. Because of the problems in getting in touch with his colleagues during the war, Freud, himself, had to take care of the editorship of both journals entirely on his own.

There were no events of particular interest in 1917. Living conditions were still disastrous and Freud's creative output was more limited than in the previous year. Moreover this was the worst year in terms of the future expectations of psychoanalysis.

The year 1918 was even worse, with respect to living conditions – the rise in prices, the lack of food and heating fuel – and scientific productivity. To these problems were added as well the preoccupations for the health of both Rank, who during the period he spent in Krakow underwent two serious crises of depression, and Ferenczi, who had contracted pulmonary tuberculosis and Graves's disease. However, 1918 was also a watershed year because two important things happened, two events that contributed a sense of hopefulness to the future of the psychoanalytic movement.

The first was a large financial donation from a rich Hungarian brewer, Anton von Freund, a doctor of philosophy, and a one-time patient of Freud and Ferenczi. The donation was earmarked for the creation of an independent publishing house, a place for the management of psychoanalytical publications. The *Internationaler Psychoanalytischer Verlag* became a reality in 1919, but unfortunately von Freund died in January of 1920 and the Hungarian political situation made it impossible to access a great deal of the money that he had allocated for the cause of psychoanalysis. This left the fledgling publishing house in financial distress. (A few days after the death of the Hungarian patron, who, it seemed, was supposed to become a member of the Secret Committee, Freud suffered an even greater sorrow – the death of his own twenty-six-year-old daughter Sophie, who left behind two children.) *Verlag* was however destined to have a prosperous life, initially thanks to Rank's enormous commitment and to the generous donations of Eitingon. From the time of its establishment in 1919, it published around one hundred and fifty books, five journals, and the collected works of Freud in twelve volumes. Its English branch, the *International Psychoanalytical Press*, headed up by Jones, published more than fifty books, including many translations of the best texts that *Verlag* had published in German.

The second happy occasion was the decision to hold the fifth International Psychoanalytical Congress during the summer holidays, a Congress that was held on September 28–29 in Budapest, the city that Freud saw as the new centre of the psychoanalytic movement (Freud and Abraham, 1907–26, pp. 381–382). Forty-two psychoanalysts (one came from Poland, two from Holland, three from Germany, the rest from Hungary and Austria) participated at this Congress, and for the first time, as proof of the growing attention that military circles were attributing to 'war neurosis', some official representatives of the governments of Austria, Germany, and Hungary took part. The presentations in this instance created such an excellent impression on the high-ranking medical officials of the army that the setting-up of psychoanalytical hospitals for the treatment of war neurosis was immediately planned. Unfortunately the defeat, which the Central Empires were soon heading for, quashed these plans. The political changes of the post-war period extinguished any hope that Budapest would become the new capital of psychoanalysis. This was because a short while later, Hungary, which became independent of Austria in October 1918, fell to the Bolsheviks (after this event would follow the Romanian occupation in August 1919), and for many long months, communication across the new borders was extremely difficult. For these reasons, the centre of the psychoanalytic movement had to move westward, and Ferenczi, who had been elected the president of the IPA, but was unable to execute his responsibilities, had to pass the presidency on to Jones, who, from England, was in a better position to advance the cause.

Finally the war ended. Between the end of September and the first half of October 1918, various armistices were decided upon, and in order to establish the conditions for peace, the Paris Conference of 1919 was convened, as a result of which, various peace treaties were signed between June of the same year and

August of the next. But it would take quite a few years before Europe in its entirety would recover from the human loss, the destruction, and the economic debts caused by the war.

As we have seen, for Freud the war years represented a period of work-related inactivity, which however forcibly left him free time to think and write. Thus began a long period of theoretical-clinical reflection and reconsideration of his vision of the psychic apparatus and functioning, as well as that of the etiopathogenesis of the disorders that might relate to it. The first product of this effort of deep reflection and rethinking is *Beyond the Pleasure Principle* (1920), a work which set in motion the 'turning-point of 1920'. This turning-point doesn't only refer to the introduction of the conflict between the life instinct (*Eros*) and the destructive instinct (*Thanatos*), but also to certain concepts that were introduced in later years (such as that of id, ego, and superego), or to the greater importance attributed to already existing concepts (such as that of ambivalence, object relations, identification, sense of guilt, anxiety, etc.) As André Green (1990) writes, the 1920 turning-point can be encapsulated in this threefold statement: first we have the insistence, through the concept of repetition compulsion, on the demonic force of the instinct; then we have the dualism of the ego, whose structure reveals that it is for the most part unconscious, since the development of its defences is conditioned by the same blindness that characterises desire; and ultimately we have the unmasking of the principal force that constitutes an obstacle to the creative potential of the libido: the destructive instinct.

This accounts for what pertains to the new theoretical configuration that psychoanalysis was taking on in the mind of Freud, but what exactly was the post-war situation of the psychoanalytic movement? The first International Psychoanalytical Congress, after the Great War, was held in The Hague in September 1920, and it definitely had a more international character than the previous one, in that sixty-two psychoanalysts attended: two were from America, seven from Austria, eleven from Germany, fifteen from England, sixteen from Holland, one from Poland, seven from Switzerland, and three from Hungary. Moreover fifty-seven guests were present, including Anna Freud, James Glover, and John Rickman. On this occasion the Swiss Society and the British Society were formally admitted into the IPA and Ernest Jones was elected president. It was the first time that the Secret Committee was fully reunited.

Therefore even the IPA survived. As a matter of fact, through communications, which began to flow normally by the end of the war, Freud became apprised of the news of the great progress made by the psychoanalytic movement in Berlin, London, and New York.

With respect to Berlin, of exceptional importance was the opening on February 14, 1920, of the Psychoanalytic Polyclinic, the first such centre in the world, offering free care, and treating patients according to the psychoanalytic method, and the first Training Institute for aspiring psychoanalysts. The inaugural ceremony was presided over by Eitingon (who generously financed the centre until 1930), with

Ernst Simmel and Anna Smeliansky at his side. Abraham was another fundamental figure within the Polyclinic and the Berlin Institute.

Eitingon had been the first doctor at the Burghölzli Clinic to meet Freud. Eugen Bleuler had told him to contact Freud for a consultation about a patient, with a deeper interest in verifying what psychiatry could learn from the nascent psychoanalytic discipline. Eitingon was also the first analyst to do a training analysis, an analysis over a period of five weeks between 1908 and 1909, done with Freud during their evening walks. It is said of him that, as an analyst, he intervened (interpreted) much more than the majority of his contemporaries did. Within the Institute he was mainly devoted to clinical supervisions. With the death of Abraham in 1925, it was Eitingon who became the guarantor of the formative standards for the training of analyst-candidates. On the occasion of the 1926 International Congress in Bad Homburg, following a preliminary conference dedicated to a discussion on the subject matter of the training of candidate-analysts, the International Training Commission was established, and Eitingon was elected its president. In 1927 Vienna, Berlin, and London represented the three main centres for training, and since the training organisation in each of them was so similar, it was possible to begin one's educational programme in one of them, continue on in a second city, and complete it in the third. They all followed the Eitingon model (cf. Schröter, 2002), at one time the only one, and today still the most widespread training model of all. Currently the IPA recognises the French and the Uruguayan, all based on the tripartite structure: the personal analysis of the aspiring analyst, supervisions, and theoretical seminars. However, there were some differences, and therefore Freud was doubtful that the systematic and structured educational model adopted in Berlin was the ideal solution (Sterba, 1982). A less rigid model was the one adopted in Budapest, where they did not separate the personal analysis from the initial supervisions: the rule specified that the candidate would undergo the supervision of his first case with his own training analyst (Haynal, 1987).

Given the important representative role that the incipient Berlin Institute had assumed for the psychoanalytic movement, in the months before the Congress of The Hague, it was prearranged that Sachs would be transferred to Berlin, where he would undertake the work of teacher and training analyst. Thus in the summer of 1920, after having ended a two-year sojourn in Switzerland where he had gone for a tuberculosis cure, Sachs transferred to Berlin instead of returning to Vienna. Even though Sachs, a Doctor of Law and a practicing lawyer, driven to psychoanalysis out of his interest in literature in general, and Fëdor Dostoevsky in particular, did not have clinical experience and had never been analysed, he became the first training analyst (he analysed Franz Alexander, Michael Balint, Edwing Boring, John Dollard, Erich Fromm, Karen Horney, Rudolf Löwenstein, Sylvia Payne, and Gregory Zilboorg, among others). It is said of him that he was a very silent analyst, and that he could go for weeks and even months without offering any interpretation. In 1932 he was sent to Boston to undertake the job of training analyst. He remained there until his death.

In 1927 Theodor Reik transferred from Vienna to Berlin in order to work at the Institute as a training analyst. The main reason that led Reik to move was an accusation of abusive practice of the medical profession (Reik was not a doctor) made against him in 1925. A year later he was charged with 'charlatanism'. Reik was fully absolved of the charges by a Viennese court in 1927, but the icy reaction of almost all his colleagues, except for Freud, Oskar Pfister, Ferenczi, and the Hungarian contingent, as well as the newspaper attacks generated by Stekel and Karl Kraus, prompted him to leave the Austrian capital.

Meanwhile, in London, Ernest Jones had disbanded the London Psychoanalytical Society, which he had founded in 1913 and which initially consisted of a dozen people interested in discussing psychoanalysis, because of the outbreak of war and the subsequent breakdown of communications with Vienna, but not with Zurich. For this reason, many of the English members drew closer to Jung and his ideas. Jones and those members who had remained close to Freud's ideas founded the British Psychoanalytical Society in February 1919. Anyone carrying out the profession of psychoanalyst, whether a doctor or not, could join. Up until the Second World War, this new Society was exclusively made up of persons originating from Great Britain, but most of these spent periods of training and work in Vienna or Berlin. By 1925, the Society already had fifty-four members, many of whom were destined to write the history of British psychoanalysis. These included: Douglas Bryan, David Eder, John Flügel, Joan Rivière, James and Edward Glover, Susan Isaacs (Brierley as she then was called), Sylvia Payne, John Rickman, Ella Sharpe, Adrian and Karin Stephen, William Stoddart, and James and Alix Strachey. Within a five-year period, these next joined up: Melanie Klein, Donald Winnicott, and Marjorie Brierley, while during the 1930s more members entered upon the psychoanalytical scene, including John Bowlby, Ronald Fairbairn, and William Gillespie.

The year after the establishment of the British Psychoanalytical Society, the *International Psychoanalytical Press* commenced its publication in translation of certain books published by *Internationaler Psychoanalytischer Verlag*. Furthermore, Jones founded the *International Journal of Psychoanalysis*, destined to become the 'official' organ of the IPA.

Also important were the events that marked the ensuing years. In 1924, the Psychoanalytical Institute was created for the commercial management of publications, and a little later, a contract for a collaboration with Hogarth Press Publishing was drawn up for the publication of the *International Psycho-Analytical Library* series. The International Psychoanalytical Library, managed by Jones and Rickman, was also opened. In 1926 the London Clinic for Psychoanalysis was inaugurated. Headed up by Rickman, it was set up to care for an affluent clientele. A Training Committee composed of Jones, Rickman, Glover, John Carl Flügel, and Douglas Bryan was formally instituted in the same period. From 1925 on, the first news about Melanie Klein's work with children reached London, via the members of the British Society who had gone to Berlin to do their analysis with Abraham or Sachs. In the same year, Alix Strachey organised this German colleague's first trip to London for a series of conferences on child analysis and play technique, recently developed in Berlin, conferences that were held in July in Adrian Stephen's home, where the Bloomsbury Group usually met. In the beginning, Jones had not welcomed the organisation of conferences given by Klein, but he changed his mind. In the following year, 1926, having seen the strong opposition that Klein's work was receiving, especially after the death of Abraham, on the part of her Berlin colleagues (primarily from the Hungarians Franz Alexander and Sándor Rado, who had emigrated to Berlin at the beginning of 1920), he successfully invited her to move to London.

It is clear that the above-mentioned invitation represented a precise stance on Jones's part with regard to the Vienna school. In more general terms, during the 1930s, despite the fact that a 'Viennese' sense of identity persisted in some analysts, most of the British Society members no longer identified with the Viennese group's way of thinking. This situation for the most part was due to the growing influence that studies on child analysis conducted by Klein had had on a large part of the London colleagues, studies that brought about different results in relation to those Anna Freud had reached in Vienna. Freud's official position was a defence of his daughter's work and criticism of Klein's, who, he maintained, ascribed excessive importance to early childhood phantasy life to the detriment of external reality.

Here I will confine myself to mentioning that Anna Freud (1926) completely excluded the parents from the therapy of the child, seeing their actual presence as an obstacle to the creating of a transference neurosis. This does not mean that she was not aware of or that she undervalued the importance of the family environment, to the extent that she claimed a double source at the origin of infantile neurosis: internal and external (the family environment). For her part, Melanie Klein (1927) maintained that it was possible to establish a transference neurosis in the therapy of a child, just as it was in that of an adult. This is because those that 'enter' the playroom are the imaginary parents, the parents of the internal world, while the real parents remain in the waiting-room. Furthermore, since the real parents accompany the child throughout the therapeutic journey, Klein was certain that it was essential to establish and maintain good relations with them (and that the relationship on the part of the parents should be a kind of passive collaboration, neither interfering nor obstructive). Klein's paper was presented on the occasion of a Symposium on child analysis, organised by Jones against Freud's advice. In it, the author expressed all of her concerns, as well as those of many of the British Society (including Isaacs, Rivière, Sharpe, and Nina Searl, to some extent), about the possibility that the position maintained by Anna Freud was more than anything an obstacle to the development of child analysis.

Such differences of a theoretical-clinical nature did not stimulate a potentially enriching debate, but rather brought about a long period, lasting almost a decade, in which the contact and the exchanges between the two Societies became more and more infrequent. The situation remained like this until the years just prior to the Second World War.

Note

1 Initially *The Development of Psychoanalysis* was favourably received by Freud, to the extent that on June 1, 1923, Freud wrote to Ferenczi that: "His [of Rank] finding is great indeed" (Freud and Ferenczi, 1920–33, p. 106). But after the publication of *The Trauma of Birth*, which occurred without prior consultation on the part of Rank, with any member of the Committee, about the ideas contained within the book, the criticisms coming out of the psychoanalytic community were such that in the end Freud himself had to distance himself from both works. On October 29, 1924, he wrote to Ferenczi that Rank: "probably wouldn't have written the book if he had been analyzed" (Freud and Ferenczi, 1920–33, p. 166).

3

THE CONTRIBUTION OF THE EARLY PIONEERS

In years when a great deal of energy was expended on the rational aspects of the *talking cure* to the detriment of the element of affective interaction, some analysts emphasised the importance of the emotions they experienced in the therapeutic relationship. Included among these are Sándor Ferenczi and Carl Jung, who, in perhaps being less fearful than other colleagues with respect to their affective responses, placed a proper value on the interpersonal dimension in the analytical situation. It is no coincidence that we are referring to two analysts famous for being accessible to their patients, and whose positions on this topic are comparable.

Ferenczi distanced himself a great deal from classical psychoanalysis in his anticipation of this discipline's future developments on certain issues. Think of the value he assigned to the role of interpretation of non-verbal communication, and not only of its content, interested as he especially was in assessing the specific weight of the stronger partner in a couple (analyst, caregiver, etc.), knowing full well that the weaker (patient, child, etc.) is extremely attentive and sensitive to the other's moods, primarily conveyed via a non-verbal means of expression (Borgogno, 1999b, 2005). What incited Ferenczi to experiment with innovations in technique were the patient typology of those he treated (borderline and psychotic) and the influence from the studies on children conducted by Melanie Klein,[1] a protégé of his. An important factor was also the stormy and gap-filled analysis he underwent with Freud (three short *tranches* of analysis: in October 1914, mid-June to early July 1916, and the second half of September 1916), whom he mostly accused of not having analysed his negative transference and his reactivated primary depression. In fact, it seems that Ferenczi made an effort to devise for his patients what he wanted Freud to devise for him (Dupont, 1985). Furthermore the distress, confusion, and hate engendered by the non-working-through of his maternal fixation during the analysis led "Ferenczi [to] introduce new concepts in the hope of extricating himself from this transference impasse. His helplessness led to the wise baby; his confusion yielded the confusion of tongues; and, lastly, his hate produced the introjection of the adult's guilt, arousing in the child the terrorism of suffering, splitting and fragmentation" (Bokanowski, 1996, p. 354).

Ferenczi viewed the analytic situation as an intersubjective terrain, a field where two people may meet and where a certain climate may be generated. In order for this possibility to manifest itself there must be an empathic-maternal attitude on the part of the analyst towards a patient who is also always a child. At the Budapest International Congress of 1918, Freud presented a work, entitled 'Lines of Advance in Psychoanalytic Therapy', that called into question the advancements linked to the psychoanalytic technique. This paper can be seen as the precursor to the active technique later developed by Ferenczi (it should be remembered that the 'active technique' devised by the Hungarian initially had to do with frustration, and only later on did he also take into consideration gratification as a therapeutic factor). The idea that the analyst must not maintain a 'passive' attitude grew gradually stronger in Ferenczi's mind. Rather the analyst must be flexible and adapt his/her personal technique to the specific patient. Thus, following the example of Freud (1918), who had already produced important modifications to psychoanalytical technique, for instance by establishing a time limit for the 'Rat Man's' analysis (Freud, 1908), or by prescribing a visit to the place of one's phobia in the case of phobic patients (Freud, 1910a), Ferenczi, three months after the Budapest Congress, presented at a Hungarian Society meeting his work, 'On the Technique of Psychoanalysis', in which he writes:

> As a doctor, however, is always a human being and as such liable to moods, sympathies and antipathies, as well as impulses . . . he has constantly to perform a double task during the analysis: on the one hand, he must observe the patient . . . and construct his unconscious from his information and his behaviour; on the other hand, he must at the same time consistently control his own attitude towards the patient, and when necessary correct it; this is the mastery of the *countertransference.*
>
> *(Ferenczi, 1918, pp. 186–187, emphasis in original)*
>
> For the analyst this means "understanding how to *graduate* his sympathy. Indeed he may not even yield inwardly to his own affects; to be influenced by affects, not to mention passions, creates an atmosphere unfavourable for the taking up and proper handling of analytic data."
>
> *(ivi, p. 186, emphasis in original)*

During the analytical session, it is not only the patient who is addressing emotional changes. The therapist participates as well in an emotional reciprocity. (What Ferenczi asserts is completely in line, and will be up until 1933, with the principles upheld by Freud, 1913b, at the moment in which he had declared that the primary responsibility of the analyst is to bind the patient to the person of the analyst, by showing a serious and sincere interest in him and by assuming an attitude of sympathetic understanding.) By ascribing to the analyst the natural existence of positive feelings besides negative ones,[2] both having been elicited by the relationship, Ferenczi restored wholeness to the clinician, while preserving at the same time the elements of responsibility. Thus the way was paved for the possibility of analysing the transference and countertransference of the analyst. In Ferenczi's case, we no longer have unanalysable patients, just analysts more or less capable of taking care of a specific patient. What this means is that, for him, countertransference arises out of the couple's affective interaction, and precisely for this, it can be utilised as a tool for understanding what is happening between analyst and patient: it is the experience one goes through in the transference-countertransference relationship that nourishes the therapeutic process. The *counter*transference thus loses the oppositional meaning of the prefix. It manifests itself together with the patient's transference, sometimes even preceding it. As Giannakoulas and Fizzarotti Selvaggi (2006) suggest, for Ferenczi, the essential characteristic of countertransference is that the patient becomes affectively important to the therapist, in a subjective way, rather than in an objective way. Here the freely fluctuating mental processes have a fundamental importance – processes that would become limited by efforts to defend oneself from the countertransference. Such importance assigned to countertransference, for which Ferenczi was not concerned about formulating a definition, together with the recognition of the patient's ability to intuitively recognise the emotional responses of the analyst, brought this theorist to conclude that, in certain circumstances, the analyst could communicate to the patient his personal feelings in order to create a more human relationship (Ferenczi, 1920). Ferenczi's student, Alice Balint (1936), in an essay that she presented in Vienna on the occasion of the first Four Countries' Conference, and in which she dealt with the problems associated with the transference-countertransference dynamics, maintained that, at least in some cases, expressing one's own feelings openly and honestly is useful to the patient, and that it is, in any case, in line with the respect for truth, so dear to psychoanalysis. In any event, affirms Alice Balint (and with her, her husband, Michael, as we shall more fully see later on), the analyst must always perceive and analyse his own actions as well as those of the patient.

The vision Ferenczi was developing of countertransference was closely associated with the conception of trauma he had reached, a conception that persuaded him to move the *focus* of analysis from the phantom to the real, from the endogenous-driven to the relational-environmental, from the intrapsychic to the interpersonal. As Franco Borgogno (1999a, 2005) specified, according to Ferenczi, trauma, which can only be revealed in analysis if the analyst is disposed to accommodate it within himself (role reversal), does not simply pertain to what has taken place, but also what has not taken place: the meeting of minds which is the foundation of a healthy development. Therefore there are always two aspects: "an intrusion as well as a complementary and concomitant extraction, an implantation and an explanation, a graft and an excision, a non evolutive subtraction and a projection alimented by double bond" (Borgogno, 2007, p. 146).

Ferenczi's reflections on the concept of countertransference led him to also engage in the subject of touch, intended as *Einfühlung*: the "capacity for empathy" (Ferenczi, 1927–28, p. 89). These two elements are indispensable for the carrying out of the analysis, elements which, if worked through by the analyst (who must maintain a continuous fluctuation between empathy, self-observation, and the activity of judgement, the latter intended as a conscious evaluation) will guide him/her in his/her choice of the timing and the formulating of his/her interpretation, more than in the choice of its content. The limits of Ferenczi's approach were closely related to the analyst's tendency to pass on to the patient his/her own emotions and thoughts, due to a sometimes indiscriminate use of countertransference. Like Freud, and Jung before him, Ferenczi was convinced that 'the best analyst is a cured patient'. According to Michael and Enid Balint (1968), this new Ferenczian technique led to two great discoveries: the first concerns the enormous effect that the 'usual', 'customary', or 'classical' attitudes of the therapist towards analytical practice have both on the transference relationship that is being created and on the course of the treatment; the second relates to the technical possibilities of the interpretation of the countertransference.

In perusing the literature of this period, one discovers that other psychoanalysts were beginning to doubt or sometimes were aiming to improve on the 'classical' vision of countertransference. From this point of view, a rather unknown but hugely relevant contribution to the subject came from the American neurologist and psychoanalyst Adolph Stern (cf. Stefana, 2015), analysed by Freud in three different periods between 1920 and 1921. At the American Psychoanalytic Association Congress of June 3, 1923, he spoke extensively on the countertransference phenomenon or of "the transference that the analyst makes to the patient" (p. 167). He writes:

> Theoretically, the counter-transference on the part of the analyst has the same origin as the transference on the part of the patient; namely, in the repressed, infantile material of the analyst. By the same law, it may manifest itself in any form that the transference does. Practically, however, owing to the previous training that the analyst has undergone, his theoretical knowledge and his actual clinical experience reduce considerably the field of activity of the counter-transference in comparison with the protean forms which the transference takes in patients.
>
> *(Stern, 1923, pp. 168–169)*

Furthermore, he identified two types of countertransference: one, an impediment to understanding, resulting from the analyst's neurotic vestiges; the other, useful to the analysis, in response to the patient's transference. According to Stern, the analyst should use his/her own transference to get closer to the patient's transference, and in so doing seek a more sensorial rather than cognitive understanding (an experience that implies that the clinician comes into contact with his/her own feelings and phantasies), and a communication between unconsciouses. It is in this conceptualisation that originates the idea, upheld by Joseph Sandler (1976), that a good analyst is one who, beyond his/her freely fluctuating attention, is capable of resorting to a complimentary fluctuating behavioural resonance (which is the clinician's ability to allow himself to be used, to accept the role that the patient assigns to him via the transference; cf. Stefana, 2011).

During these same years, Helene Deutsch, who, after a brief period of analysis with Freud in 1918, was analysed by Karl Abraham in 1923–1924, while investigating the ways in which the analyst might receive and use the patient's material, reached the conclusion that, in order to have affective communication within the analytical situation, a communication from unconscious to unconscious must take place. This type of connection would occur thanks to a (partial) identification, which she called a 'complementary position', of the analyst with the image of the patient's infantile objects (in other words, the analyst feels like the patient's mother or father depending on the feelings that the patient is reliving towards whichever parental image in that moment). This identification is made possible because the development processes of both participants in the analytic duo are totally alike and they represent therefore the common basis for the harmonisation of the impulses and desires of each. Deutsch (1926) maintained that: "The affective psychic content of the patient, which emerges from his unconscious, becomes transmuted into an inner experience [of fantasies and memories] of the analyst, and is recognized as belonging to the patient . . . only in the course of subsequent intellectual work [thoughtful: What makes me feel this patient now?]" (p. 136). What transpires is that the analyst's own emotional resonance would allow him/her to reconstruct what happened to the patient there and then, and what is happening, in a re-creation produced by the transference-countertransference, in the here and now of the session. According to this author, in order for the identification to remain partial, and therefore therapeutic, one must not run into unresolved infantile conflicts that could induce the analyst to seek gratification, thus fixating on 'total' countertransference identifications, which, rather than allowing him/her to understand the patient, would lead the clinician to unconsciously play a specific role.

A year later, at the Symposium on child analysis, Ella Freeman Sharpe (1927) explored the notion of the analyst's making him/herself accessible to the possibility of entering into a dialogue with his/her own emotions. Sharpe was an analyst for adults, but at the Symposium she reported on her treatment of an adolescent (the second non-adult patient she ever treated; the first experience had happened six years before). She conducted her analysis, based on the technique of interpretation of symbolic play set forward by Melanie Klein. She reached the conclusion that "the necessity for immediate analysis of my reactions in this case, has illuminated the difficulties that beset child analysis" (p. 384). Later on we read:

> The problem of child analysis seems more subtly implicated with the analyst's own deepest unexplored repressions than adult analyses. Rationalizations that the child is too young, that the weakness of the child's super-ego makes an admixture of pedagogy with analysis indispensable, and so on, are built upon

> the alarms of that very same infantile super-ego in the analyst that he has to deal with in the child before him. That infantile 'super-ego' in the last resort becomes the dictator in the situation between analyst, child and parent, and only so far as that deepest level is analysed in the analyst can we look for scientific accuracy in the matter of child analysis.
>
> *(Sharpe, 1927, p. 384)*

The importance of the self-analysis of one's own emotional reactions to a young patient would be even more necessary when mechanisms of negation and projection into the patient or the parents are in play within the analyst.

Returning twenty years later to the countertransference issue, Sharpe (1947) maintained that admitting that an analyst has complexes, blind spots, and limitations simply means saying that he/she continues to be a human being, and "when he ceases to be an ordinary human being he ceases to be a good analyst" (p. 4). A few lines later we read:

> 'Countertransference' is often spoken of as if it implied a love attitude. The countertransference that is likely to cause trouble is the unconscious one on the analyst's side, whether it be an infantile negative or positive one or both in alternation. The unconscious transference is the infantile one, and when unconscious, will blind the analyst to the various aspects of the patient's transference. . . . We deceive ourselves if we think we have no countertransference. It is its nature that matters. We can hardly hope to carry on an analysis unless our own countertransference is healthy, and that healthiness depends upon the nature of satisfactions we obtain from the work, the deep unconscious satisfaction that lie behind the reality, ones of earning a living, and the hope of effecting cures.
>
> *(Sharpe, 1947, p. 4)*

It should also be mentioned that Sharpe associated the difficulties in managing countertransference with its unconscious nature.

On the subject of Sharpe's training, it is interesting to note that she came to psychoanalysis as a patient (she turned to the Medico-Psychological Clinic of London, where she was first treated by Jesse Murray and later by James Glover), and that in 1920 she temporarily moved to Berlin to enter into analysis with Hans Sachs.

In the same year, 1927, Edward Glover, also analysed by Sachs in 1920 (during the time he lived in Berlin, he studied with Sharpe), highlighted the influence that the patient material has on the analyst, an influence that particularly concerns the emergence of memories of similar psycho-affective experiences. Glover specifically reveals that the patient's psychosexual conflicts can also create analogous conflicts within the clinician. On the basis of this finding, he outlines a distinction between countertransference (traditional view) and counter-resistance. The latter "is more often than not a manifestation of *negative countertransference*" (1927, p. 514, emphasis in original). In other words, countertransference is seen as the source of counter-resistance, similar (in type and intensity) to the patient's resistance in the situation. What actually happens to the analyst is the acquisition of a systematic awareness, reached through a continuous self-investigation of the various types of counter-resistance, and the ability to immediately grasp the specific form afflicting him/her in any given moment.

Now we come to the person who probably preceded everyone on the issue of countertransference: Carl Gustav Jung. His clinical experience, accumulated, alongside Bleuler, in his work with psychotic patients at the Burghölzli Clinic, soon gave rise within him to the conviction that the clinician's personality is the basic element of the therapeutic process. The reflections this belief triggered brought him to propose the necessity of training analysis for every psychoanalyst and, above all, influenced his conception of the analytical situation: a bi-personal situation, in which the clinician him/herself is influenced by the patient in front of him/her, and in which the here and now assumes great importance. Thus, this Swiss psychiatrist placed less emphasis on clinical work, with respect, for example, to Freud, on the reconstruction of the patient's past and on the recuperation of representations repressed in the unconscious, in favour of a greater concentration on the treatment of the 'current conflict'. It should also be remembered that Jung modified the psychotherapeutic setting, reducing the sessions to one or two per week, and abandoning the couch in favour of the face-to-face.

It is evident that for Jung the analytic relationship is above all a relationship, in which the patient "will turn to the doctor . . . as an object of purely human relationship" (Jung, 1921–28, par. 286), a partner who exercises an absolutely indispensable influence on the patient, an influence that he "would rather call . . . human interest and personal devotion" (ivi, par. 271). From this, Jung is led to the conclusion that what counts for him in the treatment (whose aim is to enable the process of 'individuation' in the patient) is the flowing together of the personalities of the analyst and the patient, between whom there exists a subtle unconscious relationship. The use of countertransference is crucial, enhanced as it is by the self-awareness reached through the experience of a training analysis and a continuous self-analysis. It is a countertransference that is received and controlled, in that it is a foundation for the transformative reciprocity that characterises analysis. Jung maintained that:

> It is futile for the doctor to shield himself from the influence of the patient and to surround himself with a smoke-screen of fatherly and professional authority. The patient influences him unconsciously none the less, and brings about changes in the doctor's unconscious which are well-known to many psychotherapists: psychic disturbances or even injuries peculiar to the profession, a striking illustration of the patient's almost 'chemical' action. One of the best known symptoms of this kind is the countertransference evoked by the transference. But the effects are often much more subtle, and their nature can best be conveyed by the old idea of the demon of sickness. According to this, a sufferer can transmit his disease to a healthy person whose powers then subdue the demon – but not without impairing the well-being of the subduer.

> Between doctor and patient,[3] therefore, there are imponderable factors which bring about a mutual transformation. In the process, the stronger and more stable personality will decide the final issue. I have seen many cases where the patient assimilated the doctor in defiance of all theory and of the latter's professional intentions – generally, though not always, to the disadvantage of the doctor.
>
> *(Jung, 1929, par. 163–164)*

By means of the acceptance of the doctor's vulnerability – a kind of mediator in the therapeutic process – Jung took a step forward in the development of the concept of countertransference as a fundamental tool towards awareness and participation in the analytic treatment (according to David Sedgwick, 1994, it was precisely Jung who used countertransference for the first time as a therapeutic technique). It is obvious that from this point of view, training analysis becomes necessary for acquiring a knowledge of one's own limits, in order to treat one's own infantile aspects that would risk colluding with some of the patient's necessary work if one considers that: "every treatment that probes at all deeply consists in the doctor's examining himself, for only what he can put right in himself can he hope to put right in the patient. It is no loss, either, if he feels that the patient is hitting him, or even scoring off him: it is his own hurt that gives the measure of his power to heal. This, and nothing else, is the meaning of the Greek myth of the wounded physician" (Jung, 1951, par. 239).

Previously I hinted at the fact that, according to Jung, it is the clinician's personality that represents the necessary therapeutic factor (cf. Stefana, 2016). At this point, it would be interesting to hear what Jung himself had to say. In 1929, he wrote:

> Hence the personalities of doctor and patient are often infinitely more important for the outcome of the treatment than what the doctor says and thinks (although what he says and thinks may be a disturbing or a healing factor not to be underestimated). For two personalities to meet is like mixing two different chemical substances: if there is any combination at all, both are transformed.
>
> *(Jung, 1929, par. 163)*

> [Thus we can say that:] the doctor is as much 'in the analysis' as the patient. He is equally a part of the psychic process of treatment and therefore equally exposed to the transforming influences.
>
> *(ivi, par. 166)*

> [Or again, in 1957:] Fairly narrow limits, however, are set to the psychotherapy of severe cases. . . . The thing that really matters is the personal commitment, the serious purpose, the devotion, indeed the self-sacrifice, of those who give the treatment. I have seen results that were truly miraculous, as when sympathetic nurses and laymen were able, by their courage and steady

> devotion, to re-establish psychic rapport with their patients and so achieve quite astounding cures. . . . But even so one can bring about noticeable improvements in severe schizophrenics, and even cure them, by psychological treatment, provided that 'one's own constitution holds out'.
>
> *(Jung, 1957, par. 573)*

It is to be added that: "The consensus is that Jung was an unusually skilled psychotherapist who took a different approach with each one of his patients according to their personality and needs" (Ellenberger, 1970, p. 681).

Allow me to digress here, in order to point out how close Jungian thought is to that of Ferenczi, who, a few years before, had written: "How many famous doctors owe their successes to the dependable, calm, gentle or even energetic behaviour that they knew how to adopt with their patients? All of us have been able to ascertain how much a similar psychological help, delivered by friendly, stimulating, and benevolent words, or even simply from the doctor's appearance, might have a greater effect on the patient than drugs themselves, even in the case of organic illnesses" (Ferenczi, 1923, p. 187; my translation from Italian version). This shows how much in agreement Jung and Ferenczi were in their endorsement of the vital importance that the analyst, and his way of working, has in the interpersonal relationship with the patient, in terms of the therapy's results.

Purely as a matter of information, I would like to point out that in 1930, William Healy, Augusta Bronner, and Anna Bowers also dealt with the concept of countertransference, even if in a rather cautious manner. According to these authors:

> What is spoken of as 'countertransference' must also be reckoned with in connection with the analytic situation. By this is meant impulses on the part of the analyst to respond to the patient's affective trends. Schilder thinks that there is operative here an important psychological law regulating human relations and that the patient's feelings will of necessity call for complementary ones on the part of the analyst.
>
> *(Healy, Bronner, and Bowers, 1930, p. 444)*

In these same years, Theodor Reik (1932, 1935), having been analysed by Abraham in 1913 (an analysis paid for by Freud, with whom he underwent analysis in 1935), was hard at work on developing the theory of the analyst's 'insight', based on the idea that the clinician must be able to allow him/herself to be surprised by his/her own unconscious. He theorised, in agreement with Freud (1915a), that the unconscious of each member of the dyad was in communication with the other, and therefore that the clinician could gather in this way the unconscious material of the patient. For Reik, the analyst must maintain a receptive attitude towards the material the patient brings, as well as towards his/her own internal voices, and must also pay attention to the correspondences between the two. This provides greater space to intuition than to logical-rational thought, which means being able to trust in the unconscious and allowing oneself to be surprised, convinced that this may lead to an 'insight' into what is going on in the unconscious of the other. It must be specified that Reik believed that, whatever conjecture the analyst arrived at through intuition, it had to be repeatedly and critically verified in light of the material preceding it, and in light of what was to follow.

Here, too, we see how Reik was in keeping with Freudian thought, even if in reality we can delineate a substantial difference. Freud (1912b) maintained that the best therapeutic results are obtained "proceed[ing], as it were, without any purpose in view, allow[ing] oneself to be taken by surprise by any new turn in them, . . . submitting the material obtained to a synthetic process of thought only after the analysis is concluded" (p. 114), but only because in its present state psychoanalytic science is not "already possessed of all the knowledge (or at least the essential knowledge) about the psychology of the unconscious and about the structure of the neuroses that we can obtain from psychoanalytic work" (Freud, 1912, p. 114). For his part, Reik believed that the aspects of awareness that are offered up to the mind of the analyst or of the patient in the form of a 'surprise' are unique and unrepeatable products in that they are the result of that particular experience of dialogue from unconscious to unconscious. For Reik, "the analyst's reluctance to entrust him/herself to a fluctuating attention [to abandon him/herself to his/her own free associations inspired by those of the patient, and to listening to what the patient is saying] is a reluctance to accept the emotional turmoil that evolves out of the process, but the potential to understand and help the patient can only come from listening to this internal reaction to the patient's communication" (Sacchi, 2010, p. 29; my translation).

It is quite conceivable to think that, in speaking about the analyst's intuition and his/her freely fluctuating attention, Reik intuited the role of countertransference, at least to a certain extent. Yet he never spoke of transference or countertransference, probably because for him such a dynamic was not involved in the intuitive process of the clinician. In fact, the principal tool of the analyst was intuition (clinical intuition, seen as independent of the analyst's conflicts, to which he/she was attempting to give order), not countertransference. Nevertheless, as we will soon see, he used the term 'response'. Reik's (1915) official position on the phenomenon of countertransference was the classical one – namely a resistance to overcome by means of self-analysis.

Finally, it is important to remember that in 1948, stimulated by a diatribe on psychoanalytical technique that at this time had taken root in America, where he had emigrated in 1938, Reik wrote *Listening With the Third Ear*, a work in which he again took up and developed the themes already hinted at in 1932 and 1935. It concerns an introduction to psychoanalysis from the perspective of self-observation and self-analysis, the primary characteristic of which consists of bringing to the fore, in this discussion on technique, the clinician's behaviour, closely associated with his/her character traits (Reik saw the technical difficulties of analysis above all as psychological difficulties), as a vehicle which facilitates or impedes the freely fluctuating attention and the dialogue between one unconscious and another. The basic idea is that the psychoanalytic process is founded on the interaction between one unconscious of the analytical duo and the other. Thus in clinical work with the patient, the analyst must listen with the third ear, or rather must listen (without filtering through his/her own theories) to both what the patient says and to his/her own inner voice (usually covered up by the noise of rational thoughts). Psychoanalytic listening is therefore associated with the clinician's subjectivity and his/her willingness to get in touch with his/her own feelings besides those of the patient. Every type of impression, emotion, and thought that reaches the analyst's conscious, following the unconscious working out of the introjected stimuli coming from the patient, Reik defined with the term 'response':

> The analytic response is thus the emotional and intellectual reply to the speech, behavior, and appearance of the patient, and includes awareness of the inner voices of the analyst. Every interpretation, all that the analyst says, the form of his explanation and exposition, are all preceded, and to a great extent determined, by this response. The response is, so to speak, the inside experience of that which the analyst perceives, feels, senses, regarding the patient. It is clear from the preceding chapters that the main part of that response is in its nature unconscious or, to put it otherwise, that only a small part of it become conscious.
>
> *(Reik, 1948, p. 269)*

It is not difficult to see in this 'response', caused by the patient in the analyst, the equivalent of the concept of countertransference. Generally speaking, it is possible to see the 'third ear' as a new version of the 'telephone receiver' about which Freud spoke in 'Recommendations to Physicians Practising Psychoanalysis' (1912b), a work in which the father of psychoanalysis dealt with analytic listening, a particular characteristic of the work of the analyst that for many years was little studied (except in the case of Ferenczi and Reik. The latter was undoubtedly influenced by the Hungarian on the issue of 'tact', the 'dialogue of unconsciouses', the processes of introjection and identification, etc.). In this work, Freud proposed six recommendations with regard to analytic listening: listen without worrying about remembering; do not take notes during the sessions; avoid speculation and pondering, keeping the mind open and free of preconceptions in order to allow oneself to be surprised; maintain a cool demeanour and be free of therapeutic ambition; direct one's unconscious as an analytic instrument in order to listen to the communications of the patient's unconscious; undergo a personal analysis. Besides these recommendations Freud also provided three pieces of advice, inspired by historical circumstances: do not speak about oneself with the patient, but limit oneself to revealing to the patient only that which concerns the patient; do not be guided by pedagogical ambition, but by the patient's capacities; use wisely the patient's intellectual collaboration, and avoid advice on psychoanalytic reading.

The debate between Theodor Reik and Wilhelm Reich (1926, 1933) goes back to the 1930s. Even in the clinical cases of the latter do we find affective reactions to the patient's transference, intuitions that he saw as being linked to the clinical knowledge and skill that the analyst must possess, not to the use of countertransference. The fact that within the theoretical-clinical perspective of character analysis (understood as resistance analysis) Reich never thoroughly dealt with the issue of countertransference, is not surprising if we consider that even though character analysis might have involved a transferring of attention from the symptom to the patient's personality, it did not lead to the consideration of the clinician-patient interaction. Therefore, in the writings of Reik and Reich, the concept of countertransference as a psychoanalytic tool is totally absent, even if it seems that they used it in clinical work. It was Heinrich Racker who subsequently recalled and developed the data provided by these two scholars in order to make use of it in the formulation of his own theory of countertransference (Etchegoyen, 1986). The Reikian intuitions around the concept of the 'third ear' would be taken up and developed in an original way by other authors, which include Paula Heimann and Wilfred Bion.

In terms of Reich, who was the director of the Vienna psychoanalytical technical seminar from 1924 to 1930, it is interesting to point out that his clinical experience led him to reject the 'passive technique' that the analysts of the Berlin school (unlike those of the Vienna-Budapest school) maintained was the only possible way to help the patient. Moreover, he believed that the analyst-blank-screen led to the reinforcement of neurotic patients' sexual taboos. Furthermore, while classical technique called for the analysis of the transference at the moment in which it became a resistance to treatment, Reich, for his part, believed that the transference should be constantly analysed. It is not by chance that Reich recognised, in advance of Ferenczi and Rank, the merit of going beyond passive technique, and the therapeutic limits that it entailed. It is useful to recall here that Freud himself took the opportunity to complain with both Oskar Pfister (letter of October 22, 1927) and Ferenczi (letter of January 4, 1928) about the fact that some analysts tended to take literally, sometimes to an exaggerated extent, his 'recommendations' on psychoanalytic technique in general, and on passive technique in particular.

A few years later, James Strachey, who spent a period of time in Vienna to undergo analysis with Freud (who later chose him to be the official translator of his works into English), provided a very important contribution to the development of the concept of countertransference, even if his work was not specifically concerned with it. Influenced by Kleinian thought, Strachey (1933) played his part in introducing an intersubjective vision of the analytic process, one contained in the recognition of the reciprocity that is established between patient and analyst within the analytic situation. For this author, the source from which the 'mutative interpretations' of transference (formulated by the clinician from his double position as object of the patient's id and auxiliary superego drives) get their effectiveness is the affective relationship created between the participants of the analytical duo. It would be the introjections of some aspects of the real analyst, with which the patient has repeated experience during the course of the analysis, that might make a structural change possible: the psychic change thus consists of a long series of small changes caused by the mutative interpretations, which, when connecting the real object-analyst with the patient's primitive objects, make possible the discovery of the difference between phantasy and reality on the part of the patient – an outcome constantly jeopardised because: "The analytic situation is all the time threatening to degenerate into a 'real' situation" (ivi, p. 146), in the sense that "the patient is all the time on the brink of turning the real external object (the analyst) into the archaic one" (Strachey, 1933, p. 146). When the patient projects into the analyst his/her own primitive introjected images, the analyst becomes for the patient: "like anyone else that he meets in real life – a phantasy object" (Strachey, 1933, p. 146). The point is that, if the object-analyst becomes transformed into the archaic object, the analytical situation ceases to possess the advantages emblematic of it, and the patient relives the experience of an implacable superego instead of living a new experience of a tolerant object, an object 'without anxiety and without anger'. In this sense, the psychoanalytic experience differs in a positive way from the original one in the patient's history.

Another figure who had a great influence on British psychoanalysis and, in more general terms, on the psychoanalysis of object relations was the Scottish psychiatrist Ian D. Suttie (cf. Cassullo, 2010), who in 1928 moved to London and began to work at the Tavistock Clinic. The value of his contribution to the birth and the composition of a total theory of object relations has been recognised only recently, even if Ernest Jones admitted that in 1923, when he was the director of the *International Journal of Psychoanalysis*, he had to take the difficult decision of not publishing an article by Suttie because of the revolutionary principles contained in it (Brome, 1982). Suffice it to say that Suttie, strongly influenced by Hungarian psychoanalysis (his wife, Jane Robertson, also a psychiatrist, translated into English, under the supervision of John Rickman, the second volume of the works of Ferenczi), provided an important work on the transition from the Freudian theory on instinct towards an intersubjective vision of the analytic process, on the basis of whose (therapeutic) success he envisioned the reciprocity of interests and feelings. Suttie (1935) writes that "The Freudian conception of self-expression as a 'detensioning' process or emotional evacuation now seemed to me false and in its place I imagined expression as an offering or stimulus directed to the other person, designed to elicit a response while love itself was essentially a state of active harmonious interplay" (p. 4). For Suttie, the therapist must not inhibit his/her own feelings of tenderness (he speaks of the 'taboo on tenderness' that was developing in our culture). Otherwise the price to pay would be the waning of hope and of the possibility for the patient to see his/her own affective needs embraced. In a more general way, he believes that the most important therapeutic factor is the therapist's love for his/her patient.

In this same year, 1935, the English psychoanalyst Barbara Low, analysed by Hans Sachs in Berlin, and by Jones in London, and influenced by Ferenczi's work, aligned herself on the side of the analyst making use of his/her feelings in his/her clinical work, believing that understanding the patient was only possible through the consciousness of one's own subjective experiences and the freedom to use the feelings encountered in the psychoanalytic situation. According to Low, it is only through his/her own affective activity that the analyst can arrive at the correct translation of the patient's material and its subsequent interpretations. Furthermore, she is precise about the fact that giving space to one's own affective response to the patient's material is very different than reacting to the patient's emotions; the first is an effective modus operandi for good analytical work; the second is detrimental. Thus Low saw the mutative interpretations (Strachey, 1933) as a product of the vision of the analyst who has entered into direct contact with his/her own feelings. She also maintains that it is equally important that the analyst set free his/her own phantasies because it is only through the fusion of the analyst's unconscious and the patient's unconscious that he/she can first shape and illuminate the material received from the patient, and then return it in a form that takes into account both external reality and the patient's unconscious.

In the following year, during a series of lectures held at the Vienna Institute, the Viennese psychoanalyst Otto Fenichel, a psychoanalyst first analysed by Paul Federn, and then once he had moved to Berlin in 1920, by the Hungarian Sándor Rado (who in his turn had been analysed by Abraham), emphasised that the analyst, through his/her personality, has an influence on the patient's transference, and that if he/she wishes to be able to formulate correct interpretations must pay attention to 'not enter into the transference game'. He also pointed out how little was written on this rather important 'countertransference' phenomenon. Fenichel writes:

> The analyst like the patient can strive for direct satisfactions from the analytic relationship as well as make use of the patient for some piece of 'acting out' determined by the analyst's past. Experience shows that the libidinal strivings of the analyst are much less dangerous than his narcissistic needs and defenses against anxieties. Little is said about this subject probably because nothing can act as a protection against such misuse of analysis except the effectiveness of the analyst's own analysis and his honesty with himself.
>
> *(Fenichel, 1936, p. 73)*

Fenichel did not provide a definition of countertransference, but he underlined that training analysis and supervision help the analyst to acquire the ability to observe what is happening inside him/herself (keep in mind that in a work published in the previous year, 1935, Fenichel had asserted that the analyst's unconscious is *the* tool of psychoanalytic technique). Sympathies and antipathies, ennui and pleasure, are inevitable experiences that cannot be eliminated, but from them one can arrive at a certain awareness and control thanks to which the clinician can keep observing the patient and understand his/her resistances in the light of personal history. By adopting this perspective, he warned his colleagues against the risk of misunderstanding the recommendation that the analyst should be a 'mirror' because the fear of countertransference incited many of them to repress any spontaneity, freedom, and naturalness in the relationship with the patient, when instead: "the patient should always be able to rely on the humanness of the analyst" (Fenichel, 1936, p. 74).

The American psychoanalysts O. Spurgeon English and Gerald H.J. Pearson (analysed by Wilhelm Reich), on the other hand, provided an explicit definition of countertransference. They said that: "It is impossible for the physician not to have some attitude toward the patient, and this is called countertransference" (p. 303). Out of this comes a broader vision of countertransference, in which the clinician's every feeling towards the patient is included. Similarly, all the elements of the relationship are included in the transference – a perspective similar to one held by Michael Balint (1933), when he equated countertransference to the therapist's transference towards the patient (cf. also Balint and Balint, 1939; Balint, 1949).

In the same year, Freud published *Analysis Terminable and Interminable*, a work in which, as we have seen in the first chapter, the Viennese Master recognised the impact, not only of the analyst's weak points, but of the whole of his personality, of all of his personal traits, of all that that makes him/her what he/she is – the good and the bad – on the evolution of the psychoanalytic treatment. Freud writes:

> It cannot be disputed that analysts in their own personalities have not invariably come up to the standard of psychical normality to which they wish to educate their patients. Opponents of analysis often point to this fact with scorn and use it as an argument to show the uselessness of analytic exertions. We might reject this criticism as making unjustifiable demands. Analysts are people who have learned to practise a particular art; alongside of this, they may be allowed to be human beings like anyone else. After all, nobody maintains that a physician is incapable of treating internal diseases if his own internal organs are not sound; on the contrary, it may be argued that there are certain advantages in a man who is himself threatened with tuberculosis specializing in the treatment of persons suffering from that disease. But the cases are not on all fours. So long as he is capable of practising at all, a doctor suffering from disease of the lungs or heart is not handicapped either in diagnosing or treating internal complaints; whereas the special conditions of analytic work do actually cause the analyst's own defects to interfere with his making a correct assessment of the state of things in his patient and reacting to them in a useful way. It is therefore reasonable to expect of an analyst, as a part of his qualifications, a considerable degree of mental normality and correctness. In addition, he must possess some kind of superiority, so that in certain analytic situations he can act as a model for his patient and in others as a teacher. And finally we must not forget that the analytic relationship is based on a love of truth – that is, on a recognition of reality – and that it precludes any kind of sham or deceit.
>
> . . . It almost looks as if analysis were the third of those 'impossible' professions in which one can be sure beforehand of achieving unsatisfying results. The other two, which have been known much longer, are education and government. Obviously we cannot demand that the prospective analyst should be a perfect being before he takes up analysis, in other words that only persons of such high and rare perfection should enter the profession. But where and how is the poor wretch to acquire the ideal qualifications which he will need

> in his profession? The answer is, in an analysis of himself, with which his preparation for his future activity begins. For practical reasons this analysis can only be short and incomplete. Its main object is to enable his teacher to make a judgement as to whether the candidate can be accepted for further training. It has accomplished its purpose if it gives the learner a firm conviction of the existence of the unconscious, if it enables him, when repressed material emerges, to perceive in himself things which would otherwise be incredible to him, and if it shows him a first sample of the technique which has proved to be the only effective one in analytic work. This alone would not suffice for his instruction; but we reckon on the stimuli that he has received in his own analysis not ceasing when it ends and on the processes of remodelling the ego continuing spontaneously in the analysed subject and making use of all subsequent experiences in this newly-acquired sense. This does in fact happen, and in so far as it happens it makes the analysed subject qualified to be an analyst himself.
>
> . . . Every analyst should periodically – at intervals of five years or so – submit himself to analysis once more, without feeling ashamed of taking this step. This would mean, then, that not only the therapeutic analysis of patients but his own analysis would change from a terminable into an interminable task.
>
> . . . I am not intending to assert that analysis is altogether an endless business. . . . Our aim will not be to rub off every peculiarity of human character for the sake of a schematic 'normality', nor yet to demand that the person who has been 'thoroughly analysed' shall feel no passions and develop no internal conflicts. The business of the analysis is to secure the best possible psychological conditions for the functions of the ego; with that it has discharged its task.
>
> *(Freud, 1937a, pp. 247–250)*

It is abundantly clear that with this statement, Freud not only confirms the position held by Ferenczi (1927), but goes beyond it and transforms it, recognising as he does the impact that the analyst's personality has on the analytic relationship and, consequently, on the therapeutic process.

The subsequent contribution to the subject comes from the United States, from Karen Horney, who emigrated to the U.S. in 1932, at forty-seven years of age, after being trained at the Berlin Institute (she was in analysis with Abraham and then with Sachs). According to Horney (1939), Freud's most important discovery was that of transference and of the related possibility of using, for therapeutic ends, the emotional reactions of the patient towards the analyst and the analytical situation. She saw the entirety of the patient's actual personality (and his/her feelings around these emotions due to his/her character – like those of anxiety and uncertainty) as an essential factor. She saw therefore transference as much more than the mere transferring of infantile feelings onto the analyst. Horney was critical of those colleagues who followed the recommendation of the analyst as a 'mirror' and who assumed an aloof, cold, and authoritarian attitude, to the point of denying any feelings towards the patient, instead of trying to understand them: "Fortunately the analyst's spontaneity usually prevents him from adhering too strictly to the ideal of being a mirror" (p. 165). For this author, this does not mean that the clinician must offer up his/her own problems to the patient, or that he/she must become emotionally involved with the patient, thus taking the risk of losing a clear vision of the latter's problems. She asserted that:

> The principle that the analyst's emotional reactions should be understood as a 'countertransference' may be objected to on the same grounds as the concept of transference. According to this principle, when an analyst reacts with inner irritation to a patient's tendency to defeat his efforts, he may be identifying the patient with his own father, and thus repeating an infantile situation in which he felt defeated by the father. If, however, the analyst's emotional reactions are understood in the light of his own character structure as it is affected by the patient's actual behavior, it will be seen that his irritation may have arisen because he has, for example, the fantastic notion that he must be able to cure every case and hence feels it a personal humiliation if he does not succeed.
>
> *(Horney, 1939, p. 166)*

For Horney the analytic relationship is a special form of human relationship. She identified three factors characterising this relationship, factors that allow the analyst to work psychoanalytically with the patient. The first is the clinician's detachment from the patient, one that is greater than that of the people who are part of the patient's life; and since the clinician's attention is centred on the reactions of the patient in order to understand them, his/her reaction will not be spontaneous and subjective. The second is that the analyst has been in analysis, a fact which should have provided him/her with a greater capacity for self-observation and control of his/her own reactions. And finally, the third is the analyst's awareness that the patient reacts with him/her in the same way that he/she reacts in every other relationship and this allows the analyst to remove any personal trace from the patient's responses.

A view of countertransference, like Horney's, as we have seen, had already been envisaged to some degree by others: like Ferenczi, Glover and W. Reich in Europe, and Stern in America.

At the beginning of this chapter, I hinted at Ferenczi's clinical experiments, ones which his student and friend Michael Balint continued with, in his own work. Because of the pressures of anti-Semitism, Balint moved from Hungary to Manchester (1939) and then to London (1945). He played an important role in the dissemination of Ferenczian thought (which for years floated on the fringes of the psychoanalytic mainstream), within the British psychoanalytic movement, especially among the Independents (Haynal, 1987). (Balint brought with him to England the *Clinical Diary* and all of the letters Freud had written to Ferenczi, material entrusted to him for safekeeping by Ferenczi's wife, Gizella, until the right moment to publish it came along. Eventually he entrusted this material to his niece, Judith Dupont, who edited its publication.)

The Balints[4] (Balint and Balint, 1939; Balint, 1949) focussed on the analyst, who, with his/her own style and personality plays a crucial role in the development and termination of treatment. Within this conception, the people involved in the transformations happening within analysis are two: the analysand and the analyst. Balint preferred the observation of the analyst by other analysts to Ferenczi's idea of mutual analysis because if one conceives countertransference as normal transference towards the patient, it follows that, like the patient, the clinician, as well, experiences transference. The difference lies in the fact that the clinician must be capable of understanding what is happening and what is being created in the relationship with that patient in that moment. In the words of Alice and Michael Balint: "[T]he analytical situation is the result of an interplay between the patient's transference and the analyst's countertransference" (p. 228), and in this process

> a patient analysed in any of the many individual ways shall learn to know his own unconscious mind and not that of his analyst. . . . Returning to Freud's metaphor, we see that the analyst must really become like a well-polished mirror – not, however, by behaving passively like an inanimate thing, but by reflecting without distortion the whole of his patient. The more clearly the patient can see himself in the reflection, the better our technique; and if this has been achieved, it does not matter greatly how much of the analyst's personality has been revealed by his activity or passivity, his severity or lenience, his methods of interpretation, etc.
>
> *(Balint and Balint, 1939, p. 229)*

It seems evident that with the contribution of the Balints the conception of countertransference has broadened to include not only the pathological emotional reaction, but every emotional reaction of the clinician with respect to the client (embracing as well his/her professional attitude). It is necessary to point out that six years earlier another Hungarian analyst, Fanny Hann-Kende (1933), analysed by Deutsch and a pupil of Ferenczi, when considering Freud's thoughts on telepathy, had spoken of the positive function of countertransference, defined by her as a function of the patient's and the analyst's transference. In this period, other analysts were also occupied with telepathic phenomena. For example, the Hungarian psychoanalyst István Hollós (1933), first analysed by Freud and then by Paul Federn, believed they represented a reciprocal unconscious action (an experience jointly worked through) and not a mere isolated perceptive action on the part of one or the other.

It is worth highlighting that various aspects of Winnicott's theorisations and those of the theories of many analysts belonging to the Independent group are connected to many of Michael Balint's conceptions, such as the central position assigned to the mother-child relationship and the recognition of the key role played by an environment which facilitates the emotional development of a child towards health rather than pathology.[5] According to Balint: "The ill-ness' of his patient . . . is largely the result of early environmental factors in the patient's life" (Khan, 1969b, p. 238). The importance that he attributed to the role of primary object relations is easily observed where the clinician-patient relationship is placed at the centre of the analytic situation (seen as a process): "a situation where relations to an object – admittedly a very peculiar object – are of overwhelming importance" (Balint, 1949, p. 120). The relational-interpersonal situation, whether primary or analytical, is determined by the inseparable interweaving of transference-countertransference: this is the object relation. It will now become more evident why Balint placed at the centre of the psychoanalytic process and technique something which belongs to the uniqueness and unrepeatability of the relationship between a specific patient and a specific analyst. I should hasten to add that Balint did not speak of a precocious primary object relation, as did Ronald Fairbairn and Melanie Klein (from whose thought it differs when also considering hatred and sadism as secondary to the loss of primary love). However, instead of stopping at the object relation, Balint tried to plunge into the experiential reality of the subject in order to be able to describe its development from the 'inside'. It is significant that for Balint: "The most important field of investigation for this coming theory must be the *analyst's behaviour in the psycho-analytic situation*, or, as I prefer to phrase it, the analyst's contribution to the creating and maintaining of the psycho-analytic situation" (p. 121), since clinical phenomena "happen in an inter-relation between two individuals, in a constantly changing and developing object-relation" (p. 123). Moreover, as Masud Khan (1969b) points out, Balint assigned a reduced importance to the emergence of feelings of hate (Winnicott, 1947) and envy (Klein, 1957) in the analyst. In fact, in 1968, Balint (Balint and Balint, 1968), the then president of the British Psychoanalytical Society, criticised the psychoanalytic technique widely practiced at the end of the 1960s: he believed that the frequency and excessiveness with which aggression, envy, and hate were emerging from the material brought up in the session by the patients of some analysts (the Kleinian ones) were in part due to the type of attitude – self-assured, wise, and probably omnipresent – that such analysts transmitted through their interpretations. This would also explain why Kleinian analysts were so preoccupied with introjections and idealisation. This was the impression that Balint had after several scientific meetings with Kleinian colleagues and from reading their publications. It would be interesting to find out if that impression was shared with at least some of the patients of Kleinian analysts.

I will end this chapter by referring to the results of an empirical research study from 1938 by Edward Glover. Shortly after becoming the Director of Research of the London Institute of Psychoanalysis, and prompted by the uniformity of clinical difficulties, which over the years, his training pupils, as well as beginner and expert analysts, were reporting to him, Glover prepared a questionnaire with the purpose of investigating in direct fashion ('What are you actually doing in analysis?') the real state of affairs in terms of the technique used by psychoanalysts of the British Psychoanalytical Society. This study had "the merit of being the first and moderately successful attempt to penetrate the curtain of uncommunicativeness behind which psychoanalysts are only too prone to conceal their technical anxieties, inferiorities and guilts" (Glover, 1955, pp. vi–vii). The questionnaire was sent to twenty-nine member psychoanalysts of the British Psychoanalytical Society and twenty-four responded. This sample was representative, in both experience and theoretical orientation, of all of the British Group of the time. According to Glover, from the answers received, it could be inferred that, in some way, factors of guilt and timidity were at work, but the only way forward was to accept the answers for what they were, keeping in mind however that the consensus of opinion, on some of the questions, could be a sign of a successful defence. Glover decided to publish the results of the study in 1940 under the title of *An Investigation of the Technique of Psychoanalysis* (Glover and Brierley, 1940), and, convinced that at a distance of more than fifteen years the difficulties expressed by his colleagues in training were the same, even if expressed in a more complex language, he republished them in his book *The Technique of Psychoanalysis* in 1955.

I will now put forward some of the questions with their respective answers that I believe to be interesting in terms of our review.

> ***How far do you think the personality of the analyst plays part in the conduct of analysis?***
>
> More than half the replies agreed that the personality of the analyst plays 'a considerable part', 'a more important part than is always realised', etc., in the conduct of analysis. Amongst these some regret this influence, e.g. 'unavoidably; ideally minimum'. A small minority take the opposite view, e.g. 'Very little part', 'less than one might think'. One said 'not large unless technique faulty'. Another 'some importance but skill more important'. One answer suggested that the personality probably affects the order in which transference situations develop and the sequence of material.
>
> *(Glover, 1955, p. 306)*
>
> ***Do you find the practice of analysis acts as a therapeutic procedure for the analyst or not; does it increase or diminish his own conflict?***
>
> Answers here were varied and rather confusing, apparently because there was a tendency to equate diminution of conflict with therapeutic effect. A majority consider the total or dominant effect is therapeutic, provided that the temporary exacerbations of conflict which may be produced in the course of the treatment are appreciated, i.e. analysed. It was recognised that the analyst is subject to a process of continuous conflict-stimulation which is probably without parallel. This effect is increased in proportion to the number of cases

seen daily. A minority replied in the negative, 'not therapeutic', and regard such a notion as 'suspect'. On the other hand, some point out the wealth of opportunity for sublimation and even for direct satisfaction (e.g. of curiosity) offered by the practice of analysis.

(ivi, p. 307)

Do you ever admit to the patient the possibility of being wrong? Do you ever admit to the patient the possibility of 'not knowing'?

This is another of the few questions which produced unanimous replies. All answered in favour of admitting fallibility to the patient. Only one special reservation was made to the effect that it may be unwise to do this with patients whose deep anxieties are so strong that they still 'need' to feel the analyst is omnipotent.

(ivi, p. 308)

Do you believe in giving some indication of a positive friendly attitude as distinct from the friendliness implied in 'professional interest'?

One-third replied 'Yes', another third, 'No', i.e. should not exceed 'professional' friendliness. Of the affirmative replies one insisted that the analyst must not be afraid to be human.

(Glover, 1955, p. 306)

If you have no fixed or rigid practice in these matters, what indications do you follow? For example, even if you hold in general that the analyst should be a neutral or shadowy figure, are there instances where you believe he should be more of a 'real' figure for the patient? If so, what respects?

Two answers only were against departure from neutrality under any circumstances. About one-third favour neutrality with some qualifications, e.g. 'unless a kindly super-ego rôle is necessary in a crisis' and 'ego must feel the analyst a stand-by'. Another third insist that the analyst must be throughout human and real. Some of these think that the opposition between neutrality and reality is false and that the conditions of analysis allow the patient ample opportunity to prove the analyst's reality without the latter abandoning his neutrality by any form of self-assertion. A small minority, however, believe that the analyst should deliberately emphasise his 'reality' in some cases of acute conflict, where the ego is weak. One recognises the need that may arise for extra ego support, but thinks this can best be given by directing analysis to the most urgent problems.

(ivi, p. 309)

How far should the spontaneity of the analyst be restricted? Are there any dangers or drawbacks in such restrictions?

Only twelve answers were received. Of these, six realise some restriction (e.g. of speech) is necessary, but find it difficult to draw the line between desirable and undesirable restraint. What must be avoided is the establishment of an unfavourable 'inhibited' atmosphere. Five feel that the analyst ought to be able to trust himself to be spontaneous, and that restriction is often defensive and therefore to be distrusted. Only one sees no dangers in restriction.

(Glover, 1955, p. 306)

How far do you think the patient's unconscious capacity to read the analyst's psychological tendencies should be allowed for? (This involves the problem of how far the transference situation is solely a projection or displacement on the part of the patient, or how far it is a (conscious, unconscious) recognition of the real (conscious, unconscious) attitudes of the analyst.)

Quite a large majority appeared to believe that patients observe or read the analyst's unconscious. There was a tendency to regard the transference as a mixed product, but to estimate its 'projection' components as variable but high in proportion to the 'perceptual'. One said 80 per cent. Several remarked that the projection elements are the only ones of fundamental importance for analysis.

(ivi, p. 310)

Would you admit change of mood, anxiety, or personal illness to the patient?

Most of those who answered are willing to make admissions to patients, in answer to questions, confirming observations or under pressure of necessity, e.g. to account for missing appointments. A small minority do not, as a rule, confirm or deny patients' suppositions, or make admissions. Others regulate their admissions by consideration of the probable effect on the patient.

(Glover, 1955, p. 306)

Do you communicate personal opinions (e.g. cultural, social, or political views)?

The majority do not communicate personal opinions (two 'not consciously', 'unless by implication'). One makes a special point of not doing so. Others do so 'rarely' or 'at times'. Ones answer was a definite 'Yes'.

(ivi, p. 311)

Notes

1 Before Klein, those who dealt with the psychoanalytic treatment of children were the team of Freud/Max Graf (the father of Herbert Graf, *alias* 'Little Hans') and the Austrian psychoanalyst Hermine Hug-Hellmuth (she was killed by her eighteen-year-old nephew whom she had previously tried to psychoanalyze). At the same time as Klein, Anna Freud had also begun to psychoanalytically treat children, but these were older than Klein's patients, who were sometimes less than three years old.

2 In 1923 Ferenczi and Rank, in considering the problem of the analyst's narcissistic component, wrote that: "The narcissism of the analyst seems suited to create a particularly fruitful source of mistakes; among others the development of a kind of narcissistic countertransference that provokes the person being analyzed into pushing into the foreground certain things which flatter the analyst and, on the other hand, into suppressing remarks and associations of an unpleasant nature in relation to him. . . . The anxiety and the sense of guilt of the patient can never be overcome without this self-criticism, requiring indeed a certain overcoming of himself on the part of the analyst; and yet these two emotional factors are the most essential for bringing about and maintaining the repression" (p. 41). It is evident that Ferenczi, similarly to Freud (1937a), saw the analyst as a 'real' person, who influences the analytical situation; thus differentiating between a countertransference as a response to the patient's transference and the transference of the analyst onto the patient. According to Ferenczi, it is the clinician's narcissism and his resistance to the analytical process that cause the patient's resistance and negative therapeutic reactions.

3 Henri Ellenberger has clearly shown that the relationship between patient and 'clinician' (healer, witch doctor, shaman, hypnotist, psychoanalyst) is the common basis of the various therapeutic techniques, and the dynamic of the path to recovery (in which the influence of the clinician always depends, even though to varying degrees, on the qualities that the patient attributes to him/her).

4 I use the plural because Michael Balint's psychoanalytic thought is inextricably bound up with that of his wife, Alice Székely-Kovács. It was the latter who, at the time of her university studies, lent a copy of Freud's *Totem and Taboo* to Michael. Alice and Michael married in 1921, and three years later, because of the political situation in Budapest, moved to Berlin. The atmosphere that reigned at the Berlin Institute was stimulating, but the analysis that both of them began to undergo with Sachs was unsatisfactory, too intellectual and akin to an indoctrination. Therefore after two years, they decided to return to Budapest to continue their analysis with Ferenczi (Haynal, 1987; Dupont, 2009). In order to have an idea of how each influenced the thought of the other, all that is necessary is to read what Michael wrote in 1952, in the preface to the first edition of *Primary Love and Psycho-Analytic Technique*: "Starting with our shared enthusiasm for *Totem and Taboo* till her death in 1939, Alice and I read, studied, lived and worked together. All our ideas – no matter in whose mind they first arose – were enjoyed and then tested, probed and criticized in our endless discussions. Quite often it was just chance that decided which of us should publish a particular idea. . . . We published only one paper jointly, although almost all of them could have been printed under our joint names. In fact, our development was so intertwined that this book would be incomplete, in the true sense of the word, without her contribution" (Balint, 1965, p. viii).

5 We must mention Ian Suttie (1935), Ronald Fairbairn (1941, 1944), John Bowlby (1944, 1951), and Donald Winnicott (1945, 1950–55, 1956, 1960a) as some of the British analysts who explicitly and entirely recognised the importance of this environment.

4

THE SECOND WORLD WAR, THE CONTROVERSIAL DISCUSSIONS, AND THE TRIPARTITE DIVISION OF THE BRITISH PSYCHOANALYTICAL SOCIETY

On January 30, 1933, Adolf Hitler received the mandate to become Chancellor of the Reich. The National Socialist Party formed a minority government with the Nationalists – a government that from the outset was characterised by the dismantling of the democratic system and the persecution of political adversaries and entire social groups (Jews, Gypsies, etc.). For many Jewish psychoanalysts, especially after the issuing of the anti-Semitic laws in 1935, life became extremely difficult and emigration the only option. Ernest Jones, the then president of the IPA, in close collaboration with Anna Freud, endeavoured his utmost to find solutions which would allow as many analysts as possible to leave Germany and move to England, the U.S., or other countries.

In the meantime, also worried about the growing theoretical disagreements between the London School and the Vienna School, Jones strove to organise a series of exchange-conferences that eventually took place between 1935 and 1936. The first conference was held by Jones himself in Vienna; the second by Robert Woelder in London; the third by Joan Rivière, followed by a conference led by Jones in Vienna. These exchange-conferences did not have the desired effect, and with the publication in 1937 of the English translation of Anna Freud's *The Ego and the Mechanisms of Defence*, the anti-Kleinian opposition sparked by a section of the British Society, more specifically by the continental analysts, recently immigrated to England, became even stronger.

When Germany conquered Austria in 1938, the number of Jews subjected to German dominance substantially increased just as the climate of collective resentment further intensified. Jones went to Vienna and succeeded in his effort to persuade Freud to request visas for himself and his family and to leave Austria. The procurement of the visas on the part of Freud, father of an allegedly Jewish science, was not an automatic affair to be taken for granted. The interventions of Princess Marie Bonaparte, who maintained close ties with the Greek royal family, and of the

American diplomat William Bullit, were decisive. Thus in May 1938, Freud moved to London, as did many other Viennese analysts, while the majority emigrated overseas.

As a consequence, during the years just before the Second World War, the British Psychoanalytical Society was characterised by a convergence of middle-European cultures upon its ranks, a situation forced upon the organisation by the realities of war. The magnitude of continental analysts who immigrated to London was such that in 1938 they numbered one third of all members of a Society that in that year had seen the arrival of Edward Bibring, Margarethe Bibring, Dorothy Burlingham, Ludwig Eidelberg, Kate Friedlander, Anna Freud, Sigmund Freud, Hedwig Hoffer, Wilhelm Hoffer, Otto Isakower, Salomea Isakower, Ernst Kris, Marianne Kris, Barbara Lantos, Max Schur, Erwin Stengel, and Hans Thorner. Soon after, their numbers exceeded that of their British colleagues. All of this brought with it an inevitable change to the socio-cultural character of the Society, creating more than a few difficulties in communication between the various members (difficulties due in part to a poor knowledge of English on the part of many continental analysts, a circumstance that generated ambiguity and confusion). It should be clear that, within this prevailing situation, a mutual enrichment prompted by scientific exchange was practically non-existent.

The outbreak of war had the further effect of scattering the various groups: some analysts were called to arms as doctors, while others left London to protect themselves from the aerial bombardments. For example, Jones went to Sussex, leaving the management of the Psychoanalytical Society to Edward Glover, while Klein withdrew to Pitlochry. Upon their return to London, they found a Society divided not only by profound theoretical discordances, but also by the dissatisfaction circulating among the members over the handling of political-administrative aspects of the organisation, and by struggles over the management of the training of the analyst-candidates.

By 1940 the Society's internal tensions were fierce enough to prompt James Strachey to write the following letter:

> Dear Glover,
>
> . . . I'm afraid there's no chance of my getting to London for the Training Committee tomorrow. I should rather like you to know (for your personal information) that – if it comes to a show-down – I'm very strongly in favour of compromise at all costs. The trouble seems to me to be with extremism, on both sides. My own view is that Mrs K. has made some highly important contributions to PA, but that it's absurd to make out (a) that they cover the whole subject or (b) that their validity is axiomatic. On the other hand I think it's equally ludicrous for Miss F. to maintain that PA is a Game Reserve belonging to the F. family and that Mrs K's ideas are totally subversive.
>
> These attitudes on both sides are of course purely religious and the very antithesis of science. They are also (on both sides) infused by, I believe, a desire to

> dominate the situation and in particular the future – which is why both sides lay so much stress on the training of candidates; actually, of course, it's a megalomaniac mirage to suppose that you can control the opinions of people you analyse beyond a very limited point. But in any case it ought naturally to be the aim of a training analysis to put the trainee into a position to arrive at his own decisions upon moot points – not to stuff him with your own private dogmas.
>
> In fact I feel like Mercutio about it. Why should these wretched fascists and (bloody foreigners) communists invade our peaceful compromising island? – But I see I'm more feverish than I'd thought. Anyhow, I feel that any suggestion of a 'split' in the society ought to be condemned and resisted to the utmost.
>
> (Strachey, quoted in King and Steiner, 1991, pp. 24–25)

At the beginning of the 1940s, the atmosphere that permeated the Society's scientific meetings was so tense that Eva Rosenfeld, who had been in analysis both with Freud and Melanie Klein, remembers them as 'nightmare years' (Rayner, 1991). This was going on while 'on the outside' a world war was in full swing, one which some analysts seemed hardly to be aware of, so taken were they by the discussions on theoretical issues. An episode that perhaps can shed light on the situation is the one that took place during the meeting of February 17, 1943. It so happened that there was an air raid going on over London at the precise time that the members were engaged in a heated discussion. They did not seem to notice what was happening outside because they were so involved in the battle taking place inside. Each of them remained glued to their chairs until Winnicott at a certain point had to intervene in order to restore a sense of reality, saying: "I should like to point out that there is an air raid going on" (Grosskurth, 1986, p. 321).

This is the panorama that encompassed the turbulent controversies involving two groups of analysts, referring respectively to Anna Freud and Melanie Klein, and relating to the temporal origin of unconscious phantasy, superego, and Oedipus, to the concept of internal objects, and to the role played by the death instinct in the intrapsychic conflict. This situation prompted Jones in 1942 to propose a series of scientific discussions supervised by a moderator. Thus it was between 1943 and 1944 that the well-known *controversial discussions* (cf. King and Steiner, 1991) took place, ones that were characterised by a large variety of theoretical-clinical papers, whose goal was to reduce the technical-political rifts that, realistically speaking, seemed irreconcilable at the time. There was a total of eleven meetings, of which only a few were presided over by Jones, who passed the burden of chairing the most important meetings onto Glover, who certainly was not neutral (one only has to remember that a little after the termination of the controversial discussions, Glover called for the expulsion of the Kleinians from the British Society, mainly because he saw the situation, primarily that of psychoanalytic training, from a scientific point of view, as desperate. He finally reached the point of resigning himself from the Society because he considered his presence incompatible with that of Klein).

We should keep in mind that each of the two factions in this struggle, the Kleinians and the Anna Freudians, had little more than a dozen analysts, while the majority of members (about sixty) did not side with either group. These then went on to form what came to be known as the 'middle group'. Some of analysts that made up the Kleinian group were Susan Isaacs, Paula Heimann, Joan Rivière, and others; among those that composed the Anna Freudian group were Willie Hoffer, Kate Friedlander, Barbara Lantos, Dorothy Burlingham, and others; while among the analysts that did not side with either of these, there were Marjorie Brierley, Ernest Jones, Sylvia Payne, Ella Sharpe, and James Strachey.

As already pointed out, a rapprochement between the two factions was not reached and thus a Commission, made up of three impartial and outstanding delegates, Sylvia Payne, John Rickman, and William Gillespie, was set up with the task of drafting a new Constitution, ultimately drawn up in 1944. It had a democratic structure and called for regular elections. In 1946, Jones resigned his position as president of the Society, one which he had held without interruption since the foundation of the organisation. Payne was elected in his place.

Since of primary importance among the reasons for the dispute between Anna Freud and Melanie Klein was the training of analyst-candidates, one of the points pertaining to a modification in organisational structure was specifically about training norms. Two separate courses for the training of candidates were set up: the 'A Group' was open to Kleinians and to the analysts from the 'middle group', while the 'B Group' was reserved for the students of Anna Freud and her collaborators (those who today are identified as contemporary Freudians). Moreover, each candidate could choose the first supervisor of his or her own clinical cases from among the Kleinian group or the Anna Freudian group, while the second supervisor did not have to belong to either of the two (and thus the middle group came into being). This stipulation concerning the agreement over the student's choice of supervisor lasted into the 1950s, but at that point most of the analysts and students clearly identified with one of the three groups, and so a 'gentlemen's agreement' was arrived at, one that was never formalised in writing, but which divided the Society into three groups, each with their respective training programmes and each having the right to equal representation within the Administrative Commission.

The analysts of the middle group called themselves 'the Independents', a name chosen to indicate a common philosophical attitude on the part of the members making up the group – an attitude characterised by an openness to ideas from different sources, without any relinquishing of freedom of creative and original thought and style, in addition to a descriptive and empirically explorative method. The Independents have therefore carried forward that mental attitude which prevailed before the tri-partition of the British Psychoanalytical Society (Rayner, 1991). Albeit with each member having his/her own original approach, the Independents have always shared, and still do to this day, the belief in the importance attributed to environmental factors (mental and emotional, besides the physical), to external reality, in the psychic-physical development of the human being, without adopting a rigidly environmentalist position. Out of this comes the value attributed to precocious traumas on the subsequent development of the individual and the resulting influence that a facilitating environment can exercise over a healthy development. The analytical situation, seen as facilitating a healthy development, is defined as a symbolisation, a metaphor for the parent-child relationship in which the latter can introject the healing modalities (holding, handling, and object-presenting) of the therapist.

Over the course of time, the three groups have become more clearly defined, but the number of members is still higher in the middle group.

5

THE WORK OF MELANIE KLEIN AND HER INFLUENCE ON THE DEVELOPMENT OF THE CONCEPT OF COUNTERTRANSFERENCE

Melanie Klein can be placed among those scholars who have most contributed to the development of psychoanalysis. She has done this while keeping true to Freud's vision, but, at the same time, playing the role of key figure in the transition from the classical drive/structure model to the relational/structure model (Greenberg and Mitchell, 1983). She places the psychogenesis of manic-depressive states (Klein, 1934) at the foundation of her entire theorisation – a theorisation influenced by the misfortunes, which had a decided influence on her life at the time. Among these events that marked Klein's life in this period, we can enumerate the death of her oldest son, Hans, in a mountain-climbing accident, the decline of her relationship with her daughter, Melitta (who immigrated to London in 1927 and contributed much to psychoanalysis, even if her work is little known or recognised; cf. Cassullo, 2016) – a relationship that, within a few years, ended in total estrangement – and the death of Ferenczi. It should be remembered here that Klein moved to Budapest in 1910 in order to follow her husband whose work took him to the Hungarian capital. Here she came into contact with Freudian thought and, in the aftermath of a bout of depression, she decided to enter into analysis with Ferenczi in 1914. This analyst played a significant role in encouraging and supporting Klein in her interest in child psychoanalysis. Subsequently, at the conference held in The Hague in 1920, Klein met Karl Abraham. He made a profound impression on her and urged her to continue her work in child analysis. Ultimately this meeting persuaded her to move to Berlin, where, after a lengthy and sustained attempt at persuasion, she convinced Abraham to accept her as a patient in analysis. This second analysis began in 1924 and lasted only nine months because of the premature death of the German analyst. Hanna Segal (1979) tells us that

> Melanie Klein's relation to her two analysts was very different. She felt grateful to Ferenczi for the encouragement he gave to her work and she also felt that she derived from his analysis a conviction about the importance of

> unconscious dynamics. But Ferenczi did not analyse the negative transference (hostile feelings towards the analyst), and she felt that this analysis did not give her any lasting insight. . . . For Abraham she had unmitigated gratitude and admiration. The nine months' analysis she had with him gave her, she thought, a true understanding of psychoanalysis. His premature death was one of the great losses of her life. . . . Although she took from Ferenczi the concept of introjection, Abraham's work, particularly on melancholia, was the more important influence. She considered herself his pupil and her work a contribution and development of Freud's and Abraham's.
>
> *(pp. 32–33)*

Thus, despite recognition of her debt to Ferenczi, who had initiated her into psychoanalysis, helping her to understand its real essence and importance, making her aware of her aptitude for child analysis, and spurring her on to develop her capacity to understand the psychology of young children (cf. Klein, 1932), the psychoanalytical contribution of Ferenczi has almost been totally excluded from Klein's work, and even, to a great extent, from the Kleinian tradition.

Reading her treatise on the psychogenesis of manic-depressive states we realise how, from the moment of writing this work, Klein began to distance herself from Freud's (for example 1905) and Abraham's (for example 1924) theoretical structure, a structure from which her previous writings emanated (and yet it is also true that the embryo of her theory of object relations can be found even in her earliest writings). Elizabeth Spillius (1994), in fact, identifies two phases in Klein's theoretical work: the first entails the articles written between 1920 and 1933; the second, those written between 1934 and 1960 (especially 1934, 1938, 1946, and 1957), in which she deals with paranoid-schizoid and depressive positions.[1] These latter positions include specific anxieties, defence mechanisms, and internal and external object relations. It is clear that the real watershed is 'A Contribution to the Psychogenesis of Manic-Depressive States' (1934), from which point Klein began to recognise the importance that the external environment also played in the process of child development. The internal world and internal objects are established at the time the child makes use of the mechanisms of splitting, introjection, and projection primarily, and secondarily of those of idealisation, devaluation, and denial. What follows is that the internal world is not formed as a faithful reproduction of the external world. The latter contributes to a modelling based on the former, while the former represents a lens for perceiving the latter.

It was precisely within such a theoretical framework that it was possible to develop a theoretical-clinical concept, destined to hold a key position in Kleinian and post-Kleinian thought, namely, projective identification. More precisely, one could say that the characteristic and distinctive concept of Kleinian psychoanalysis is not one of projective identification, but that of paranoid-schizoid and depressive positions (Spillius, 2012b).

It is important to point out that projective identification as a specific concept was made famous by Melanie Klein, but as in the case of all concepts, it didn't just appear out of nowhere. There was already much research material dealing with the same phenomenon, but other linguistic terms of classification were in use. Invaluable contributions on this subject can already be found in Sigmund Freud's work (for example 1895, 1905, 1910a, 1910b) and in those of some analysts of the first generation like Karl Abraham (1911) and Sándor Ferenczi (1913), or of the second generation like Anna Freud (1936). I will not delve into these roots for the moment, but will concentrate my attention on Klein's elucidations and on the developments generated by the British Kleinian analysts. That said, despite the fact that the date of the first description of the mechanism of projective identification is usually considered to be 1946 with Klein's 'Notes on Some Schizoid Mechanisms', in reality, as Giovanni Massidda (1999, 2009; cf. also Steiner, 1999; Spillius, 2007, 2012a) has alluded to, the Trieste-born Edoardo Weiss had already introduced the concept of *projektive Identifizierung* (projective identification) in 1924–25. Klein was aware of Weiss's work, which focusses on the explanation of the choice of sexual object, and she even cites it in her essay *The Psychoanalysis of Children* (1932), without however emphasising the term *projektive Identifizierung*. Massidda, exclusively referencing the United Kingdom, mentions that it is also possible to find another writer that dealt with the issue before Klein, namely Marjorie Brierley, who spoke about projective identification in relation to the "capacity to put oneself in other people's shoes" (1945, p. 96), and in relation to "empathy" (1947, p. 91). It is odd that even though both Brierley's and Klein's articles were published in the *International Journal of Pychoanalysis*, and both psychoanalysts belonged to the British Psychoanalytical Society, no one for over sixty years seems to have noticed this fact. Moreover, as Phyllis Grosskurth (1986) points out, it seems that Klein asked Herbert Rosenfeld, who was in analysis with her at the time, to postpone the publication of his 'Analysis of a Schizophrenic State of Depersonalization' (1947), so that she could first publish an article that she was then working on 'Notes on some Schizoid Mechanisms' – a request that would seem to have been made precisely because Rosenfeld was dealing with projective identification in that article (Steiner, 1999). Such behaviour does not sound foreign to Klein, who it seems told Rosenfeld that, when she was in analysis with Abraham, he usually refrained from formulating similar interpretations, if he thought that she would have been able to use them before him in some essay (Grosskurth, 1986). The underlying psychological dynamics obviously have something to do with the issue of taking precedence in the formulation of ideas, of cryptomnesia and plagiarism, as Massidda (2009) indicates.

This being said, let us see what Klein writes on the subject of projective identification:

> The phantasied attacks on the mother follow two main lines: one is the predominantly oral impulse to suck dry, bite up, scoop out and rob the mother's body of its good contents. . . . The other line of attack derives from the anal and urethral impulses and implies expelling dangerous substances (excrements) out of the self and into the mother. Together with these harmful

> excrements, expelled in hatred, split off parts of the ego are also projected on to the mother or, as I would rather call it, into the mother. These excrements and bad parts of the self are meant not only to injure the object but also to control it and take possession of it. In so far as the mother comes to contain the bad parts of the self, she is not felt to be a separate individual but is felt to be the bad self.
>
> Much of the hatred against parts of the self is now directed towards the mother. This leads to a particular kind of identification which establishes the prototype of an aggressive object-relation. I suggest for these processes the term projective identification.[2]
>
> It is, however, not only the bad parts of the self which are expelled and projected, but also good parts of the self. . . . The projection of good feelings and good parts of the self into the mother is essential for the infant's ability to develop good object relations and to integrate his ego.
>
> *(Klein, 1946, p. 102)*

It is important to keep in mind that in the section of the article that precedes the above quote, Klein says that "the vital need to deal with anxiety forces the early ego to develop some primary mechanisms and defences" (p. 101), in keeping with the hypothesis that "one of the driving forces of projective identification is the ego's need to survive" (O'Shaughnessy, 2012, p. 161).

Klein continues to deal with the issue of projective identification in the essays 'On Identification' (1955) and in *Envy and Gratitude* (1957). It is also possible to find passing references to this phenomenon in other of her writings. If it seems that this concept does not figure prominently in Klein's work, we must remember what Spillius (2012a) has pointed out that if we take into consideration her unpublished material, consistent with her theoretical reflections and clinical examples, found in the Klein Archive (donated by the Melanie Klein Foundation to the Wellcome Library of the History of Medicine in 1984), we find valuable and substantial contributions to the subject. Documents B98 (1946–47) and D17 (1950s) (cf. Spillius, 2007, 2012a) are especially relevant to this treatise. Moreover, we are well aware that Klein often referred to the concept of projective identification in her reflections on what was happening in her clinical work with patients (Gammill, 1989; Spillius, 2012a).

Thus we can see that:

> Klein uses the term 'projective identification' to describe a complex set of processes: part of the self is split off and projected into an object, the individual reacts to the object as if it were the self or the part of the self that has been projected into it. The individual who projects in this way will then in phantasy introject the object as coloured by what he or she has projected into it. It is through such constant interplay that the inner world of self and internal objects is built up.
>
> *(Spillius, 1994, p. 336)*

In the Kleinian vision: "the analyst must simply be a medium in relation to whom the different imagos can be activated and the phantasies lived through, in order to be analysed" (Klein, 1929, pp. 203–204), and the analyst: "must have no preference for any particular rôle; he must accept that which comes to him naturally from the analytic situation" (ivi, p. 204). Thus it is clear that the 'analytic situation' takes on a unipersonal character, in which the unfolding of transference is understood as a dynamic to which the clinician (the 'external' observer) does not contribute (because the conception of defence mechanisms, including that of projective identification, fundamentally remains connected to the drive model, without acquiring a true intersubjective value). Transference is here understood as an "expression in the analytic situation of the forces and relationships of the internal world"[3] (Spillius, 1994, p. 348), or rather of that dynamic product (the result of a continuous process) of the interaction between unconscious phantasy, defence mechanisms, and experiences from external reality.

It is obvious that for Klein projective identification played a fundamental role in the analytic process, while countertransference – which would have great significance for post-Kleinian analysts – was seen as something that interferes with the analytic process, for example by intensifying the analyst's identification with the patient, thus preventing the uncovering of the mind's deepest layers (Klein, 1957). Such a view of countertransference is anything but surprising, especially if one considers the role that the analysis of transference played within the Kleinian theoretical-clinical structure: it is the patient's inner world in its entirety that must be analysed, not just the analytical relationship. This is because, with object relations seen as existing from the child's birth (the relationship with the breast), and not the result of an evolving maturation process, beginning with a primary phase of autoeroticism and narcissism, transference (comprising that which is established in relation to the analyst) "originates in the same processes which in the earliest stages determine object-relations" (Klein, 1952, p. 436). Despite this, Klein never publicly rejected the concept of countertransference, even if she tried to impede its diffusion, as when she asked Paula Heimann not to present her work 'On Countertransference' to the 1949 International Congress of Psychoanalysis in Zurich. Heimann responded in this manner: "Do you think it gives me such great pleasure to stand in your shadow my whole life long?"[4] (Grosskurth, 1986, p. 378). In addition, there was no shortage of attacks on those who attempted to make countertransference an implement useful to the analytical process. One of these episodes occurred during a scientific meeting held in 1956 under the auspices of the British Psychoanalytical Society. During the discussion that followed Margaret Little's presentation of her work on countertransference, Klein acidly commented that the only thing the work demonstrated was Little's need for more analysis.[5] At this point, Winnicott, who was presiding over the meeting, angrily addressed Klein, telling her she had no right to speak like that, and adding that: "We *all* need more analysis. None of us can get more than a certain amount, and the same could be said of anybody: they need more analysis" (Little, 1986, p. 270, emphasis in original). Not even Winnicott was spared the criticism of his colleague. In fact it would seem that he is Klein's (1957) interlocutor when she writes that: "It makes great demands on the analyst and on the patient to analyse splitting processes and the underlying hate and envy in both the positive and negative transference. One consequence of this difficulty is the tendency of some analysts to reinforce the positive and avoid the negative transference, and to attempt to strengthen feelings of love by taking the rôle of the good object which the patient had not been able to establish securely in the past" (p. 225).

Klein believed that it was projective identification that played a fundamental role in the analytical process. As already mentioned, Klein did not publically contest the concept of countertransference. However she did work to deter its dissemination, and she never missed an occasion to deliver this saying, which was circulating around Berlin in the 1950s: "If you feel like that about your patient, go in a corner and think it out carefully: what is wrong with you?" (Grosskurth, 1986, p. 442). She was however very careful that not all of the material brought to her by a patient be interpreted on the level of projective identification by her pupils: when supervising Sonny Davidson, a psychoanalytic candidate-in-training, after he had reported having submitted to a patient an interpretation of a state of mental confusion concerning something that the patient had divulged to him, Klein responded: "No, dear, that's not it, *you* were confused" (Grosskurth, 1986, p. 449, emphasis in original). Klein "evidently wanted to keep the definition of countertransference as the analyst's unanalysed transference to the patient, but [she also wanted] to add the idea of empathy as the analyst's awareness and understanding of the patient's projections" (Spillius, 1983, p. 326). In more precise terms, empathy, for Klein (1955), is the product of normal projective identification (Hinshelwood, 1989). In this way, the analyst may have different emotional reactions to the fact of projecting him/herself into a patient, or of the patient's projecting him/herself into the analyst (Klein Archive, D17, frames 805–806; cf. Spillius, 2007), but if the analyst possesses a strong enough ego, he or she will not be overly disturbed by the anxiety that such projections create within, and will be able to analyse them (Spillius, 2007).

It is worth pausing here to remember, as did Paolo Migone (1988), that at a certain point many psychoanalysts felt the need to abandon classical terminology, based on the concepts of transference-countertransference, and to use the terms projective identification/projective counteridentification. Migone (1988, 2013) suggests that this probably happened because these analysts were tired of having to always think that it was 'their fault', if with certain patients they felt bad or had distressing, violent, or primitive feelings (it is no coincidence that these analysts worked mostly with seriously ill patients). They were tired of hearing their supervisors tell them that they themselves needed more analysis and things of that nature. For this reason they found it easier or more reassuring to think that it was the patients (or certain patients, those more seriously ill, among others) who made them feel bad. And so the season of projective identification came into being. Ultimately it shared the same fate as the one of countertransference, in the sense that projective identification was deemed useful for the same reason – its heuristic power. It thus became a habitual term, and was applied to almost every patient or clinical situation. This had the result of causing a similar harmfulness, just as countertransference had: the 'guilty' ones became the patients and not the therapists. The same error was being committed, just in contrary fashion.

The emphasis placed by Klein on the use of paranoid-schizoid mechanisms and on projective identification on the part of patients, especially the more disturbed ones, implies an underlying image of the analyst, who, in his/her clinical work, inevitably finds him/herself invested with these primitive mechanisms and his/her own responses (subjective experiences) to them, the recognition of which, including the ability to cope with them, represent key aspects of psychoanalytical treatment. The post-Kleinian development of the concept of countertransference therefore begins with the presupposition that the patient's projective identifications represent the chief but not exclusive feature of psychoanalytical treatment. It is clear that projective identification (which is an interpersonal process) and countertransference are indissolubly interwoven.

Regarding the post-Kleinian development of the concept of countertransference, it is useful to recall that Robert Hinshelwood (1989; cf. also Spillius, Milton, Garvey, Couve and Steiner, 2011) identified five phases which developed over the years, thus outlining what has been the evolution of the concept. The first phase was that in which the feelings of the analyst began to be seen and used as an important indicator of the psychic state of the patient. The second is linked to the distinction between two types of projective identification, one pathological and one normal. The third is characterised by the hypothesis that the basis for an intrapsychic understanding of the situation (interpersonal) of transference-countertransference may lie in the alternation of cycles of projective identifications and introjective identifications (here the analyst is intended as a maternal container). The fourth is that of 'normal' countertransference, and lastly the fifth phase is that in which the analyst's mind (an important element of the patient's environment) is considered fundamental. In a subsequent study, Hinshelwood (1999) resorts to a different subdivision of the phases in the Kleinian development of the concept of countertransference: (a) projection and introjection, (b) containment, and (c) enactment.

Finally, it is interesting to compare the above-mentioned developmental stages of the concept of countertransference, as identified by Hinshelwood, with the stages into which Joseph Sandler subdivides the development of projective identification. Sandler (1984) identifies three conceptually distinct phases, but with areas of overlap, in which the aspects of the previous phase are preserved alongside the new ones of the subsequent one. The first phase coincides with the conceptualisation of projective identification as developed by Melanie Klein, specifying that, even though she expressed herself "in very concrete terms, it can be understood as referring to processes which occur *in fantasy*, processes of change in the mental representation of self and object occurring at various levels of unconscious fantasy. The concreteness of the formulations can be taken to refer to processes *imagined* as concrete, i.e., involving images of literal incorporation or of 'forcing' something into an object" (p. 16, emphasis in original). It is evident that here projective identification is "a process that occurs *in fantasy*" (Sandler, 1984, emphasis in original), and involves modification of the internal object representation, not the transformation of the real external object. The second phase begins with the studies of Heimann, Racker, and others who "made a significant extension of projective identification by bringing it into conjunction with the analyst's identification with the self- or object representation in the patient's unconscious fantasies, and with the effect of this on the countertransference. The countertransference reaction could then be a possible source of information for the analyst about what was occurring in the patient" (p. 18). The third phase is closely related to the concept of container-contained developed by Bion: in that phase "it is no longer one or the other aspect of the unconscious fantasies that is identified with by the analyst. Projective identification is now described as if the externalization of parts of the self or of the internal object occurs directly *into* the external object" (Sandler, 1984, emphasis in original). With this third phase, projective identification is no longer conceptualised as a pathological mechanism, but as a pathogenic mechanism.

Notes

1 Initially Klein spoke of 'paranoid position'. 'Schizoid' was added later, on the basis of Ronald Fairbairn's (1941, 1944) original formulation.

2 This last proposal was added in the 1952 version, published in *Developments in Psycho-Analysis*, edited by M. Klein, P. Heimann, S. Isaacs, and J. Rivière (London: Hogarth Press); however, the expression 'projective identification' appeared, two pages after, and was also in the 1946 version: "I have referred to the weakening and impoverishment of the ego resulting from excessive splitting and projective identification" (p. 304). It seems that, in reality, Klein was never fully convinced of the validity of the expression 'projective identification' inasmuch as, in her viewpoint, it could be misused (Segal, 1982), being that it is an expression that would indicate the specific unconscious phantasy that expresses the mental mechanism of projection (Segal, cit. in Spillius, 2012a), whose only usefulness would be that of helping the study of the relationship between projection and introjection (*ibid.*).

3 Currently most London Kleinians see: "Transference . . . as based on projective identification, using that term in the widest sense as I have suggested earlier" (Spillius, 1994, p. 352), "broad enough to include both cases in which the recipient is emotionally affected and those in which he is not" (ivi, p. 340; cf. also Spillius, 2012b).

4 Heimann at the time was fifty years old. She was an ambitious and competitive person, but despite the image of strong intellectual independence that both women demonstrated, "Possibly they were both basically frightened, lonely, and vulnerable, and clung to each other in a state of mutual dependence, although Klein was undoubtedly the stronger of the two" (Grosskurth, 1986, p. 384). It should be remembered that the relationship between the two, both of German origin, began in 1934 when Heimann sent Klein a letter of condolences on the death of her second son. A year later the budding friendship was overlaid by a relationship of analysis (the second for Heimann, who had done an analysis with Theodor Reik in Berlin), one that extended until 1953, broken

as it was by various interruptions. As Giorgio Meneguz (2011) highlights, "the experience of analysis that Paula Heimann did with Melanie Klein represents a good example of accepted dominance in the interaction between patient and analyst, in a case where patient and analyst are both psychoanalysts" (pp. 156–157; my translation), a dominance that, as we have seen, led to estrangement.

5 It seems that: "Klein thought that such extension [of the concept of countertransference] would open the door to claims by analysts that their own deficiencies were caused by their patients" (Spillius, 1992, p. 61).

6

1947–1950

The 'watershed' years

Despite the pioneering work of the analysts discussed in the previous chapters, countertransference had a similar fate to that of transference, for it was considered for years to be the blind spot of the analyst, an error of technique whose interpretation was believed to be dangerous, and therefore to be avoided. Up until 1950 not much was written about countertransference, and the little that was written hardly deviated from some conceptions of Sigmund Freud, or more exactly from a 'narrow' and 'rigid' reading of the papers on technique written by the Master. However, between the forties and fifties, analysts began to write about countertransference in works that did not lack in profound differences, and which made of it a central concept in psychoanalytic technique. Some of these authors, writing in English, besides those who will presently be more fully examined, are, for instance: Alexander and French (1946), Leo Berman (1949), Maxwell Gitelson (1949), Annie Reich (1949), Frieda Fromm-Reichmann (1950), Mabel Cohen (1952), Robert Fliess (1953), Harry Sullivan (1953), Edward Tauber (1954), Lucia Tower (1955), René Spitz (1956), and others. The following circumstances contributed to this developmental turning-point: the growing quantity of clinical experience, the increase in the curability of seriously ill patients[1] (borderline and psychotic: which caused strong emotions in the analyst), the resulting gradual rise in attention afforded to the here and now of the psychoanalytic situation in relation to the reconstructive aspects[2] of psychoanalytic work, the initial data being gathered from the burgeoning activity in infantile psychoanalysis, the greater rigour assigned to the surroundings of the psychoanalytic setting, and the improvements in education and training (analysis and supervisions, which undoubtedly helped to circumscribe the countertransference enactments – countertransference that however would have very little place in seminars frequented by the analyst-candidates during the course of their training within the Institutes at least until the years between 1970–1980). The work of Winnicott, Racker, Heimann, and Little are considered milestones within this nascent perspective. These authors were probably influenced by the descriptions of splitting and projective identification, developed by Melanie Klein (1946), and which, as we have seen in the preceding chapter, are revealed as split-off and projected parts of the patient, possibly finding expression in the feelings and phantasies of the analyst, more than in the words of the patient him/herself. As Thomas Ogden (1991) says, projective identification is a universal trait of the interpersonal externalisation of an internal object relation (transference); consequently "just as projective identification can be understood as an aspect of transference, the recipient's response to the projective identification constitutes an aspect of countertransference" (p. 72).

The first author whose thoughts on countertransference I will now examine in this historical account is Donald W. Winnicott, a pre-eminent exponent of the British Psychoanalytical Society. He was the president of this organisation for two mandates (1956–1959 and 1965–1968) and had been in analysis, first with James Strachey and then with Joan Rivière, and under the supervision of Klein. In 1947, Winnicott presented his paper 'Hate in Countertransference' – the result of his work experience with borderline and psychotic patients. In this paper, he dealt with countertransference not as a technical tool, but as a specific aspect of ambivalence[3] on the part of the analyst: hate in countertransference. In this way, he evokes, without naming him, Sándor Ferenczi (1932a), who in his *Clinical Diary* dealt with one of the main problems associated with countertransference. After having listed a series of reasons for which a mother hates her own baby, Winnicott concludes that if she cannot tolerate hating him/her, the child will suffer in his/her development. The good enough therapist is the one who can love a patient, and hate him/her at the same time. If one cannot freely experience one's own feelings, these (denied) feelings will develop into a negative countertransference. It will then become difficult to achieve complete awareness which could enable one to act. The inevitable involvement of the analyst – says Winnicott – increases to the same degree as the patient's regression increases. Much as in the classical view, the analyst should maintain a position of relative objectivity in the disclosure of the countertransference. According to Winnicott, the therapist can accept ambivalence towards his/her own patient, and can allow the patient to tyrannise him/her, knowing that he/she will not be destroyed (except in the patient's phantasy). After having established the relationship of omnipotence, what becomes necessary is a phase in which the object, no longer under omnipotent control (cause and effect of that destruction), may be destroyed by the subject in his/her unconscious phantasy. From the patient's point of view, the object (the therapist) survives when he more or less stays the same and does not react with rejection or punishment. Thus the patient can achieve the recognition of a sense of self and of external reality. Under certain conditions, such countertransferential experience could be communicated to the patient.

Winnicott differentiated between three possible meanings of the term 'countertransference': first he identified the feelings of abnormal countertransferences, as well as the repressed relationships and identifications in the analyst (in this case, the analyst should resume his/her own analysis); then he cited the tendencies towards identifications of that specific analyst (having his/her own particular developmental experiences), ones that make his/her being with that patient qualitatively different than that of any other analyst (a point also recognised by Alice and Michael Balint, 1939); and finally, intimately associated with the analyst's personal idiom and thus connected to the previous point, he indicated the type of countertransference that is authentically objective in direct response to the patient's objective personality and behaviour. It proves to be very important to recognise whether the countertransferential emotional response evolves out of the patient's projections into the analyst or, rather, out of the analyst's transference onto the patient. By means of the three above-mentioned types of countertransference, Winnicott expressed a rather comprehensive conception of this phenomenon, which contain within it the unresolved conflicts of the analyst, his life-experiences, and his personality, as well as his actual (objective) emotional responses. However it seems inevitable to ask oneself up to what point a person, however adequately trained in the psychoanalytical profession, is able to objectively evaluate the nature of the emotions caused within him/her during the interaction with the patient without being influenced, to a greater or lesser degree, by mechanisms such as rationalisation, which can lead to justifying the hate reaction as an objective response.

A decade later, Winnicott suggested distinguishing between countertransference, as understood in the 'classical view' that "can only be the neurotic features which spoil the professional attitude and disturb the course of the analytic process as determined by the patient" (1959, p. 162), and the analyst's total response to his patient's needs (Little, 1950). According to Vincenzo Bonaminio (1991), Winnicott's intention, by insisting on the theme of hate, was to bring attention to the theme of the feelings of the analyst as a person with respect to the patient. It was all about being authentic during the session, a situation which would allow the patient to recognise the analytical relationship as a true one.

The first detailed publication on the use of countertransference was that of Paula Heimann in 1950. It contained her lecture given at the Zurich Congress the year before,[4] a work later enlarged upon in 1959, and one which did not differ substantially from what Winnicott had presented. Heimann trained at the Berlin Institute, where she had done her analysis with Theodor Reik, and then emigrated from there to London in 1933. Here she underwent a second analysis with Klein. She believed that Freud's (1910a) warning to analysts to know how to recognise and exercise control over countertransference was not meant to be translated into detachment and the absence of feeling on the part of the analyst, but rather it was meant to push the clinician to: "use his emotional response [covering all the feelings which the analyst experiences towards his patient] as a key to the patient's unconscious" (p. 83). Heimann returned to the subject of the analyst's neutrality in a paper from 1978, and in it she pointed out that if the analyst doesn't want the analysis to fail then he/she must not be unnatural, must not put aside his/her feelings, or pretend to be neutral, there being a great difference between a neutral analyst and a neuter-analyst. Thus she conceived the analytical situation as a relationship between two people (one of which is competent – the analyst), each with his/her own feelings that differ in intensity, in range, and in the use which is made of it. The analyst, no longer a blank page, is the user of his/her own emotions and feelings, the normal responses to the patient; in this context, it is possible to see a part of Heimann's work as the development/expansion of the idea of free-floating attention explored by Freud. These countertransferential responses are an important indicator of the patient's unconscious processes (transference), insofar as the clinician, during the times in treatment that he/she finds it difficult to cognitively understand the material the patient brings up, thanks to the exploration of his/her own countertransference, is able to discover when (rather than just comprehend) he/she has unconsciously introjected something of the more hidden aspects of the patient's communications; this is what has caused the emotional response. Countertransference is therefore a crucial tool for searching within the other's unconscious and for formulating suitable interpretations; it is not countertransference, but the obstacles in the way of the analyst's perception that must be overcome. The countertransference "is not only part and parcel of the analytic relationship . . . it is the patient's *creation*,[5] it is a part of the patient's personality" (Heimann, 1949, p. 83, emphasis in original). Thus one can see the clinician as a receptive and resonating instrument of the patient's overwhelming anxieties. In this way it becomes clear that, despite the fact that this work by Heimann represented an important step forward in terms of technique, it still did not take into account the complexity of the relational interweaving, since she saw the analyst only as the receiver of the patient's projections; it is therefore possible that the clinician does not recognise the countertransferential feelings as his/her own, seeing them instead as representing aspects of the mind of the patient to whom he returns them as such. Countertransference is something distinct from the personal neurosis of the clinician, as well as something different from the neurotic transference of the clinician towards the patient.

Heimann (1949) argued that "the analyst's immediate emotional response to his patient is a significant pointer to the patient's unconscious processes and . . . helps the analyst to focus his attention on the most urgent elements in the patient's associations and serves as a useful criterion for the selection of interpretations" (p. 83) that can offer to the analysand a reflection of him/herself. Heimann (1980) vigorously contended that these interpretations must not be based on the simple affective state experienced by the therapist: "A student in supervision presented interpretations that were totally off the mark, totally unrelated to the patient's material. I asked him for an exact quote to justify what he had said to the patient. The student casually answered, 'I felt it in my countertransference'. I said to him very firmly that his feelings did not absolve him of the obligation of thinking sensibly" (p. 123; my translation). A few lines later she continues: "I have based my theory that countertransference serves as a cognitive tool for recognising the unconscious processes of the patient on my clinical observations. . . . In contrast, the transference on the part of the therapist does not improve his/her way of thinking, but it obscures and falsifies the patient's perceptions. We expect that during training the therapist may acquire enough self-knowledge to be able to practice his/her own profession with the necessary self-discipline" (ibid.).

This author narrows the concept of countertransference, a very distinct one, yet closely related to the analyst's transference onto the patient, to those situations in which a temporal variance between the unconscious comprehension and the conscious one is present. Therefore, the countertransferential feelings are a clue to the fact that the analyst has not been able to understand the patient's communication at the right moment. What follows from this is that the goal of the analyst's personal analysis is to be able to work through his/her own infantile conflicts and (paranoid and depressive) anxieties, thus being able to enter into a relationship with his/her own unconscious that otherwise would lead him/her to attribute to the patient what actually belongs to him/her.

Despite the fact that Heimann's work from 1949 was seen as a fundamental contribution within the Kleinian *corpus*, and that it resonated with authors like Bion, Money-Kyrle, and Rosenfeld, it is evident that the view of countertransference that she outlined could not have pleased Klein who, strongly influenced by Freud's (1910a) warning, held firm to the idea that countertransference was something that interfered with the analytical process, and that, if such a phenomenon presents itself, what the analyst must do is undergo immediate analysis. With the presentation of the paper 'On Countertransference', Heimann's sliding towards the Independents had definitely begun. As has been said, Klein remained sceptical until the end over the role played by countertransference within the British school, but she never publicly refuted her colleague's work.

Finally it must be noted that Heimann had two afterthoughts on the subject. Beginning in 1970, Heimann retracted her position of outright rejection of the possibility that any form of disclosure could be useful to the patient, ultimately maintaining that sometimes attributing countertransferential thoughts and/or emotions caused by the analytical relationship onto the patient can be of help both in showing the patient from where interpretations originate and in making him/her feel an active and important participant in the therapeutic couple (Borgogno, 1992). Moreover, towards the end of her life, Heimann (1978a) reached the point where she formulated the therapeutic use of countertransference without referring to the concept of projective identification and, more generally speaking, to the Kleinian theory, thus taking a position in which she: "so distanced herself from the thesis that countertransference is the patient's creation that she expressed amazement at having ever made such an assertion (in a private conversation with B. and H. Thomä on August 3, 1980)" (Thomä and Kächele, 1985, p. 84). It is quite probable that the first theory of countertransference Heimann formulated was an attempt to reconcile Reik and Klein: "Through his countertransference the analyst hears with Reik's 'third ear' and the patient's creation allegedly reaches him via the mechanisms described by Klein" (Thomä and Kächele, 1985, p. 86).

At the same time as Heimann was developing her theory on countertransference, Margaret Little, too, was independently fostering her own conception of countertransference. It is to be remembered that Little, after undergoing a personal analysis with a Jungian analyst, did her training analysis with Ella Freeman Sharpe; this latter experience, stretching between 1940 and 1947, proved most unsatisfactory for Little, who therefore turned first to Sylvia Payne, and then, on her suggestion to Marion Milner, with whom she undertook a year-long period of analysis. Ultimately, in 1949, she entered into analysis with Winnicott and stayed with him until 1957, a long course of treatment that was broken by various interruptions (cf. Little, 1990).

Little (1950) defined countertransference as "the analyst's total response to his patient's needs, whatever the needs, and whatever the response" (Little, 1956, p. 241) and reserved the term *countertransference* for "the specific part of the analyst's total response to his patient's need that has remained unconscious and under repression" (Little, 1959, p. 29). She did not participate in the Zurich Congress, but when she read Heimann's paper, published in the *International Journal of Psychoanalysis* in 1950, she ascertained that many of the conclusions, at which she had arrived personally, were entirely similar to the ones expressed by her colleague. Little however made some steps forward, since she did not stop at seeing countertransference as a 'mere sign', but instead as an essential tool of every analysis and an indispensable guide for interpretations. In her mind the driving force of this whole response came entirely from the analyst's love and hate for his/her patient. For her, such feelings contain the fundamental and invariable elements which lie at the heart of the analyst's participation in the analysis, to the extent that the analyst is able to face (on a conscious or unconscious level) his/her own paranoid anxieties and his/her own depression, usually awakened by seriously ill patients. The impersonal analyst is a myth. He/she does not exist. It is clear that this author viewed the analytical situation as an interaction between two persons to such a degree that she maintained that any analysis that finished without having induced or at least initialised some sort of growth (or cure) within the analyst, could not be considered successful for either of the pair.

According to Little, strongly influenced by the ideas of Ferenczi, besides those of Winnicott, transference and countertransference are "products of the combined unconscious work of patient and analyst" (Little, 1950, p. 40). What follows from this is that the relationship of transference-countertransference is composed of the conscious and unconscious, normal and pathological elements of both. In her paper from 1956, she added that the success of the analysis is linked to the satisfying working through of the analyst's pathology. We find another connection with Ferenczi's thought when Little speaks of the ability of the patient to enter into contact with the emotions of the analyst and the ability to respond to the unconscious countertransference even before the clinician realises it (a theme which would be developed by Robert Langs, 1976). Since "the analysand is naturally sensitive to any insincerity in his analyst, and will inevitably respond to it with hostility" (Little, 1950, p. 38), it is essential for a good outcome to the analytic process that the analyst recognises his/her own feelings. This will prevent the analysand from identifying with the clinician in this insincerity, through an identification that is "a means of denying his own feelings" (Little, 1950, p. 38).

If Little presumes that mistakes on the part of the analyst are inevitable during the course of treatment, and one of the patient's rights is the expression of the possible feeling of anger that can ensue, she also believed that Heimann was wrong in maintaining that communicating to the patient the reasons for one's own absence of attention could be detrimental. Little was however not of the idea that one had to explain the countertransference explicitly to the patient (something that Ferenczi thought was useful to do, or, at the very least, sometimes was); she believed instead that it was necessary to acknowledge one's own mistakes and integrate them into the interpretation in the light of one's own countertransference, which, effectively speaking, enters into the analytical space. It seems to me that in Little's vision, the acknowledgement of one's own mistakes is necessary to the analyst so that he/she does not stay entangled within his/her own unconscious, while the integration of such mistakes into the interpretation is necessary so as to produce effects in the patient. The quantity of such interventions would depend on the type of patient. Neurotic patients and borderline or psychotic patients cause different types of emotion and anxiety in the clinician in terms of both quantity and quality; moreover, when one works with the first, the unconscious countertransference may not present difficulties to the expert analyst, as Winnicott (1959) maintained, since he/she can work "with easy but conscious mental effort. Ideas and feelings come to mind, but these are well examined and sifted before an interpretation is made" (p. 161). But when working with the second group, the outcome of treatment may remain uncertain for a long time.

Lastly, I would like to briefly describe Heinrich Racker's point of view, even if his contribution, from a temporal standpoint, fits somewhere in between that of Winnicott and Heimann. Racker was an analyst who greatly influenced and at the same time was influenced by certain thinkers of the English school, although he was actually never part of it. One has only to recall that Racker was not only very influenced by Kleinian ideas on unconscious phantasy and the mechanisms of introjection and projection, but also by Ferenczi's ideas on the analytic relationship, and by the writings of Balint, Heimann, and Little (de Bernardi, 2000). It must be pointed out that, after a first analysis with Marie Langer, Racker underwent analysis with Ángel Garma, who had been in analysis with Reik in Berlin, and who in Argentina had promoted Ferenczian thought. Broadly speaking, it should be noted that between 1940 and 1950 Argentine psychoanalysts had been enormously interested in the work of Melanie Klein and her school, and during this decade, various British analysts (for instance, Segal, Rosenfeld, and later Bion) visited South America. We cannot be sure that these British visitors influenced Racker, or vice-versa, or if a combination of these two factors is at work.

Racker, an analyst of Polish origins, and an immigrant to Buenos Aires in 1939, presented to the Argentine Psychoanalytic Association, in September 1948, a work entitled 'Aportación al problema de la controtransferencia', whose English translation was published in 1953 in the *International Journal of Psychoanalysis.* The contents of the article caused some dissent among the analysts present at the meeting. Horacio Etchegoyen remarked (1986, p. 265) that an important analyst said haughtily that "the best thing for an analyst to whom 'those things' happened was for him to re-analyse himself!". It must also be highlighted that Racker was very young and had little clinical experience when he presented this paper (Etchegoyen, 2014). In this pioneering work "that would establish him as one of the most original and creative analysts in the history of our discipline" (ivi, p. 88), Racker, re-evoking and expanding upon Helene Deutsch's (1926) intuitions on the subject, maintained that countertransference could be a valid indicator of what happens within the patient. So for him countertransference was a useful tool, but also something that, in a certain sense and to a certain degree, determines the analytic field, upon which, and due to which, changes in the patient take shape. Similarly to what Freud (1915–17) had expressed in terms of transference, Racker believed that countertransference operates as an obstacle, a tool, and a field (where the patient can live out a new experience, one therefore different from the original one). In this way, the Argentine analyst created a theory in which countertransference is closely related to transference, a theory maintaining that "the analyst is not only the interpreter but also the object of the transference" (Etchegoyen, 1986, p. 266).

Racker introduced a very valuable distinction between 'concordant countertransference' and 'complementary countertransference'. In the case of concordant countertransference, the analyst is consciously identified with some aspects of the analysand's personality; more specifically, in some cases, the clinician identifies his/her own parts of the psychic apparatus (id, ego, and superego) with the patient's respective parts, while in other cases he/she identifies his/her own ego with the patient's internal objects. This type of countertransference lies at the basis of one's empathic and intuitive abilities to understand what the patient felt as a child in relation to an early object. On the other hand, in the case of complementary countertransference,[6] the analyst is identified with the internal objects projected by the patient and takes on the role that the latter 'assigns' to him. We are talking about a non-empathic perception, from the patient's point of view, of what an important childhood object of the patient had felt towards him/her. It is obvious that if the analyst is not aware of what is happening he/she could behave in a way that would represent a repetition of an experience that has already been harmful to the patient; while in a situation where the analyst would be able to be attentive to his/her own countertransference experience, he/she could break the vicious cycle of the patient's neurosis, by making use of an interpretation instead of acting (as the objects of the patient's childhood had done), proving in this way that external reality is not identical to internal perceptions.

These two classes of countertransference described above, distinct on the basis of the type of identification, are indissolubly linked to a decrease in the concordant identification which corresponds to an increase in the complementary identification, and vice versa. The model of psychic apparatus to which Racker alludes is that of the second topographical model, while the dynamic of identifications is related to the mechanisms of projection and introjection (but not of projective identification, to which other analysts of the Kleinian school would refer). As Etchegoyen (1986) reveals, this perspective leads to some problems in internal theoretical consistency;

for example, concordant identification with the superego is an identification with an internal object, and a concordant identification with a patient who self-reprimands might not be of the most empathic kind.

Racker (1948, 1953) – starting from the hypothesis that "Just as the whole of the patient's personality, the healthy part and the neurotic part, his present and past, reality and fantasy, are brought into play in his relation with the analyst, so it is with the analyst, although with qualitative and quantitative differences, in his relation with the patient" (Racker, 1948, p. 105) – also introduced the concept of 'countertransference neurosis', implying a vision of the analytic process on the basis of the members of the therapeutic dyad. This countertransference neurosis consists of three aspects which should be examined in detail: a) concordant countertransference and complementary countertransference; b) direct countertransference and indirect countertransference; and c) countertransference thought and countertransference position. We have already considered the first of these. On the subject of the second, it may be said that the clinician experiences a direct countertransference when the object, upon which the countertransference depends, is the patient (countertransference as a response to the patient's transference; similar to the countertransference described by Annie Reich, 1949), whereas he experiences an indirect countertransference when it depends on an object other than the patient (for example, a colleague with whom one discusses the case and from whom one desires some sort of appreciation; this refers to the use of countertransference for the purposes of *acting-out* about which Reich speaks). Finally, in terms of the third, we are looking at the thoughts and position as related to countertransference. The first are the thoughts which the analyst suddenly discovers himself having, without however being able to find a rational connection to the patient and the material he has brought up. These are linked to very deep conflicts and so it is not unusual for them to appear both in the material of the patient, as well as in the clinician's mind. The clinician should not fall into the error of impulsively trying to push them aside. He/she must instead examine them with careful consideration, until their confirmation or negation emerges from the patient's material (in the first case, such thoughts could be profitably used in the formation of an interpretation; in the second case they cannot, since they are probably linked to the analyst's neurosis or, at any rate, they are far from a possible understanding on the part of the patient). On the other hand, the countertransference position often, but not always, implies deeper conflicts and a greater disturbance in the clinician (the feelings and phantasies of the countertransference can be ego-syntonic and therefore pass unobserved). For those cases where the pathology of the patient is very serious, ones entailing severe regression and the reawakening of archaic neurosis in the clinician (colluding with that of the patient), Otto Kernberg (1963) speaks of 'chronic countertransference fixation', in which the countertransference response is a function of the patient: the more the patient is situated at the psychotic extreme of the continuum, the more intense and detached will be the clinician's countertransferential reaction from his/her own personal conflicts (but linked to the patient's transference). In all cases, the therapist always has his/her own personal conflicts, and during the conducting of a psychotherapy process he/she inevitably makes mistakes; what becomes necessary is that the therapist recognises his/her own errors and conflicts – recognises them within him/herself, without explaining them openly to the patient, because such a behaviour would be equivalent to burdening the patient with something that does not belong to him/her.

Notes

1 The Second World War brought to the analysts' consulting rooms patients with a rather large variety of mental disturbances, ones which went beyond the neurotic; there were a great deal of patients suffering serious traumas.

2 Reconstruction must however maintain its importance so as not to risk cancelling out the role of *Nachträglichkeit* (deferred action, *après-coup*), a basic co-construction for the repetition of the interiorised object relations, which only in this way may be able to be relived within the analytical situation, and then be analysed and worked through there.

3 Differently from Klein, who believed hatred to be innate, a manifestation of the death drive, Winnicott saw the capacity to hate, as distinct from the capacity to love (ambivalence), as an indicator of the realisation of a certain level of emotional development, more precisely that of relative dependence and the preoccupation phase.

4 It is important to realise that precisely in that year – 1949 – the 'Sándor Ferenczi Issue' of the *International Journal of Psychoanalysis* was published. In this issue some of Ferenczi's works, hitherto unknown to the Anglophone public, appeared in English translation. Reading Heimann's work, the influence of Ferenczi's (1915) notion of the 'dialogue of the unconsciouses' becomes obvious.

The evident delay in the publication of Ferenczi's works in English was due to Ernest Jones's attempt, in agreement with Freud, to impede the spreading of his thought. Jones (1953) believed that the Hungarian analyst was psychotic, and that his last works were the result of his mental deterioration. It was due to the efforts of John Rickman (analysed by Freud and Klein; and in turn the analyst of Wilfred Bion and Pearl King) and Michael Balint, both students of Ferenczi, motivated by the hope (which later proved to be illusory) of rehabilitating the name and thought of their Master, that the publication of the 'Ferenczi Issue' was made possible. It would be necessary to wait another six years to have the English translation of the entire works of Ferenczi. In fact, it is in 1955 that the third volume of the writings of Ferenczi, entitled *Final Contributions to the Problems and Methods of Psychoanalysis*, came out. The volume was edited by Balint, with the preface, however, being written by another of the Hungarian Master's students, Clara Thompson (it is interesting to note that at the time she had already left the IPA; it is also reasonable to contemplate whether Balint chose her because the other eminent members of the Association had refused).

5 Many authors see this 'creation' as projective identification, and it seems to be Heimann's position in the period between 1950–1960, even if she does not make any direct reference to projective identification and to its role within the transference-countertransference dynamic. Others instead believe that this 'creation' is linked to the "work of the analyst with respect to the patient, his/her feelings, and those thoughts that cannot yet be thought or represented" (Bonaminio and Di Renzo, 2003, p. 66; my translation), and they associate it with the evocative or expressive use of the countertransference described by Bollas (1987) as a transferring of the unthought-known, or rather "a form of knowledge that has not yet been dreamed or imagined as it has not yet been mentally realized" (p. 241).

6 Here an expression of Deutsch's (1926) has been adopted. She spoke of a particular type of partial identification, calling it a 'complementary attitude'.

7

THE CONTRIBUTION OF THE BRITISH SCHOOL OF OBJECT RELATIONS

First phase

The Winnicottian view of the concept of countertransference, one which we have seen was strongly influenced by Kleinian theory, was further developed by William Ronald Dodds Fairbairn (1952, 1958) and Harry Guntrip (1961) (first analysed by Fairbairn and later by Winnicott). These two treated countertransference in the same way as any other clinician's response, or rather as fully dependent on the introjection within the inner world of the internal objects projected by the patient; not coping with the countertransference means communicating to the patient that the analyst does not feel any authentic interest in him/her as a person. (The influence of the Hungarian school is apparent here.) According to Fairbairn, the decisive factor in analytic treatment is the relationship between patent and analyst, understood not simply as a transferential relationship, but as a global relationship that evolves between the patient and the analyst as people. This prompts the idea that countertransference takes on a prominent function in promoting the development of a 'genuine emotional connection' within the analytical situation. It should be recalled that Fairbairn, perhaps because of his geographical and academic 'isolation' from the psychoanalytic world (he was living in Edinburgh), came close to a systematisation of a relational-structure model, and that central to his theory is the hypothesis that "libido is not primarily pleasure-seeking, but object-seeking" (Fairbairn, 1946, p. 30), or rather: "the *individual in his libidinal capacity* (and not libido) . . . is object-seeking" (Fairbairn, 1957, p. 335, emphasis in original).

During this same period, the 1950s, Herbert Rosenfeld, a psychiatrist of German origin who immigrated to England in 1935 and had been in a training analysis with Melanie Klein and been supervised by Sylvia Payne and Joan Rivière, also saw the use of countertransference as an effective cognitive tool (Heimann, 1949). He hinted at the difficulties that are encountered in dealing with countertransference reactions, ones which in and of themselves are disturbing. According to Rosenfeld (1952), "the unconscious intuitive understanding by the psycho-analyst of what the patient is conveying to him is an essential factor in all analyses, and depends on the analyst's capacity to use his countertransference as a kind of sensitive 'receiving set'" (p. 116). He goes on to say that this intuitive understanding is even more important in one's work with schizophrenic patients (who usually have great difficulty verbalising), in that it helps the clinician to establish what is important in that given moment. The analyst must then be adept at formulating in conscious terms what he/she has understood on the unconscious level, in order to be able to communicate it to the patient in a form that becomes comprehensible to him/her, helping him/her to understand in this way on a conscious level what he/she feels in such an intense way only on the unconscious level.

Rosenfeld wrote the above-mentioned work in honour of Melanie Klein's seventieth birthday, and it was published in an issue of the *International Journal of Psychoanalysis* entirely dedicated to this primary figure. In the same issue of the journal, Marion Milner (1952b) also expressed her own vision of countertransference as a beneficial tool in the therapeutic process. The patient of the clinical case about which she speaks in this article, Simon, in reality was Michael Clyne, nephew of Melanie Klein and son of Erich Klein (Eric Clyne from 1937 onwards). In the beginning, the analysis was supervised by Melanie Klein herself (who provided Milner with a thorough family background), but it had already been suspended during the period in which Milner had reached awareness of the need to become the 'lovely stuff' created by the patient in order for him/her to be able to achieve a creative relationship with the world (we are referring to the analyst's mental pliability or, from the patient's point of view, to the use of the object), as well as during the period in which solemn ritual-like play was instituted. Not only is the analyst's mental pliability necessary but also something else is necessary: the ability of the analyst to take charge of his/her own negative countertransference. Due to conflicts with Klein, the patient afterwards went into analysis with Wilfred Bion.

Milner[1] realised that sometimes, in order to accommodate the patient's need to connect, the clinician has to give up on interpretations, at least until the patient reaches integration, in favour of a total presence of self during the sessions. For Milner this psychophysical presence is able to facilitate the management of one's own negative countertransference (Winnicott, 1947). This is a type of work in which the concentration of the body (not only of the mind, which would coincide with logical thought) plays a decisive role: a state, in which the direct proprioceptive body-self awareness – regarding the relationship that is taking place in the here and now of the session – that develops out of observing one's own thoughts and not forcing them, moves from the preconscious background to the conscious foreground, in both patient and therapist. This psychic and somatic concentration, even though it could appear as a distraction with respect to the patient, seems to help the patient to allow his own material to surface, and the clinician to understand, share, and experience it. Such concentration in the self and the body is not only to be seen as a regressive path, but also, if not mainly, as a pre-logical subject-object fusion, besides a mind-body fusion (Milner, 1952b, 1960, 1969).

The important work of Roger Money-Kyrle also fits within the Kleinian mould. Money-Kyrle had been in analysis with Jones in 1919, with Freud during the period spent in Vienna, and with Klein in 1936. Money-Kyrle (1955) starts from the recognition that while in the past countertransference was believed to be a symptom of a personal ailment in the analyst, one to be eliminated through a further *tranche* of analysis, in the present – or rather in 1955 – one is aware that it has causes (Heimann, 1949) and effects (Little, 1950) in the patient, and must therefore be analysed in the latter. For this author, countertransference has a dual aspect: it is potentially both a useful tool for and an impediment to analytical work. Money-Kyrle talks about a 'normal countertransference', or rather a countertransference that is *normally* present in the analytic process, at least when there is a continuity in the process of understanding the patient on the part of the analyst. What emerges from this is that to a certain extent it is an ideal – something not realistically achievable. By means of a partial identification, the clinician assumes a parental role countertransferentially (unconsciously he/she feels like the patient's father or mother), complementary to that of the patient (who unconsciously considers the analyst a parent); what allows the clinician to maintain an analytical stance and to respond to the patient's transference in a therapeutic way is the setting (with a particular emphasis on one of its components, the relational asymmetry).

According to Money-Kyrle we can speak of countertransference in the classical sense for all of those situations in which the non-collaboration of the patient, or the presence of his/her problematic areas, begins to overlap with a blind spot of the analyst, causing slow-downs or worse – stumbling blocks in the process of understanding. In order for the process to function well, the analyst must make a dual identification: one with the subject, the other with his/her object; or rather a concordant identification and a complementary one (Racker). This comes about through the projective identification of the childhood ego of the analyst in the patient, and with the introjective identification of the internal parental object projected by the patient. Should, for instance, only the first type of identification manifest itself, the reason could lie in the clinician's attempt to get rid of an aspect placed inside him/her by the patient, an aspect which closely touches upon some of his/her own unconscious conflicts. Based upon what has been said, it follows that the analysis is going well when there is, from an intrapsychic point of view,

> a fairly rapid oscillation between introjection and projection. As the patient speaks, the analyst will, as it were, become introjectively identified with him, and having understood him inside, will reproject him and interpret. But what I think the analyst is most aware of is the projective phase – that is to say, the phase in which the patient is the representative of a former immature or ill part of himself, including his damaged objects, which he can now understand and therefore treat by interpretation, in the external world.
>
> Meanwhile the patient is receiving effective interpretations,[2] which help him to respond with further associations that can be understood. As long as the analyst understands them, this satisfactory relationship – which I will call

> the 'normal' one – persists. In particular, the analyst's counter-transference feelings will be confined to that sense of empathy with the patient on which his insight is based.
>
> *(Money-Kyrle, 1955, p. 361)*

This oscillation is blocked if during the introjective phase in the clinician there is an obstacle in recognising that a given emotional pattern that he/she is 'absorbing' (and which stirs up specific problems in his/her life) expresses a particular phantasy from the unconscious world of the patient. If the clinician cannot identify what belongs to him/her and what belongs to the patient, he/she will not be able to provide valid interpretations, because these would only be supported by his/her theoretical knowledge, and not by the indispensable element of his/her intuition as well. Nevertheless, a similar obstruction of the oscillation process can immediately be recognised by the analyst, who becomes aware of a "feeling that the material has become obscure, and that we have somehow lost the thread" (Money-Kyrle, 1955, p. 361). This obscuring of the material causes in the analyst (and also in the patient) a state of tension that leads to a further compromising of the capacity for understanding; a vicious circle sets in, one to which all the deviations from a normal countertransference are linked. Money-Kyrle believed that for the countertransference to really function as a sensitive receiving set, the analyst has to consider three factors: his/her own emotional troubles (that necessitates a silent self-analysis), the role played by the patient in triggering this turmoil, and the effect that this all has on the patient. It should be noted that for Money-Kyrle the emotional turmoil is primarily connected to the severity of the superego, which, in response to the non-immediate comprehension of the patient's emotional processes on the part of the clinician, could cause the emergence of a sense of failure in him/her (an unconscious, persecutory, or depressive sense of guilt), or could make him/her blame the patient (a defence against the sense of guilt). Ultimately, for this author, in contrast to Racker, it is the complementary countertransference that is more appreciably linked to the analyst's empathy.

The following year, in Argentina, Leòn Grinberg (1956) – who underwent analysis with Arnaldo Rascovsky and Marie Langer – presented a paper entitled 'Magical aspects of transference and countertransference: Their technical implications' to the Argentine Psychoanalytic Association. Even if he does not belong to the British school, this author made such an important contribution to the development of the concept of countertransference, and he influenced to such a degree the theorisations and the clinical work of so many analysts around the world, that he cannot be overlooked. In his paper from 1956, Grinberg introduced the concept of 'projective counteridentification' "to refer to a specific and differential aspect of countertransference, based on the unconscious analytic interaction between the patient and the analyst, and which is brought about by the particularly intense use of and psychopathic modality of the mechanism of projective identification of the patient" (1979, p. 226). Grinberg's work can be considered an expansion of Racker's (Grinberg was in supervision with him right at the time of his initial theoretical-clinical formulation on countertransference), but it diverges from the latter because Grinberg includes the mechanism of projective identification and places it at the centre of his own theory. He hypothesised a *continuum*, at one extreme of which one finds concordant transference, and at the other extreme, passing through complementary countertransference, one finds projective counteridentification. At this second extreme of the *continuum*, countertransference plays no role because while in complementary countertransference, the analyst responds to the patient's transference, identifying as he/she does with the patient's internal objects (objects that are experienced as his/her own), in projective counteridentification there is a kind of coercion taking place within the clinician to represent/assume that part introduced inside him/her by the patient's projective identification.

According to Grinberg, in projective counteridentification "the analyst's reaction turns out to be largely *independent of his own conflicts and corresponds predominantly or exclusively to the intensity and quality of the analysand's projective identification*" (1963, p. 117, emphasis in original) in that it is only the patient who affects this process. In this way, he in fact excluded the contribution of the clinician, herein understood as a passive receiver, unaware of the patient's projections, unable to recognise what is happening in the analytic situation, and unable to actively introject the projective identification and restore it, after it has been processed, to the patient. It is evident that for Grinberg, this progression begins with the patient and only subsequently, if perhaps quite soon after, is a specific reaction evoked in the analyst, in response to the patient. We are dealing with a particular form of countertransference, which has nothing to do with the reactions associated with the clinician's neurotic residue, reactivated or intensified by the material brought up by the patient (it should be clarified that Grinberg believed that during the work with the patient the analyst is subjected to both mechanisms, sometimes even simultaneously, but he keeps them distinct). It is as if the clinician has ceased to be him/herself in order to be transformed, coercively, into what the patient on an unconscious level wants him/her to be (Id, Ego, or an internal object). The product of the patient's projective identification consists of the insertion into the analyst (recipient 'passive object') of roles, affects, and phantasies that he/she is unconsciously drawn to take on and experience; in this way one can say that projective counteridentification refers to a specific and differentiated aspect of countertransference.

In conclusion, we can say that for projective counteridentification Grinberg (1979) meant "the analyst's specific response to the violent projective identification from the patient, which is not consciously perceived by the analyst" (p. 231), whose "specific reaction . . . is due to the way in which the patient projected, lodged or 'forced' into the analyst his projective identification" (p. 236), which "will have different modalities related to the respective modalities of the projective identification, coloured by the qualitative shading which gives it a functional specificity" (Grinberg, 1979, p. 236). For Grinberg it is the degree and the quality of the projective identification that, once a specific critical threshold has been crossed (one belonging to that specific analyst), produce a projective counteridentification rather than a countertransference resonance. Such a situation, one which corresponds to the failure of the analyst's *alpha*-function (Bion, 1961b), usually makes the clinician resort to the mechanism of rationalisation, in an attempt to find a justification for the disturbing state of affairs in which he/she finds him/herself (Grinberg, 1962). Once the clinician becomes the object of the patient's violent projective identifications he can react in two ways: therapeutically, interpreting the material the patient has brought up and showing him that he/she has not been destroyed by the violence of the projective identification; or non-therapeutically, if he has not been able to tolerate what the patient has forced into him, by passing his/her own reaction onto another patient or in other different ways.

Let us go back now to London, but this time not to discuss the contribution of a psychoanalyst, but of an analytical psychologist: Michael Fordham. But before we delve into his thinking, it must be noted that one of the great merits of Fordham, a personal friend of Carl G. Jung and Donald W. Winnicott, was to promote, within the British arena, debates and conferences with spokespeople belonging to both the Jungian and Freudian (the object relations theorists) camps, but also to traditional psychiatry. Among the various symposia that Fordham organised, the one dedicated to countertransference must be especially remembered. It was held in London on October 28, 1959, and Heimann, Little, and Winnicott all participated as speakers.

Fordham agreed with Jung that the entire personality of the analyst (his/her ego) is the fundamental therapeutic factor and that, whatever the clinician's attitude or behaviour (verbal and non-verbal), he/she expresses his/her global personality, which therefore is destined to emerge during the course of the analysis (understood, in essence, as the dialectic exchange between two deeply involved individuals who influence each other). For Fordham, transference and countertransference are two closely related processes, both originating in the unconscious and involving mechanisms such as projection and introjection. As he states: "because of the archetypes, the analyst inevitably becomes sooner or later involved with the patient in an unconscious process, which is first experienced as a projection and then further analysed" (Fordham, 1957, p. 96).

On the basis of his clinical experience, Fordham came to the conclusion that often, during a session, what he believed to be a part of himself, in reality, represented the introjection of a part of the patient that the latter had projected. (It becomes clear that we are dealing with a conception similar to concordant countertransference as described by Racker.) Fordham (1957) understood countertransference as including both "the analyst's reactions that emanate from the repressed unconscious" (p. 89), as well as "the analyst's conduct in his analytic work" (Fordham, 1957); he therefore came to identify with the analyst's spontaneous archetypal response to the patient's transference. His original contribution to the subject is linked to the concept of 'syntonic countertransference', which he distinguished from 'countertransference illusion'. Such a distinction would find justification in the need to identify the path to take in order to increase the level of awareness. While some syntonic countertransference reactions can contribute to an increase in the patient's awareness, the countertransference illusions can provide such a contribution only if the analyst is disposed to self-analyse his/her own personal reaction.

Let us start from the countertransference illusion. It consists of an unconscious (approaching vaguely conscious) reactivation of a past situation, which completely overwhelms the analyst in relation to the patient and makes analysis impossible. "Illusion springs from projections arising out of the repressed unconscious, the anima, and also indirectly from the animus-anima conjunction. Repressed elements are particularly important in stabilising the illusions" (Fordham, 1959, p. 244). Even if these represent a serious obstacle to the development of analytical procedures, they can still be corrected by tearing down the defences upon which they are based. If the analyst will allow them enough space inside of him/her, and undergo continuous self-analysis, he/she may be able to make use of them as a valuable tool for connecting to his/her own unconscious processes.

Let us now look at Fordham's original idea – syntonic countertransference:

> [In the case of syntonic countertransference, the analyst can choose between] two ways of behaving: (1) trying to isolate oneself from the patient by being as 'integrated' as possible; and (2) relinquishing this attitude and simply listening to and watching the patient to hear and see what comes out of the self in relation to the patient's activities, and then reacting. This would appear to involve de-integrating; it is as if what is put at the disposal of patients are parts of the analyst which are spontaneously responding to the patient in a way that he needs; yet these parts are manifestations of the self. . . . Analysis depends upon the relatively greater experience of the analyst in de-integrating so as to meet the patient's disintegration.
>
> *(Fordham, 1957, p. 97)*

> [Therefore] it can be just as valid for the analyst to know of the projection through registering its impact upon himself and perceiving it first within himself, as it is by listening to the patient and realizing it as an inference from what the patient says.
>
> *(ivi, p. 98)*

> At this stage in the transference the affective stability of the analyst is crucial; he must be able to rely on the de-integrated knowing that consciousness will inevitably arise from them. It follows that he *will inevitably find* the right form or response so long as countertransference projections do not obstruct its development.
>
> *(ivi, p. 99, emphasis in original)*

> [What the analyst must do is take] notice of the irrational experience: realization of a syntonic countertransference can start with a sense that the analyst is doing or feeling something that he cannot at first explain; it will later become understandable when the unconscious content becomes related to the main ego nucleus, which can perceive and moderate its activity.

> . . . When the analyst's ego is trained to relax its control, then another centre can be sensed and symbolized . . . the self. To it the ego can relate as a part to the whole, as part of the whole . . . as part of the whole the ego can allow for the activity of an unconscious that it cannot understand but that is, as it were, understood by the self; and this makes a great deal of difference.
>
> *(Fordham, 1959, p. 249)*

> [In this light the interpretations are construed as an] end product of the analyst's syntonic countertransference. They stand, as it were, on the basis of less definable affective preconscious experiences out of which they are distilled.
>
> *(Fordham, 1957, p. 99)*

> [Thus] giving a good interpretation is an expression of a syntonic interchange in which psychic contents pass unconsciously from the patient into the analyst. Intellectual or intuitive inference is only of minor importance because it is the affective process that gives rise to certainty in the analyst; this can then be conveyed to the patient.
>
> *(Fordham, 1959, p. 248)*

If we compare this definition of the concept of syntonic countertransference with the Jungian definition of 1929, quoted in the chapter dedicated to the pioneers, it becomes evident that Fordham's conception is derived from the idea that there is therapeutic potential in the introjection of the patient's psychopathology on the part of the clinician. Generally speaking, we can see many overlapping points between the ideas expressed by Fordham and a part of those expressed by others that we have already taken into consideration. However, it must be highlighted that Fordham (cf. 1970) believed that he had reached a conceptualisation of syntonic countertransference all the while unaware of contributions of psychoanalytic origin; but he was aware of those of other analytical psychologists such as Robert Moody (1955) and Alfred Plaut (1956). Only subsequently did he come into contact with theories that his psychoanalyst colleagues had formulated around the countertransference phenomenon, acknowledging "many of my propositions were considered before I thought of them" (Fordham, 1979, p. 630). From that moment on, Fordham deepened his study of psychoanalytic authors, and in his works he cites Bion, Heimann, Langs, Little, Meltzer (with whom he underwent analysis at the age of seventy-nine), Money-Kyrle, Racker, Searles, Winnicott, and others. Conversely, his name also began to be cited by a number of psychoanalyst colleagues.

Notes

1 This essay by Milner, written between 1950 and 1951, is a milestone of psychoanalytic theory on symbol formation; in it the concept of the transitional phenomenon, thoroughly developed by Winnicott (1951, 1971b), is anticipated. It is worth noting that the friendship and professional relationship between Winnicott and Milner was crucial and creatively stimulating for the both of them, to such an extent that it would be totally impossible

to determine what belonged to one and what to the other, being that their theoretical development is inextricably intertwined (Letley, 2013). It is also interesting to consider that when Milner, dissatisfied by the training analysis with Payne, asked Winnicott to suggest a colleague to whom she could turn in order to cure her own 'madness', her friend offered himself up as analyst (by 1943 he was already her supervisor). The analysis began in 1945 and was held in Milner's office. One could surmise that behind the practical reasons for choosing to use Milner's office lay Winnicott's unspoken desire to be taken into treatment by his colleague. Some years later, not content with this analysis either, Milner consulted Clifford Scott who suggested to her to stop analysis and find a lover. In 1949 Milner began her analysis with Scott.

2 According to Money-Kyrle (1955), the interpretation formulated for the patient in some cases would be correct even if the analyst is addressing it to him/herself. To this possibility may be added another, that by "discovering new patterns in a patient, the analyst can make 'post-graduate' progress in his own analysis" (p. 365, footnote 4).

8

THE DEVELOPMENT OF THE CONCEPT OF PROJECTIVE IDENTIFICATION

A medium of communication

We have now reached the late 1950s and early 1960s, a period in which some of the major innovative contributions to Kleinian theory and technique first appeared in England. I am referring to the work of Wilfred R. Bion, the director of the London Clinic for Psychoanalysis from 1956 to 1962, the year in which he was elected president of the British Psychoanalytical Society.

In view of the above-mentioned writings, beginning with those of Klein, with whom he had been in analysis at the end of the Second World War, and of the collaboration – and subsequent discussions – with Hanna Segal and Herbert Rosenfeld in their work with psychotic patients during the 1950s and 1960s, Bion (1957, 1961, 1962) modified the concept of projective identification and introduced a derivative of it, that of 'container↔contained'. It should be remembered that projective identification was originally described by Klein as an evacuative projective mechanism in close conjunction with splitting, and the goal of this schizoid defense was the immediate relief of an anxiety. (In the case of schizoid mechanisms, splitting is the basic defence upon which the other defensive mechanisms are based). As we shall see below, Bion's communicative projective identification is significantly different from Klein's evacuative projective identification; however, he did not really develop the idea until after Klein's death in 1960.

In Bion's mind, projective identification is certainly an unconscious intrapsychic omnipotent phantasy, but it is also a normal and real form of intersubjective communication. He therefore thought it extremely simplistic to interpret projective identification merely as an unconscious phantasy, because this was not what clinical experience had taught him: sometimes the patients behaved as if in reality – and not on the phantasy level – they were splitting off parts of their own personality and thrusting these into him. In these cases, Bion started asking himself why he was beginning to feel angry or worried during the session. He couldn't rid himself of the sensation that the patient was really doing something that was affecting him. In other words, Bion was feeling "that what I am exposed to in my office is just a phantasy of the patient's. . . . perhaps something really takes place when two people are so closely associated as they are in the psychoanalytic experience" (Bion, 1978–80, p. 269). Thus the analyst becomes the container of 'thoughts without a thinker' (Bion, 1959–78, 1975–78, 1978–80) – those of the patient.

By developing and expanding on a point that Klein merely hinted at, Bion was able to clearly distinguish two forms of projective identification: normal and pathological, with the difference between the two lying in how intensely the subject resorts to this mechanism (it is the psychotic part of the personality which resorts to excessive projective identification, while the neurotic part uses the mechanism of repression). Normal projective identification, as opposed to the pathological variety, is characterised by the fact that it is not a form of pure evacuation, but rather a way to communicate a mental state. I open a parenthesis here to indicate something to which Bob Hinshelwood (2016, personal communication), has directed our attention: it is never very clearly put that the significant difference between communicative and evacuative projective identification is that in the former the person does not lose the part of his experience and so has not completely split himself. Whereas in evacuative projective identification, the split is complete. So the baby cries with anxiety/terror, and needs mother's attention when desperate, but it does not stop crying even when mother has heard the distress and introjected the anxiety. Only when she has given it meaning, and communicated the meaning, then the baby's communicative projective identification stops. Therefore, the communicative form is not a defence, it is communication – the beginnings of symbolisation, or sublimation perhaps. Going back to Bion's normal projective identification, it should be added that within it the aspects of omnipotence are reduced in favour of "behaviour reasonably calculated to arouse in the mother [or in the analyst] feelings of which the infant [or the patient] wishes to be rid" (Bion, 1967b, p. 114), feelings that, if all goes well, the mother works through and restores to the child in a new, tolerable, and conceivable form inasmuch as the form now makes sense; if this is not the case, normal projective identification will progressively give way to the pathological variety. From this perspective, the newborn's crying is a communication (of sensations and feelings) that through projective identification can be received and introjected by the mother. In the case of the psychoanalytical relationship, this reception-introjection of the object's projection is what Money-Kyrle (1955) called introjective identification. If the mother is a good enough mother, she is capable of tuning into the emotional experience of her child and of performing mental work (the alpha-function), thanks to which she makes sense of the newborn's feelings, and then she will adopt behaviours (which are communications) directed at alleviating the suffering and anxiety of the baby (for example nursing him/her, changing his/her diaper, cuddling him/her, etc.). It is from this *rêverie*[1] that the baby may begin to acquire the means to think thoughts. In other words, "if the relationship between infant and breast permits the infant to project a feeling, say, that it is dying into the mother [rêverie] and to reintroject it after its sojourn in the breast has made it tolerable to the infant psyche [alpha-function]. If the projection is not accepted by the mother the infant feels that its feeling that it is dying is stripped of such meaning as it has. It therefore reintrojects, not a fear of dying made tolerable, but a nameless dread" (Bion, 1967b, p. 116). The reasons why the alpha-function can turn out badly are many. But the main ones are two: the first is an absence of rêverie on the part of the caregiver because of an inability or impossibility on her part to perform such a function (in this case the subject's projections will always grow more violent, just as the reintrojections will also be violent); the second reason is the subject's envy of that caregiver who is able to do something that he/she cannot do, a situation the child feels is unacceptable.

The introduction of the concept of projective communicative identification, and of what directly ensues from 'container↔contained', brings to the fore the fundamental importance and the irreducibility of the mother-child *relationship* and, by extension, that of the analyst-patient,[2] introducing the intersubjective approach into both classical and Kleinian psychoanalysis, whose theoretical-clinical horizon had been up to this moment quite restricted to the intrapsychic and unidirectional approach (from the one who projects to the one who receives: child→mother, patient→analyst). It is clear that Bion was convinced that "the patient does something to the analyst and the analyst does something to the patient; it is not just an omnipotent phantasy" (1977, in Bion, 1975–78, p. 283).

Nonetheless, this does not mean that there was no criticism of an intersubjective approach based on projective identification (implying that the subject projects and the object receives and contains). For example, according to Merton Gill (1994), great danger lies in the possibility that "the analyst, in regarding his feelings as necessarily 'put into him' by the analysand, would fail to recognize the contribution from his own personality. This view is in fact a variant of the blank-screen conception of the analyst's role" (p. 102). Furthermore, according to Irwin Hoffman (1998), "Instead of being a blank screen, the analyst becomes an empty 'container' . . . into which the patient deposits various parts of himself or herself. Although the emphasis is on interaction, the metaphor of the container lends itself, ironically, to yet another asocial conception of the situation, since somehow the analyst's personality has once again been eliminated from the field" (p. 123).

The ideas of projective identification and container↔contained, just as those relative to the transformations in O and from O to K (Bion, 1965), had a strong impact on the technique of post-Kleinian analysts, especially those from London, who began to place particular attention on the here and now of the session and on the evolution that the transference-countertransference situation continuously undergoes (Grotstein, 2007). Think of the premature and quick interpretations that, if up until then were the norm, from this moment began to be considered potentially harmful, inasmuch as they were a sign of the emotional difficulties of the clinician in containing the projections of the patient[3] (Robert Langs will speak of 'dumping interpretations', in which the analyst seems to say to the patient: "This problem is not mine, it's yours, and I don't want anything to do with it!"). This is a similar position to the one behind the concept of 'holding', belonging to the Independent analysts. Bion also warned analysts against the risk of collusion with the patient in the (human) attempt to avoid pain.

As we have seen, Bion's essay 'Attacks on Linking' (1957) changed the view on projective identification, which from here on in became more and more regarded as the subject's means of communicating non-verbally with a recipient object, capable of working through the projection. Subsequently the subject could reintroject it in an amended form. For Bion, the patient-therapist bond, or that of newborn and breast, is the projective identification mechanism. We are speaking of a bond based on the capacity of the clinician to introject the patient's projective identifications. This means that the creation of a bond with an object and the role it then plays depends first on the projective identification and, second, on the capacity of the caregiver to introject it. When dealing with the norm, projective identification and introjective identification constitute the basis for a healthy evolution of the subject (Bion, 1967b).

In order to have a more complete view of what was happening within the British Psychoanalytical Society, it is important to keep in mind that, since the 1950s, the concept of projective identification began to appear in every discussion among the London psychoanalysts, and in a great many papers. The spreading of 'projective identification fever' was such that Winnicott wrote in a letter addressed to Bion and dated October 7, 1955:

> I do feel that the Society gets awfully bored with the plugging of terms. In the last six months the words 'projective identification' have been used several hundred times. Of course we are in for a few months in which the word 'envy' will be brought in everywhere. As you know, the words 'internal objects' came across in every communication right up to the time when projective identification took their place. There is something wrong here and I believe and hope that you will take part in the attempt we must make if the Society is to survive to get behind these disruptive tendencies, which are of the nature of a plugging of theme-songs. Incidentally, I am very doubtful about the value of the words 'projective identification' when applied to the parking out of the minute particles of the personality since the word identification rather implies a whole human being somewhere. I would have thought that nearly the whole development of the projective identification theory was contained in the ordinary analytic theory of paranoid anxiety, but perhaps you can put me right here if I am wrong.
>
> *(Winnicott, 1987, p. 92)*

Winnicott's comment is an important testimony to the type of situation characterised by the London group of psychoanalysts, and it brings us back to what Giovanni Massidda (2009) calls 'the problem of compulsion or the hunger for personal definition'.

Getting back to the historical reconstruction of the evolution of the concept of projective identification, the next significant contribution to the subject came from Herbert Rosenfeld (1971, 1983, 1987; previously 1947, 1952, 1963). He further developed the work of Bion, for whom projective identification represented a means of communication, even if he mostly concentrated on its pathological aspects.

According to Rosenfeld (1971): "For projective identification to take place some temporary differentiation of 'me' and 'not me' is essential" (p. 120). He distinguished two types of projective identification that can come into play simultaneously or alternately: one is used "for communication with other objects" (p. 120), and the other is used "for ridding the self of unwanted parts" (p. 120), or rather for subjecting psychic reality to denial. In terms of the first type, it should be mentioned that it consists of the projection of "impulses and parts of himself into the analyst in order that the analyst will feel and understand his experiences and will be able to contain them so that they lose their frightening or unbearable quality and become meaningful by the analyst being able to put them into words through interpretations" (p. 121). Patients (Rosenfeld was referring to psychotics) who resort to projective identification as a means of communication are usually receptive to the clinician's ability to understand. This requires the analyst to introject, recognise, tolerate, and give back the patient's projections after a process of working through them (relapses fall within the development – healthy vs. pathological – of the introjective processes[4] and of the patient's ego). It seems as if we are dealing with a kind of distortion or intensification of the normal infant-caregiver relationship, based on non-verbal communication. This first type of projective identification is usually used in an unconscious way by the patient within transference, but, in some cases, this process can be used in a conscious way. The second type of projective identification is used to free the self, which has been subjected to splitting, both from one's own undesired or unbearable parts and from anxieties and disturbing impulses. Such an evacuation process "leads to a denial of psychic reality" (p. 135). Since the will of the patient is to evacuate and deny his/her own painful internal reality, he/she often sees the analyst's interpretations as frightening criticisms and reacts to them with violent resentment because he/she is convinced that they are an attempt by the analyst to forcibly throw back into him/her that unbearable and 'meaningless' mental content previously projected into the analyst.

In his treatise of 1971, Rosenfeld also discussed projective identification as a transferential relationship, or rather one of transference, which sets down its roots within the earliest infancy of the patient, within the earliest object relationships, the goal of which is to control the body and the mind of the other, in this case the analyst. We have here an omnipotent form of projective identification that undermines the capacity to engage in abstract and symbolic thought, leading as a consequence to thought becoming more and more concrete. "It is the excessive projective identification in the psychotic process which obliterates differentiation of self and objects, which causes confusion between reality and phantasy and a regression to concrete thinking due to the loss of the capacity for symbolization and symbolic thinking" (p. 123). Such a predominance of concrete thinking, due to a massive use of projective identification, means that words become 'symbolic equations'[5] (Segal, 1950, 1955) for the patient. What happens is that the clinician's words as well, or rather his verbal interpretations, get misunderstood by the patient.

Rosenfeld also wrote about projective identification used as a defence mechanism to deal with aggression and envy. He had already described, in 1963, and more completely in his 1971 paper, projective identification as part of an early narcissistic relationship with the mother (and with the analyst, with whom the patient lives in a state of fusion at a certain point in the therapeutic process), in whom denial plays a decisive role in the non-recognition of the state of separateness from the object, the knowledge of which would instil feelings of dependence on the object and, therefore, anxiety (with the consequent aggressive and destructive impulses, usually associated with envy of the good object on whom one depends, more than with the anger due to separation from the object). Thus, projective identification in the psychotic patient is usually construed as "a defence against excessive envy, which is closely bound up with the patient's narcissism, rather than a defence against separation anxiety" (p. 125).

Another subject Rosenfeld deals with is linked to the psychotic patient's objective relations in which he/she maintains the illusory conviction of living completely inside the object-analyst, behaving like a parasite, and taking advantage of the abilities of the host-object (who in the patient's phantasy functions as if he were his/her own ego and as the person responsible for his/her own life). According to Rosenfeld (1971), "severe parasitism may be regarded as a state of total projective identification. It is, however, not just a defensive state to deny envy or separation, but it is also an expression of aggression, particularly envy. It is the combination of defence and acting out of the aggression which makes the parasitic state a particularly difficult therapeutic problem" (p. 125). We should add that: "It is important to differentiate the very chronic forms of parasitism from the massive intrusion and projective identification into the analyst which resembles parasitism but is of shorter duration and responds more easily to interpretations. It occurs at a time when separation threatens or when jealousy or envy is violently stimulated in the transference or in outside life" (p. 126). Rosenfeld also examines the parasitic state in which seriously delusional patients live totally in an unreal world, delusional, yes, but seemingly structured in such a way as to represent the inside life of the object (and most probably, this object is the mother).

I will pause here a moment to give voice to a criticism along the lines of what Winnicott suggested in his letter of October 7, 1955, and which at the time of its formulation was ignored, despite coming from an important exponent of the Kleinian group. In 1974, Donald Meltzer, who, from the early 1960s, actively took part in developing the concepts of identification (first on his own, and then in collaboration with Esther Bick,[6] who developed the concepts of 'second skin', 1968, and 'adhesive identity', 1975) and projective identification, described the climate permeating the debates around the concept of projective identification, debates that took place between Kleinian analysts and the analysts disposed towards a different theoretical orientation. Meltzer writes:

> There was just the matter of exploring what began to look like an almost limitless field of phenomenology related to projective identification and its

> consequences. We got quite used to the term – it's not a very nice term, you know, in the sense that it isn't poetic at all – but it came easily off the tongue and we found ourselves saying, 'projective identification', 'projective identification', and we got quite blasé about it and I think quite careless about it in a way. Of course we also began to notice that the interpretation along the lines of projective identification didn't seem to carry any weight in certain situations. We were in trouble with certain kinds of patients and saw that something else was going on that certainly was connected with identification processes; it certainly was connected with narcissism, but it seemed to have quite a different phenomenology from what we had gathered together under the rubric of projective identification.
>
> *(Meltzer, 1974, p. 295)*

In 1979, Thomas Ogden, a North American intersubjective analyst, influenced by the object relations theoreticians, published an important work on projective identification with a distinct Kleinian flavour (it should be remembered that this author worked for a short time at the Tavistock Clinic in London in the 1970s and continued to maintain close personal ties with various Kleinian and Independent analysts).

According to Ogden (1979; cf. also 1991), projective identification constitutes an ensemble of phantasies and object relations in which it is possible to distinguish three (simultaneous and interdependent) elements – "first, there is the fantasy of projecting a part of oneself into another person and of that part taking over the person from within; then there is pressure exerted via the interpersonal interaction such that the 'recipient' of the projection experiences pressure to think, feel, and behave in a manner congruent with the projection; finally, the projected feelings, after being 'psychologically processed' by the recipient, are reinternalized by the projector" (Ogden, 1979, p. 358).

In the first phase, a person (the projector) has an unconscious desire to free him/herself of an undesirable part of him/herself by transferring it into someone else (the recipient). In line with Klein's thought (1946), Ogden believes that both the 'bad' and the 'good' parts of the self may be projected. In the first case the subject tries to protect him/herself by projecting parts experienced as bad and which he/she fears could destroy the self from within (in essence he/she is projecting feelings of guilt, anxieties, envy, etc.). In the second case, the subject tries to protect the good part of the self from the aggression that other parts, the bad ones, could cause (this would involve, for example, an adolescent who comes regularly to the sessions but always complains of being forced to come by the parents). What is clear here is that the projector functions, at least partly, at an archaic level of development, in which the boundaries between the self and the object representations are beginning to fail. This allows the subject to maintain contact with the object of projection, to feel deeply connected with that object, and to feel that the object is experiencing the same feelings (those projected) that he/she is and not merely analogous ones. In the second phase, the subject exercises on the object of projection some sort of interpersonal pressure aimed at making the object experience him/herself and making the object take on behaviours congruent with the projective phantasy. The emphasis here is on the need for a real/concrete interaction to take place between the one who projects and the one who receives, a behavioural interaction in which the projective phantasies may have a real impact on the recipient. If this did not happen, a simple projection would take place instead of a projective identification – an intrapsychic event rather than a psychological-interpersonal process. In the third and last phase, if all goes well, what takes place is the 'psychic processing' of the projection on the part of the recipient, and the reinternalisation of the 'metabolised projection' on the part of the projector. But what does the recipient-object experience/process? Certainly not the same feelings projected by the patient, ones that cannot be transplanted, but rather a new set of feelings which, to all intents and purposes, are similar to the projector's, and elicited within the object of the projection. The nature of this new set of feelings depends on the fact that the recipient is a human being with his/her own history, unconscious, personality, conflicts, and anxieties. And it is precisely the differences in psychological functioning that allows the therapist (who, thanks to his/her own personal analysis, should have reached a greater integration compared to the patient) to manage difficult feelings in a different way – in other words, the therapist should be better able to contain and work through them. Therefore the clinician functions as a container (Bion, 1962) that experiences the part projected into him/her by the patient, and through this alpha-function transforms (metabolises, digests, etc.) it. The result is a 'processed' version of the originally projected feelings, a version which implies the possibility of coexisting with them without damaging other aspects of the self and/or one's own internal world. Thus, for Ogden, what makes this phase therapeutic is the clinician's ability to welcome the patient's projections, contain and process them by using aspects of his/her own (more mature) personality system within the processing operation, and ultimately making the digested projection available to the patient for reinteriorisation by means of the therapeutic interaction. We are dealing with a type of work that is often long and hard, in which the processing moreover is always 'incomplete' and 'contaminated' by the pathology of the recipient. If the projection is sufficiently absorbed by the therapist (who should have a more mature personality system than the patient), the reinternalisation of what is undergone in the relationship with the analyst offers the patient a new capacity "to blend experience, memories, and emotions, previously held fiercely separate or split off" (Speziale-Bagliacca, 1994, p. 9; my translation), and this contributes to psychological growth. If instead the therapist fails to contain and/or process the projective identification, then the patient will reinternalise the feelings that he projected, mixed with those elicited within and inadequately assimilated by the clinician, thus experiencing an intensification of his/her original fears (and the related defences) and a weakening of the hope of being helped by a therapist with whom he/she shares some significant pathological characteristics.

To summarise, we can say that in Ogden's conception, projective identification is a process that serves as:

> (1) A type of defence by which one can distance oneself from an unwanted or internally endangered part of the self, while in fantasy keeping that aspect of oneself 'alive' in another. (2) A mode of communication by which one makes oneself understood by exerting pressure on another person to experience a set of feelings similar to one's own. (3) A type of object relatedness in which the projector experiences the recipient of the projection as separate enough to serve as a receptacle for parts of the self, but sufficiently un-differentiated to maintain the illusion that one is literally sharing a given feeling with another person. (4) A pathway for psychological change by which feelings similar to those with which one is struggling are processed by another person, following which the projector may identify with the recipient's handling of the engendered feelings.
>
> *(Ogden, 1979, p. 371)*

The process of projective identification, which pertains to both patient and analyst, in that "in part . . . there is never a recipient who is not simultaneously a projector" (Ogden, 1994c, p. 102), is at the centre of the subsequent theoretical formulation of the 'intersubjective analytic third' (Ogden, 1994a, 1994c, 2004): a third subjectivity created within the analytical setting by the dialectical relationship between the individual subjectivities of patient and analyst.

Two years after Ogden made his contribution to the subject matter, another American analyst, James Grotstein, who since the 1960s had been preoccupied with this issue (cf. Malin and Grotstein, 1966), published a book devoted to projective identification. This text represents the realisation of the author's commitment to clarify certain important theoretical questions by comparing and integrating different psychoanalytic stances: classical psychoanalysis, the psychology of self, and object relations. We should emphasise here the strong influence that the theories of Bion (Grotstein had been in analysis with him) and of others belonging to the British school of object relations, especially Klein, Fairbairn, and Winnicott, had on the evolution of his personal theory of mind and the analytic relationship, which Grotstein had been developing over the years.

According to Grotstein, projective identification and splitting are the primary ingredients in all defence mechanisms, and are the main mechanisms involved in perception, cognition, and object relations. They are the main components of the primary process and, at the same time, are two important components in the secondary process.

Grotstein has

> arbitrarily assumed that externalization applies to those aspects of projective identification which are nondefensive, whereas projective identification proper includes all defensive operations. Thus, disavowal of identification with the projection would constitute defensive projective identification, and acceptance of the identification with projection would constitute externalization. Externalization includes foraging, scanning, exploring, generalizing, imagining, translocating, creating 'projects', etc. Defensive projective identification includes (a) evacuation of accretions of mental stimuli; (b) dedifferentiating

> attainment of 'at-one-ment' either with the Background Object of Primary Identification or with a secondary interpersonal object (self-object); and (c) the entry of the self into an object in order to control it for omnipotently adaptive purposes. In analysis we make use of the externalizing aspects of projective identification in free association, but we also observe projective identification as the instrument for all phantasies. Thus it is responsible for the creation of the objects which comprise the inner world. Imagination is the metaphor for projective identification.
>
> *(Grotstein, 1981, p. 213)*

To better understand the phenomenon of projective identification, Grotstein applies the dual-track principle associated with the 'siamese twin' (or symbiotic) model, according to which

> there can be two states of mind simultaneously on different levels; one of separateness and the other of fusion. Thus, the infant can go back and forth between the two states or experience both states simultaneously. At the same time, this model allows for the infant to experience identification with the projection into the object and also to be able to deny it (disidentification). Projective identification is an object relationship and involves an extension of self into the object rather than a hurling of content into space. In psychosis, projective identification seems to be extending the self into an object, but it actually is a withdrawal of self away from its ego boundaries (including mind and sense organs) which then fuse with the object(s) interfacing with that boundary.
>
> *(Grotstein, 1981, p. 214)*

Grotstein also explains the relationship between projective identification and transference:

> Transference, rather than merely being a distortion of experience, represents the quintessence of projective identification in its capacity to protectively transfer mental pain from the self to the therapist in a special kind of 'siamese' bonding which allows for an 'exchange transfusion' between the sacred and the profane. The conduit of that bonding is the therapeutic alliance; the thrust of its viability is projective identification.
>
> *(Grotstein, 1981, pp. 212–215)*

The point of view expressed in this monograph would constitute the basis for a subsequent original contribution to the concept of projective identification that Grotstein would provide twenty-five years later by introducing the concept of 'projective transidentification', which we will consider later.

As we shall see in the next chapter, Joseph Sandler (1976, 1984; Sandler and Sandler, 1987) – member of the contemporary Freudian Group – preferred using the concepts of 'actualisation' and 'role-responsiveness' rather than that of projective identification to identify the process (which is not concrete, but is a phantasy) by means of which a subject establishes his own set of external objects within a situation first of feeling and then of taking action to satisfy the needs and desires that he/she has projected into them.

Some years later, in 1984, Sandler, the then chair of psychoanalysis at the University of Jerusalem, due to the ever-increasing interest that the concept of projective identification was generating, even beyond the confines of Kleinian followers, organised an international conference on this subject. The Kleinian analyst Betty Joseph was one of the speakers. She spoke of projective identification from the same theoretical position as Bion and Rosenfeld (these three analysts, along with Segal and Elliott Jaques, form a circle of people who had close professional and social contact with Klein), but referred to clinical work with seriously neurotic patients, but less severely compromised, with respect to those analysed by his two other colleagues.

Betty Joseph (1984) maintained that if the child's development moves along quite well, the greater integration, typical of the attainment of a depressive position, makes possible the forsaking of a primitive and massive use of projective identification (which allows the subject to distance him/herself, to free him/herself from the intolerable mental pain that he/she would otherwise experience), in favour of a more mature use, from which may be created a basis for empathy. However, sometimes the development doesn't allow the subject to go beyond this position in early childhood, and the use of projective identification remains so primitive and massive in adulthood, as to give the clinician the impression that the patient projects his own self into the object in phantasy, thus feeling trapped and claustrophobic. It is clear then that Joseph places the origin of projective identification at the primitive attempt of the subject to re-enter the object, lose him/herself within, and merge in an undifferentiated way with the object, thus avoiding any pain. For Joseph,

> projective identification is only one aspect of an omnipotent balance established by each individual in his own way, any interpretive attempt on the part of the analyst to locate and give back to the patient missing parts of the self must of necessity be resisted by the total personality, since it is felt to threaten the whole balance and lead to more disturbance.
>
> *(Joseph, 1984, p. 170)*

On the subject of Bion's study on the alpha-function, Joseph writes that

> projective identification is, by its very nature, a kind of communication, even in cases where this is not its aim nor its intention. By definition projective identification means the putting of parts of the self into an object. If the analyst on the receiving end is really open to what is going on and able to be aware of what he is experiencing, this can be a powerful method of gaining understanding.
>
> *(Joseph, 1984, p. 170)*

According to Joseph, there exist diverse forms of projective identification and these can act together towards a goal (unconscious) of maintaining a certain omnipotent narcissistic balance (which allows one to evade the experiencing of feelings of dependence, jealousy, envy, hate, etc., but which is however a source of strong persecutory emotions), very resistant to psychoanalytical treatment. In other words, the patient does everything to try to maintain or restore that particular system of psychic balance, which makes it possible for him/her to avoid painful or distressing feelings. Clear-cut analogies are evident here with Sandler's concept of 'actualization'. Sandler believes that the patient continuously works to modify the therapist's behaviour so that he/she might embody the unconscious fantasies and fulfil the expectations of the patient.

Joseph also highlights different aspects of projective identification: an attack on the analyst's mind; a form of total invasion; a partial invasion and appropriation of the analyst's characteristics or abilities with which the patient identifies; an introduction of parts of the self (especially the inferior or envious parts) into the analyst, parts with which the analyst has come to be identified.

> [Thus] projective identification by its very nature means the putting of parts of the self into the object, in the transference we are of necessity on the receiving end of the projections and, therefore, providing we can tune into them, we have an opportunity *par excellence* to understand them and what is going on. In this sense, it acts as a communication, whatever its motivation, and is the basis for the positive use of countertransference . . . it is frequently difficult to clarify whether, at any given moment, projective identification is primarily aimed at communicating a state of mind that cannot be verbalized by the patient or whether it is aimed more at entering and controlling or attacking the analyst, or whether all these elements are active and need consideration.
>
> *(Joseph, 1984, pp. 174–175)*

From this viewpoint, countertransference allows the clinician to grasp the nature of the patient's communication, since it develops out of the projective identification with which the patient strives to make him/her (by projecting into him/her during transference) experience specific feelings and react to them. It should be mentioned that both feelings and defences, or internal figures, may be projected (for example the internal representation of the mother).

What Joseph has described is a type of projective identification in which unconscious phantasy combines with unconscious behaviours in order to arouse specific responses in the object. However, as previously stated, today the term *projective identification* is used in such a wide sense as to include cases where the object is emotionally infected by the projection as well as cases where the object is not. For this reason, Elizabeth Spillius (1988a) suggested that it was useful to add the adjective 'evocative' in cases in which there is a presence of a type of projective identification "where the recipient is put under pressure to have the feelings appropriate to the projector's phantasy" (p. 83; cf. also Spillius, 2007).

In 1995, Michael Feldman, who was born in South Africa and trained as a psychoanalyst in England, considered the use of projective identification as a means of involving the analyst. He starts from the fact that the behaviours (verbal and non-verbal), which express the patient's fantasies, constitute conscious and/or unconscious pressures able to influence the mental state (feelings and capacity for thought) and the behaviour (actions) of the analyst. The analyst inevitably runs up against forms of enactment, which however represent a unique opportunity to get to know some of the unconscious identifications as well as the functioning levels of the patient (cf. Heimann, 1949; Racker, 1958; Sandler, 1976; Joseph, 1984), and therefore represent, at least potentially, a valuable source of information for the patient's inner world, especially in terms of internal object relations.

Feldman shows how the analyst's involvement may be, for the patient, a basic component of the defensive use of projective identification. He states that "the projection of elements of a phantasised object relationship represents an attempt by the patient to reduce the discrepancy between an archaic object relationship and an alternative object relationship that might be confronting the patient and threatening him" (1995, p. 228). The need for the analyst to experience some of the patient's phantasies (phantasies that reflect his/her internal object relations) seems to be something the patient feels more frequently than the mere desire for the analyst to be transformed inside the patient's phantasy. When projection is made into a hallucinatory object, delusional or absent, we find ourselves facing an omnipotent process that implies a total recessivity on the part of the internal object, who, in this way, allows him/herself to be transformed. This helps ensure for the patient the elimination of the separateness between self and object, and of the discrepancy between phantasy and reality. It follows that

> the patient's use of projective identification exerts subtle and powerful pressure on the analyst to fulfil the patient's unconscious expectations that are embodied in these phantasies. Thus the impingement upon the analyst's thinking, feelings and actions is not an incidental side-effect of the patient's projections, nor necessarily a manifestation of the analyst's own conflicts and anxieties, but seems often to be an essential component in the effective use of projective identification by the patient.
>
> *(Feldman, 1995, p. 228)*

There exists a relationship between the projection into the internal object-analyst within the phantasy and what actually happens when the patient and analyst meet and interact in a non-omnipotent manner. However, there is always a discrepancy, to a greater or lesser degree, between the actual mental state of the analyst (how much he/she has really been transformed by the patient's projections) and the internal object representation that the patient has created of him/her.

What happens to the analyst who has been invested with the projective identifications of his/her patient? Possible answers to this question can be subdivided into three macro-categories: a) he/she remains comfortable, keeping his/her own role and functions intact, recognising and formulating some thoughts around the pressures to which he/she has been subjected; b) he/she is disturbed by the changes in his own psychophysical state; c) the analyst gradually becomes aware of having been the object of pressures that have driven him/her towards a subtle and complex enactment (not necessarily experienced initially as egodystonic, but perhaps he/she feels totally comfortable – sure of having identified the patient's pathological nuclei). This awareness can make it possible for the analyst to experience some of the patient's internal object relations. These differences in the potential responses, on the part of the clinician, depend on the fact that, like the patient, the therapist has to contend with the anxieties and needs generated by the phantasies (or rather the object relations of his own inner world). According to Feldman, the inevitable distance between the pre-existing unconscious phantasies, which, in some measure, are reassuring or gratifying, and the phantasies stirred up by the analytical framework, phantasies which could potentially be threatening and upsetting, incites each member of the analytical couple to resort to his/her own projective mechanisms (defence) or to some type of enactment, in an attempt to reduce the distance between the pre-existing phantasies and those aroused by the psychoanalytic encounter. It is as if the patient is desperately trying to make the analyst's behaviour and the experience with him/her more familiar, to make them correspond more to his own unconscious phantasy. This effort to 'actualise' (Sandler and Sandler, 1978; Sandler, 1988) the phantasies of his/her own internal object relations corresponds to the unconscious search for the fulfillment of his/her own desires and simultaneously performs the function of reassurance. The patient really tries to transform the analyst in order to reduce the gap – the larger it is, the more deeply disturbing it is – between the representation of the internal object-analyst and the analyst of external reality; a process that "goes beyond and seems to conflict with the need to feel understood, or reassured about the capacity of the object to take in and to 'contain' the projections. The lack of this identity between the internal and external reality may not only stir up envy, or doubts about the object's receptivity, but create an alarming space in which thought and new knowledge and understanding might take place, but which many patients find intolerable" (Feldman, 1995, p. 232).

If the analyst is receptive, as he should be, to the patient's projections, these will inevitably resonate with the unconscious needs and fears of the clinician, for whom it isn't always easy or quick to recognise when he/she is being an object of projective identification (Joseph, 1984; O'Shaughnessey, 1992), also because, as previously mentioned, the analyst's responses can vary in both quality and quantity. For example, in some cases the therapist may perceive something disturbing or alien within him, to a slight rather than a pronounced degree, while in other cases he/she may feel a benign, comfortable, and impartial type of involvement. This latter state represents a situation in which the undesirable parts of him/herself, split off and projected by the patient, correspond to the analyst's unresolved aspects, and therefore an unconscious collusion occurs, a convergence of the defensive needs of the patient and analyst (who, in this way, feels that his role is congruous with some internal phantasies), which can hinder a real understanding of the patient and, consequently, cause difficulties in the restitution of the projections (after they have been worked through) of the patient, who cannot move towards real improvement. Feldman's hypothesis is that "what is projected is not primarily a part of the patient, but a phantasy of an object relationship. It is this that impinges upon the analyst, and may allow him to remain reasonably comfortable, or may disturb him and incline him to enact" (1995, p. 234). This comes as a result of the interaction between the patient's needs and those of the analyst. These examples of enactment may be in line with the phantasy projected by the patient, or they may be an attempt to distance oneself from it, inasmuch as it is too disturbing. All this depends on the fact that "the impulse towards enactment may reflect unresolved aspects of the analyst's own pathological internal object relations" (1995, p. 234). The analyst, since he is a human being, is continuously searching for a balance between a reasonably satisfying representation of him/herself and the way in which he/she experiences external relational reality. The recognition of a possible enactment derives from a modification in internal perspective, making understanding and containment possible, and therefore the formulation of interpretations, also capable of promoting healthy changes within the patient.

Feldman writes:

> I suspect that if the analyst is receptive to the patient's projections, the impact of the patient's disturbing unconscious phantasies that concern the nature of his relationship with the patient inevitably touch on the analyst's own anxieties. This may evoke forms of projection and enactment by the analyst, in an attempt at restoring an internal equilibrium, of which the analyst may initially be unaware. The difficult and often painful task for the analyst is to recognise the subtle and complex enactments he is inevitably drawn into with his patient, and to work to find a domain for understanding and thought outside the narrow and repetitive confines unconsciously demanded by the patient, and sometimes by his own anxieties and needs. While the achievement of real psychic change is dependent on this process, it is threatening for the patient and liable to mobilise further defensive procedures.
>
> *(Feldman, 1995, pp. 235–236)*

From what has already been said, it should be clear that for Feldman the projective mechanisms perform more than one function: they allow one to distance oneself from something experienced as disturbing; they allow one to engage the object, in our case the analyst, delegating to him/her the task of creating connections on the basis of how much has been communicated to him/her via the projection – in other words, the task of creating a meaning upon which to reflect; they make it possible to partially enact, for the analyst in the external world, some of the phantasies of familiar and archaic object relations, ones which are often disturbed and disturbing, gleaned from the inner world of the patient. Even though these phantasies may be the source of great suffering for the patient, reliving them has a reassuring function – Marion Milner (1952b) would say that the patient seeks and finds the familiar in the unfamiliar – which implies that our efforts to modify the situation represent a threat to the patient's defensive equilibrium, to his mental functioning.

The enactment of the analyst is, at least to a certain degree, an integral and inevitable part of the analytical process. A part of the analyst's work consists of recognising it and getting free of it, at least temporarily, in order to reach a better and deeper understanding of the patient's inner world, and of his/her self. Thus it is fundamental to identify the pressures exerted by the patient so that the analyst, in his interaction with the patient, will enact his/her unconscious relational phantasies. Recognising this allows the therapist to retrieve his/her own therapeutic function, and to reduce the discrepancy between the phantasies about his/her own role and external reality. The ability to tolerate such a discrepancy is moreover inversely proportional to the need to resort to the use of projective mechanisms and various types of enactment. This retrieval, partial and temporary, of the analyst's ability to think reflexively is fundamental to the maintenance of the therapeutic role.

A few years after the publication of Feldman's treatise, Ronald Britton proposes a useful distinction between 'attributive projective identification' and 'acquisitive projective identification'. The first indicates an attributive process of the type studied by Klein (1955), Rosenfeld (1963), and Sohn (1985), through which the subject enters (in phantasy) the object, in order to acquire certain attributes that are thought to belong to the object (a similar process to 'extractive introjection' described by Bollas, 1987). An example of the more extreme form of acquisitive projective identification could be that of a person who believes he/she has become Napoleon during the night, when a less omnipotent person would simply report having had a dream during the night in which he/she became Napoleon. The second form of projective identification indicates an omnipotent unconscious phantasy by which the subject attributes some aspects of his/her own self to the object. It is possible that this type will not resonate within the analyst, or, by means of the subject's subtle behaviours, it can evoke in the object the projected mental state (we are dealing here with the 'evocative' form described by Spillius, 1988a). In summarising Britton's (1998) classification, we can say that in acquisitive projective identification, "'I AM YOU' – that is, another person's identity or attribute are claimed for the self. The more omnipotently this is done the more delusional the result" (p. 6), while in attributive projective identification, "'YOU ARE ME' – that is, an aspect of the self is attributed to another person. This may be *evocatory*, inducing change in the other, or *non-evocatory*, when no action is taken to give effect to it" (Britton, 1998, emphasis in original).

Some years later, in 2004, the English psychoanalyst of Brazilian origin, Ignes Sodré, provides an important contribution to our knowledge of the processes of identification, by analysing how projections, introjections, and maniacal mechanisms cooperate in the creation and maintenance of pathological states of identification, characterised by a massive projective identification of the subject with the object: different states from those in which the subject projects in order to get free of a particular experience or to control the object. Projections, introjections, and identifications constitute a complex process which is the basis of every significant interaction between two people.

According to Sodré (2004), "The central characteristic of the use of 'projective identification' is the creation in the subject of a state of mind in which the boundaries between self and object have shifted" (p. 136), so that the self, especially in the case of pathological projective identification, can "dis-identify with that which is projected" (p. 135). We are dealing here with a psychic process founded on phantasies, but if the subject enters into an interaction with the object he/she will be able to perceive that "what is being projected will also affect the development of the object relationship that is taking place at that moment" (p. 136).

The fact that the subject splits off and projects aspects of him/herself (feelings, parts of one's personality, and modalities of functioning) involves a transformation in the phantasy of both the subject's and the object's identity; sometimes this transformation is also due to the acquisition on the part of the subject of particular aspects belonging to the object. In the case of a massive projective identification, the subject becomes (in phantasy) the object or a particular aspect or version of him/her, while the object becomes the self or embodies an aspect of it, one that is experienced as unbearable. Here we are facing an excessive use, and therefore a pathological one, of projection as well as introjection mechanisms (introjections that acquire a quality of concreteness) – a modality of functioning that is based on a massive use of maniacal defences. As Rosenfeld (1963) had already indicated, an omnipotent identification, whether for projection or introjection, has a profound influence on the sense of self and self-object boundaries: the subject can experience a state of confusion due to the loss of the me/not me boundaries, or can experience a substantial character rigidity, which is useful for maintaining new and stable me/not me boundaries that protect from a return of those parts of the self that were split off and projected.

For the subject, the recourse to projective identification means attributing an aspect of him/her self to the object in whom it is projected. Therefore we are dealing with a projective dis-identification – a process by which the subject loses parts of his/her own identity. Projective identification occurs at the level of unconscious phantasy, but in the case of an interaction with a receptive object, this latter person will be able to meet the intrusion into the self of something that is alien, giving rise to a partial or total 'forced projective identification'. The outcome of this interaction will depend on how massive the projection is, as well as on the ability and willingness of the object to introject and partially identify, without confusing his/her own self with what is introjected.

If the existence of pathological projective processes is very clear to all, for many, the existence of pathological introjective processes is less clear. This is probably because what one tends to interpret as projective identification has to do with the 'bad' aspects, while what one tends to interpret as introjective has to do with the 'good' aspects; thus there is a propensity "to think of projective processes as more pathological than introjective ones" (p. 137). The identification becomes pathological when, instead of being based on the subject's desire to be like the object, it is based on the desire to become the object in a 'concrete' sense: the subject swallows up the entire object who is thus robbed of the possibility of continuing to exist as a whole object with its own identity. More specifically, "Pathological introjective identification implies a phantasy of concretely taking something in, whereas a normal identification with an internal object presupposes a capacity to introject symbolically while allowing the object to retain its separate identity. The same is true of normal projection, of course: when the ego is functioning in a depressive position mode, symbolic projection into the other's mind – being able to put oneself imaginatively in the other's place – helps us to understand who the other person is" (p. 137). It is evident that, during the introjection process described above, maniacal mechanisms, which modify the self into an entity that is greater and more powerful than the object, are involved. It is the concrete nature of the projective processes, rather than a symbolic one, that make the identification pathological.

In the case of pathological identification the subject-object relationship becomes a continuous struggle for the maintenance of a personality balance that has been reached by means of resorting to splitting-off and identification – mechanisms that guarantee a distancing from an awareness of the weaker and more dependent parts of the self. In these situations, the analyst must try to put himself/herself into a third position, from which to observe what is happening in the here and now of the interaction – a position from which "it becomes more possible to see who is who and what is the object relationship which is being enacted in the transference. In this case, this could be seen to be one between somebody who is trying to get something through, something that absolutely must be seen to be of value, and somebody else who is impenetrable, unreachable, who says 'No!' to any attempt at communication" (Sodré, 2004, p. 146). The identity change that occurs in the patient, who resorts to a pathological introjective identification, does represent an obstacle in therapeutic work but, at the same time, makes it possible for us therapists to have a direct experience of contact with the objects that animate the patient's internal world.

Grotstein's paper to which we have previously alluded came out the following year. In 2005, the Californian analyst introduced an extension of the concept of projective identification in an attempt to bring order to the confusion with which the term is used by analysts espousing different theoretical orientations. The main areas of confusion identified by Grotstein are: (a) the existence of differences/similarities/discontinuity/complementarity between Klein's (1946, 1955) conception of projective identification as rigidly intrapsychic phantasy and that of Bion (1962) who highlighted the communicative and intersubjective aspects of it; (b) the existence or not of differences between projection and projective identification; (c) the question whether projection occurs within an external object or, rather, within the image of the subject's internal object, and the resulting questions on how it is possible to explain the response of the object to projective identification, and on whether other processes that contribute to allowing such a phenomenon to become communicative exist or not.

Grotstein explains his point of view on the issue by summarising it in six postulates:

(a) Intersubjective projective identification constitutes not only . . . an unconscious, omnipotent, intrapsychic phantasy . . . but also two other processes: (1) conscious and/or preconscious modes of sensory-motor induction and/or evocation or prompting techniques (mental, physical, verbal, posturing or priming, 'nudging') on the part of the projecting subject, followed by (2) spontaneous empathic simulation in the receptive object of the subject's experience who is already inherently equipped (programmed) to empathize with it. From the perspective of experience, the projecting subject feels that he has rid himself of bad (or good) emotional contents, and now believes that the object is the self or indistinguishable from it in regard to the projected parts – and, experientially, the object may concur that it has become affected.
(b) The projecting subject and the object of projection constitute two separate self-activating systems, and the interpersonal process should consequently be renamed 'projective transidentification' to designate its unique transpersonal mode.
(c) One can never project into another individual per se, only into one's image (internal object representation) of them – and then attempt to manipulate that image in unconscious phantasy as if it were the external object that was being manipulated.
(d) Consequently, projective transidentification would function by establishing an inductive resonance between the internal object images formed by the projecting subject, on one hand, and those counterpart images formed by the external object of the subject, on the other.
(e) Projective identification into the object-image is followed by an introjection by the projecting subject of the now projectively transformed image of the object, which ultimately lands in the subject's superego and ego upon introjection.
(f) Projection from the Kleinian/Bionian points of view is inseparable from and identical with projective identification, but they are distinguished from each other in various different ways in the mainstream American view.

(Grotstein, 2005, pp. 1059–1060)

What results from this is that what Grotstein calls projective transidentification comprises not only the intrapsychic projective identification described by Klein, but also, in the light of the nature of pre-lexical emotional communication between subject (child, patient) and object (mother, analyst) demonstrated by Bion, the solicitation of the object and the signalling to the object. It should be emphasised that in analysis just as in daily life, the trajectories of the transitions of projective transidentification travel in both directions.

Finally, it must be remembered that a little after the publication of the above-mentioned article, Grotstein (2007) modified his theory. He arrived at the conclusion that (during the period in which the subject normally communicates with the object), only in the moment when some kind of disintegration takes place, or when a crisis in normal non-verbal affective communication occurs, must the subject (who from the time of birth is equipped with the rudiments of alpha-function thanks to which the subject can generate alpha-elements) resort to projective transidentification with an object who in that moment is not enough of a container.

In this present historical restructuring of the evolution of the concept of projective identification, we have taken into consideration the contributions of the British Kleinian analysts. However, it is essential to keep in mind that in each theoretical and theoretical-clinical treatise contributed by an analyst from the British Psychoanalytical Society (whether Kleinian, contemporary Freudian, or Independent) one is able to discover an echo of a filiation relationship (in the case of training analysis or supervision) and one of friendship or collaboration, as well as a familiarity with, or a discussion of certain theories, the knowledge of a specific language, and an association with the same psychoanalytical and cultural milieu. In this way, not only Kleinians, but also contemporary Freudians and Independents have taken part, in different ways and to a different degree, in these conversations on projective identification.

Here I would like to briefly report on some results to a survey conducted via email by Edna O'Shaughnessy (2012). She has identified the main criticisms that contemporary Freudians and Independents have expressed against the concept of projective identification: (a) overuse of the concept of projective identification, through which the Kleinians explain all patient communication and every feeling experienced by the analyst; (b) the concept of projective identification indicates a mechanism of aggression – a fact that involves an excessive focus by Kleinians on the patient's innate destructiveness; (c) the concept of projective identification represents for Kleinians an attempt to formulate interpretations in the here and now with a speed which would otherwise not be justified, as well as with a regrettable use of the 'I-you' and the 'you-I' analytical technique. This third point is only endorsed by some contemporary Freudian analysts.

In conclusion, I would like to reiterate the definition of identification that is found in *The New Dictionary of Kleinian Thought*, edited by Elizabeth Spillius, Jane Milton, Penelope Garvey, Cyril Couve, and Deborah Steiner, a new edition of the famous *A Dictionary of Kleinian Thought* by Robert Hinshelwood (1989):

> Projective identification is an unconscious phantasy in which aspects of the self or of an internal object are split off and attributed to an external object. The projected aspects may be felt by the projector to be either good or bad. Projective phantasies may or may not be accompanied by evocative behaviour unconsciously intended to induce the recipient of the projection to feel

and act in accordance with the projective phantasy. Phantasies of projective identification are sometimes felt to have 'acquisitive' as well as 'attributive' properties, meaning that the phantasy involves not only getting rid of aspects of one's own psyche but also of entering the mind of the other in order to acquire desired aspects of his psyche. In this case projective and introjective phantasies operate together. Among British Kleinians there is a tacit assumption that 'projection' and 'projective identification' mean the same thing, and that 'projective identification' is an enrichment or extension of Freud's concept of 'projection'.

(Spillius et al., 2011, p. 126)

Notes

1 Rêverie is the maternal function of receiving, containing, processing, and restoring the child's projections in a digested, mentalised, and transformed manner; what emerges is that it is an interpersonal element before an intrapsychic and personal one (Borgogno, 1992). We are dealing with a factor of the alpha-function, thanks to which the child will be able to reintroject the sensorial experience (beta-elements) after a process of working through it (alpha-elements), and of the ability of the newborn to tolerate the absence of the object. The ability to tolerate the absence of the object, 'of a breast within him/herself', implies non-evacuation through the projection of the bad breast (which does not present differently from receiving comfort from a good breast) and not fleeing into omnipotent fantasy (able to cancel negative fulfillment).

2 This does not mean that the psychoanalytic experience ends in the binomial projective identification-rêverie. In order for it to be completed, besides the encounter, the telling of the story and the leave-taking are also essential (Di Chiara, 1992).

3 Let us be reminded that Ferenczi (1908, 1932a) had already talked about the rush on the part of the analyst to enter into a relationship with the patient (thus not respecting the patient's timing) and to interpret. This is an analyst who is not prepared "to make space within him/herself and not prepared to contain an experience that causes tension and little-known and unforeseen feelings, ones which he/she doesn't want to experience because they would require a *pro tempore* modification of his/her own mental make-up and identity" (Borgogno, 2010, p. 563).

4 "It is important to remember that it is only the sane dependent parts of the self separate from the analyst that can use introjective processes uncontaminated by the concreteness caused by the omnipotent projective identifications; the capacity for memory and growth of the ego depends on these normal introjective processes. When the dependent non-psychotic parts of the personality become stronger, as the result of analysis, violent negative therapeutic reactions usually occur as the psychotic narcissistic parts of the patient oppose any progress and change of the *status quo*" (Rosenfeld, 1971, p. 128). And again: "It is important in dealing with patients and processes of this kind to accept that much of the ['infinite'] repetition is inevitable. The acceptance by the analyst of the patient's processes being re-enacted in the transference helps the patient to feel that the self, which is constantly split off and projected into the analyst, is acceptable and not so damaging as feared" (pp. 133–134).

5 According to Hanna Segal (1955), "The symbolic equation between the original object and the symbol in the internal and the external world is . . . the basis of the schizophrenic's concrete thinking. . . . This non-differentiation between the thing symbolized and the symbol is part of a disturbance in the relation between the ego and the object. Parts of the ego and internal objects are projected into an object and identified with it. The differentiation between the self and the object is obscured. Then, since a part of the ego is confused

with the object, the symbol – which is a creation and a function of the ego – becomes, in turn, confused with the object which is symbolized" (p. 393).

6 I must point out that in dealing with the countertransference aspects in child analysis, when working with a type of patient who creates more severe countertransference stresses on the clinician compared to the non-psychotic adult patient, Bick (1961) maintained that "The intensity of the child's dependence, of his positive and negative transference, the primitive nature of his phantasies, tend to arouse the analyst's own unconscious anxieties. The violent and concrete projections of the child into the analyst may be difficult to contain. Also the child's suffering tends to evoke the analyst's parental feelings, which have to be controlled so that the proper analytic role can be maintained. All these problems tend to obscure the analyst's understanding and to increase in turn his anxiety and guilt about his work" (p. 330).

9

THE CONTRIBUTION OF THE BRITISH SCHOOL OF OBJECT RELATIONS

Second phase

Wilfred Bion's theories on projective identification and container↔contained had obvious effects on his view of the concept of countertransference as well. For Bion, countertransference comprises all the feelings and emotions experienced in the analytic situation, with the added characteristic of allowing the analyst to understand when he/she is the object of a projective identification (since in these cases he/she should feel manipulated). Bion was however convinced that an analysis based on countertransference is destined to fail because the interpretations would have more to do with the analyst than the patient. It is interesting to note that despite the fact that Bion's first training supervisor was Paula Heimann, his ideas about countertransference date back to those days in which he practiced group therapy, and he acquired these ideas from John Rickman, his first analyst (1938–1939), and their later work together in military psychiatry. On the issue of group psychotherapy, he carefully outlined what the objective experience of an analyst who is the object of a massive projective identification might be like:

> Now the experience of countertransference appears to me to have quite a distinct quality that should enable the analyst to differentiate the occasion when he is the object of a projective identification from the occasion when he is not. The analyst feels he is being manipulated so as to be playing a part, no matter how difficult to recognize, in somebody else's phantasy – or he would do if it were not for what in recollection I can only call a temporary loss of insight, a sense of experiencing strong feelings and at the same time a belief that their existence is quite adequately justified by the objective situation without recourse to recondite explanation of their causation. From the analyst's point of view, the experience consists of two closely related phases: in the first there is a feeling that whatever else one has done, one has certainly not given a correct interpretation; in the second there is a sense of being a particular kind of person in a particular emotional situation. I believe the ability to shake oneself out of the numbing

> feeling of reality that is a concomitant of this state is the prime requisite of the analyst in the group: if he can do this he is in a position to give what I believe is the correct interpretation, and thereby to see its connection with the previous interpretation, the validity of which he has been caused to doubt.
>
> *(Bion, 1955, p. 446)*

Bion (1967a) also says something else: in order for the analyst to be able to work in a therapeutic way with the patient and be able to understand[1] and interpret the material emerging within the analytic relationship, he has to approach the session with a mental attitude characterised by an absence of memory and desire (a state of *rêverie*); in other words, in approaching the patient and the material the latter has brought up during the session, the clinician must be free of preconceptions and pre-structures (linked to his/her own subjectivity), thus becoming capable of perceiving the patient's communications and responding to them.

Now would be a good time to make a general statement about the situation, and to this end, Charles Rycroft's definition of countertransference from his *A Critical Dictionary of Psychoanalysis* (1968) should prove useful:

> 1. The analyst's transference on his patient. In this, the correct sense, counter-transference is a disturbing, distorting element in treatment. 2. By extension, the analyst's emotional attitude towards his patient, including his response to specific items of the patient's behaviour. According to Heimann (1950), Little (1951), Gitelson (1952) and others, the analyst can use this latter kind of countertransference as clinical evidence, i.e. he can assume that his own emotional response is based on a correct interpretation of the patient's true intentions or meaning.
>
> *(Rycroft, 1968, p. 25)*

Rycroft, one of the leading figures of British psychoanalysis (cf. Cassullo, 2014, 2015) belonging to the Independent group, analysed first by Ella Sharpe and then by Sylvia Payne, and highly influenced by the ideas of Ferenczi and Winnicott, had expressed his personal point of view on the issue in 1957. He understood the analytic process as one that was determined by the relationship between two individuals, the patient and the analyst; in this way the communication problem between the members of the dyad could only be a problem relating to affects: which "are not only observable but also tend to evoke a response in their observer" (Rycroft, 1957, p. 415), therefore "it is the interaction of affects which is responsible for the sense of contact which is so essential in the analytical situation" (ibid.) – an affective communication that, in order to be beneficial, must pass from the acquisition of a 'common language' between the members of that specific analytic couple to the assignment of importance to the words uttered by each one to the other.

Finally, it should be remembered that in 1964 Rycroft took the decision to leave the Society, but he did not act upon this decision until 1978 after a "long-term strategic withdrawal" (Rycroft, 1984, p. 206). Among the reasons which motivated him to take such a decision, one which made him quite unpopular among a part of the scientific community, was the fact that he was tending towards a disavowal of the existence of a relationship between the particular temperament and the personal history of each analyst, and between these two elements and his/her characteristics as a clinician and a theoretician (Rycroft, 1965–73).

And now we have arrived at the dawn of the 1970s, which for London psychoanalysts were

> the heyday of the 'countertransference'. Paula Heimann's (1950) paper on the use of countertransference had borne much fruit; Winnicott's 'Hate in the Countertransference' (1947) had made disclosure of the analyst's feelings more acceptable and enlightening, and Heinrich Racker's book *Transference and Countertransference* (1968) was required reading. We, the psychoanalytic children of the 1970s, learnt a lot about *using* countertransference. . . . In those days the clinical seminars given by various illustrious members of the British Society of all three theoretical groups often explored the countertransference as a source of understanding. What had been thought of as a dangerous complication of analysis became regarded by my generation as a familiar tool. In the same period atomic fission, initially associated with the atom bomb, had become the source of domestic electricity. However, Chernobyl happened many years after Hiroshima, and Masud Khan's countertransference misdemeanours occurred many years after the erotic enactments that first led Freud to use the term countertransference.
>
> *(Britton, 2003, p. 45)*

Among these 'countertransference misdemeanours' of Khan's were those recurring erotic ones that led him to have various amorous relationships with patients. One of these was with a woman married to a psychoanalytic candidate-in-training analysis with Joseph Sandler, the then president of the IPA, and it was used as a pretext for expelling Khan from the British Society and the International Association. In reality, the decision to expel him had much deeper and older roots, in that, over the years, Khan was identified as having a lengthy series of scandals linked to his arrogant, irascible, and violent behaviour, to excesses in terms of alcohol and women, to the ease with which he violated professional secrecy, and to his oft-proclaimed anti-Semitism. Despite all this, before his excesses became intolerable, Khan, a brilliant and cultured man, was for many years admired by a good many of his colleagues. In terms of his training, it should be recalled that he did his first training analysis with Ella Sharpe, who died only a year after it had begun, and a second with John Rickman, and this, too, was prematurely ended due to the latter's death. Khan then turned to Winnicott, with whom he underwent analysis for fifteen years, becoming his main disciple (he even edited Winnicott's published works). Moreover, Khan had a close relationship with Melanie Klein and Anna Freud, both of whom had been his supervisors during training.

Beyond his eccentricities, Masud Khan made important and original contributions to psychoanalysis (for example the concept of cumulative trauma which he developed in 1963), and to the development of the concept of countertransference as well. Based on the advancements made by Ferenczi, Balint, Winnicott, Heimann, and Little, and enriched and stimulated by the exchanges intrinsic to the deeply serious relationship that he had with two of these, Balint and Winnicott, in 1969 Khan defined countertransference as "a non-pathological capacity of the analyst's affectivity, intelligence, and imagination to comprehend the total reality of the patient" (1969a, p. 206), including archaic affectivity and object relations. In his writings, Khan emphasised the fundamental importance of differentiating, without any blurring of boundaries, one's own ego from the experience of the patient inside the area of countertransference responses ('what is mine and what is the patient's?'), thus maintaining the psychic realities of the members of the dyad clinically distinct because clinical confusion could be harmful to the patient. It is therefore essential that, at least within the analyst, the psychic boundaries and process "should always be distinctly structured and defined in terms of their functions and aims" (1969a). Within this context, the prefix 'counter' acquires great importance, in that it pays heed to the difference between what belongs to the analyst and what he/she identifies with in the patient's experience. In Khan's conception, "the spontaneous emotions and feelings specific to the analyst can be useful access routes to the therapeutic dialogue, in that the analyst becomes part of the patient's world" (Giannakoulas and Fizzarotti Selvaggi, 2006, p. 98; my translation); thus the countertransference helps the clinician to evaluate the patient's needs.

A few years later, Patrick Casement (1973) spoke of the 'diagnostic response' of the analyst, one which if subject to a profound 'internal supervision' – via the internalised supervisor – could help the clinician in the choice of the most appropriate intervention in that moment of the analytical process (seen as an interactive process, in which the bidirectional unconscious communications that take place inside the analytical space have great importance). Such a 'diagnostic response' would differ from the 'personal countertransference', the latter being an endopsychic response of the analyst. As we will later see, Casement made a further contribution to the subject in 1985.

It was Joseph Sandler (1976), coordinator of the so-called Hampstead Index project held at the Hampstead Child Therapy Clinic (now known as the Anna Freud Centre), who made a further step forward, going beyond the theoretical position according to which the countertransference would be 'induced', 'aroused', 'evoked' within the analyst by the patient. His input can be considered "a later effort by an allegedly classical analyst [member of the London Contemporary Freudian, he was in analysis with Willi Hoffer[2] and then with Hedwig Hoffer] to approach a two-person view of the psychotherapeutic situation" (Gill, 1994, p. 103), by practicing an integration of the drive model with that of the relational on a theoretical level. Sandler highlighted the complexity of the interactional dynamics that develops in the analytical process between analyst and patient, underlining the explanatory inappropriateness of terms such as *exteriorisation*, *projection*, *projective identification* – terms he maintained were excessively rigid and intrinsically unipersonal. According to Sandler, the analytical couple is an interaction largely determined by the attempt of both parties to impose on the other an intrapsychic object relationship ('role-relationship').[3] Thus certain reactions manifested by the clinician are connected to the transference of the patient (a transference that actualises the internal object relations in the analytical relationship), and through these, 'role-responsiveness' (Sandler, 1976), composed of feelings, thoughts, attitudes, and behaviours, is demonstrated. This role responsiveness, a concept which, in part, overlaps the Kleinian notion of countertransference *enactment* (O'Shaughnessy, 1992; Feldman, 1993), implies that the clinician is willing to be identified as the character that the patient is trying to create as a transference partner, and to be in tune with the patient's needs and requests. In other words, some spontaneous reactions to the patient arise from the clinician's ability to allow him/herself to be used (not from his/her unresolved internal conflicts), and to accept the role that the patient assigns to him through the transference: it is the 'free-floating responsiveness', complementary to the classical 'free-floating attention', which allows the clinician to use his/her own affective and ideational reactions in the process of understanding the patient. These countertransferential responses are forms of compromise between the personal characteristics of the analyst and the role that the patient unconsciously imposes on him/her (the patient's unconscious requests); the relationship between the weight of one factor and the other varies according to the analytic couple. Sandler specified that not all countertransferential responses of the analyst are determined by the patient's demands; however, the clinician can become aware of being influenced by the patient only through the observation of his/her own behaviour (therefore awareness is possible only through a prior behaviour or a current attitude).

During these same years, Robert Langs[4] (1976, 1980, 1986, 1987; cf. Trombi, 1987), who was among the first to disseminate the new theories of countertransference within the United States and to theoretically develop this phenomenon, spoke of the analytical situation as a 'bi-personal field' (returning to the concept of Madeleine and Willy Baranger, 1961–62), in which the patient's mind is viewed as an open system in continuous interaction with the clinician (in this dynamic process, the roles of the participants in the analytic dyad are clearly asymmetric), and he fiercely maintains the fundamental importance of projective identification as a means of understanding on the part of the clinician (considered a container for the patient's pathological content). In this way countertransference comes to represent an interactional product of the 'communicative field' in which both the analyst and patient are involved (Langs, 1978a). At the same time, Langs reversed the situation by highlighting how not only the therapist, but the patient as well, experiences feelings and has phantasies that, at least in part, are triggered by the therapist's projective identifications, thus suggesting the idea of a patient's countertransference. As a consequence, what determines the patient's (conscious and unconscious) communications is not only his/her internal world, but also, if not especially, the clinician's interventions (Langs spoke of a 'spiral dialogue'); while the patient becomes an 'unconscious supervisor' of his/her own therapist (Langs, 1978b), or indeed the therapist of his/her own therapist, to the extent that he/she introjects and contains what is projected by the analyst (Harold

Searles in 1975 had already spoken of the patient as therapist to his analyst, and Irwin Hoffman in 1983 would say that the patient is the 'interpreter of the analyst's experience'). Such a profoundly interactive view of the transference-countertransference dynamic entails on the part of the clinician the need to pay particular attention to the bidirectional processes of projective and introjective identification, and to the responses that both participants feel in response to the other. In Langs's view all analytical work revolves around the psychoanalyst in addition to the patient, in that it is the quality of the countertransference that determines the evolution of treatment. Thus countertransference takes on an enormous, perhaps extreme, significance.

Hanna Segal (1977), one of the analysts closest and most faithful to Melanie Klein, with whom she had been in analysis (although during her training she was supervised by Paula Heimann), also agreed that countertransference represented a guide for the analyst in his/her work with the patient, and maintained that it would be rather unwise to ignore the feelings triggered by the patient. Moreover, she firmly believed that countertransference must not be a justification for what in reality are the enactments of the clinician (fostered by the personal pathology of the analyst and hidden behind rationalisation). The turning-point towards which the concept of countertransference was heading at the end of the 1940s echoed, according to Segal, the change in the conception of transference (which, at that time, began to be seen in a more three-dimensional manner; Enid Balint, 1954), a conception in which the patient projects his/her internal objects not *onto* but *into* the analyst, thus influencing him/her. Segal considered countertransference as a function of the patient's personality, in the sense that the way in which the patient influences the analyst – an analyst who acquires a great importance for the patient (who tries to use him/her as a part of his/her own defence structure, as he/she did with his/her real childhood objects) and becomes essential in the process of understanding what is unfolding in the analytic situation – is a function of his/her psychopathology. Between patient and analyst there is a continuous non-verbal integrated interaction, sometimes hidden by other forms of communication, through which the patient acts on the mind of the analyst. This way of viewing transference (in which deep and structured phantasies are newly mobilised, ones which from being intrapsychic become interpersonal, since their roots rise out of primitive preverbal experiences, and which only through projective identification can be communicated) shed new light on the Freudian free-floating attention, no longer just mental but also emotional openness. That does not mean that there is no difference between transference and countertransference "because at the same time as the analyst is opening his mind freely to his impressions, he has to maintain distance from his own feelings and reactions to the patient. He has to observe his own reactions, to conclude from them, to use his own state of mind for the understanding of his patient but at no point be swayed by his own emotions" (Segal, 1977, p. 83).

This capacity for containment, similar to the one described by Bion in terms of the mother-child couple (the difference resides in the work of reflection carried out by the analyst on his/her own mental state, whereas parents react instinctively;

it is evident that the object's response is crucial)[5] could however disintegrate in various ways due to both the patient's as well as the analyst's pathology. Segal emphasised that if the transference-countertransference situation is to be understood as an interaction between the members of the analytic dyad, then one must also keep in mind that not all the patient's perceptions are a reflection of projections: some are reactions towards the real aspects of personality, of the analyst's behaviours and states of mind. This entails the need for continuous self-observation and hetero-observation, in order to always be aware of both the contribution we bring to the relationship and of the effects it has on the patient. Sensitivity to everything that comes from the clinician depends on the pathology of the patient, and provides us with useful information on how the latter probably reacted to the real objects of childhood. It is therefore important that the analyst does not reject the subject's situation or sensitivity. According to Segal, when the countertransference (of which we only perceive conscious derivations, being that it is largely unconscious) 'works well', a two-fold relationship is established with the patient: a receptive one (containment and comprehension of what has been communicated), the other an active one (the genesis, through interpretation, of understanding, awareness, or organisation). Such a function of countertransference instils empathy and guides the clinician towards an understanding of the patient's internal world. At the opposite end, where cracks in the well-functioning state of the countertransference begin to appear, the analyst becomes aware of an internal pressure to identify with his/her countertransference and to act in a more or less obvious way or in a hidden way. He/she should therefore try to understand the nature of the rift by deeply analysing the material originating out of the interaction with the patient. This implies that, according to Segal, "countertransference is the best of servants but the worst of masters" (1977, p. 86).

As we have seen, Alice and Michael Balint (1939) expanded the concept of countertransference to basically include every emotional response of the analyst towards the patient. Pearl King (1978), an important exponent of the Independent group, one who from her very first published case (cf. King, 1951) had pointed out the affective response of the analyst to the patient's communications, has provided us with a significant contribution to the subject by bringing a greater conceptual and terminological clarity to the distinction between countertransference, understood in the 'classical' sense of a pathological phenomenon due to the analyst's neurotic residue and the 'affective response' of the analyst, defined as "the perception by the analyst of feelings and moods, unrelated to his personal life, and which may even feel alien to his normal way of reacting, but which when placed in the context of the patient's material and the psychoanalytical setting, illumine and render meaning to those transference phenomena that are in the process of being experienced, consciously or unconsciously, by the patient" (p. 330). King, proceeding along the path advocated first by Winnicott and then by Heimann, believed that a careful monitoring of one's own 'affective response' and an attitude of neutrality are among the principal tools at the disposal of the analyst, especially in working with patients who have suffered early (preverbal) childhood traumas that otherwise risk remaining unspoken (unelaborated). If the analyst, who constantly has to maintain awareness of his/her own affects, should perceive the presence of egodystonic feelings, he/she must necessarily investigate whether they originate in the projective identifications of the patient (countertransference) or instead whether they have a preverbal origin. In either case, these feelings must never be communicated to the patient. King imagined a splitting in the analyst's ego between one part in which he feels "free to use his own affects to understand aspects of his patient's unconscious conflicts", and another one in which he "must maintain an attitude of neutrality or 'non-attachment'" (ivi, p. 334); a 'functional' splitting totally in keeping with what Richard Sterba (1932) hoped for in terms of the patient's ego.

It appears clear that the analytic situation is defined here as a dialogue of affects, in which the analyst maintains a therapeutic distance and space. In fact it is essential that there is no excessive emotional involvement on the part of the clinician. In this regard, Adam Limentani (1977) argues that "In our actual clinical work we could hardly overlook the affects as they are often the immediate reason why patients seek treatment. . . . The vicissitudes of the affects in the analytic situation can, and in my contention are, controlled by the analyst. . . . The dissociation of his faculties of thinking and feeling will have far-reaching effects on the course of an analysis. A patient will often respond with increasing persecutory anxiety to an excessively feeling approach because it can be experienced as seduction, teasing and, finally, frustrating" (p. 172).

Limentani tackles the issue of countertransference in a clear and concise way in the presidential address that he gave to the Hamburg International Congress of 1985. First and foremost, he limited the term 'countertransference' to cases in which the analyst's personal pathology influences the ability to decipher what is happening within the analytical situation, affecting as a result the management of the analytical situation; one example is when a therapist cannot distinguish between what emerges from the patient and what emerges from his/her own inner world. Clearly, for Limentani it is not right to speak of countertransference, not even in terms of the transference of the analyst to the patient, a condition which, incidentally, only occurs when the emotions of love and/or hate towards the patient become unmanageable. In the remaining cases, Limentani preferred to use the term 'emotional response', understood as a reflection of what is occurring in the analyst, who will be able to perceive this response as appropriate or not. However the use which Limentani makes of such emotional responses to the patient's material is not immediate. Initially one is limited to making a mental record of them, and then deals with them after they have been spread over many hours of analytical work, at which point one uses them as a criteria guide for formulating an interpretation; in no way does he maintain it useful to share with the patient one's own personal experience. To do that would mean weighing down the patient with the task of analysing his/her therapist. What this signifies is that one of the fundamental jobs of the clinician is to analyse his/her own mental state, in order to be able to differentiate with sufficient certainty what is pathological from what represents instead an emotional response to the patient's associations and behaviour – a task that is sometimes made even more difficult by the analyst's lack of time to be alone during the course of his professional day, an objective condition to which he/she might react, for instance, by becoming intrusive and vomiting interpretations onto the patient. According to Limentani, the term 'emotional response' also has the advantage of underscoring the importance of evaluating and verbalising the affects with which the analytic situation is imbued, an importance not always adequately recognised.

The importance of the affects of the analyst is a leitmotif that runs through the entire opus of another significant figure in the international psychoanalytic panorama, Harold F. Searles, an American psychiatrist who was deeply involved with borderline and schizophrenic patients, and who believed that the clinician must not choose between incompatible theoretical concepts,[6] but he/she must rather establish in which phase of the patient's ego development each of these concepts may prove useful, since, for example, interpretations are only useful with a psychotic in principle. In practice they are damaging (as almost all continental European analysts reveal, not excluding Winnicott).

In 1979 Searles, whose interest in the interpersonal character of countertransference comes primarily out of the United States tradition, basically that of Harry S. Sullivan and the interpersonal school, before the arrival of the Viennese school of thought in the North American, published a monograph on countertransference in which he gathered together essays written between 1965 and 1977. However, already in 1947–1948 he had dealt with the feelings of the clinician, and how and how much the latter (a real person who participates emotionally in the relationship with the patient) with his/her own behaviour arouses in the patient projective tendencies (to which the transference phenomena are also related).[7] Moreover, in 1957 he had presented 'Oedipal Love in the Countertransference', an essay at the centre of which lies the idea that in order to analyse the patient's oedipal complex the analyst must be able to allow him/herself the possibility of freely and consciously experiencing his/her own desires and feelings of tenderness and love towards the patient, recognising at the same time that such desires will never be fulfilled in external reality. What is fundamental is that the clinician recognises that his/her own countertransference feelings represent an aspect specific to the analytic relationship, one that is useful to therapeutic work.

To put it simply, we could say that, according to Searles (1965, 1979, 1986), the analytic situation can be expressed as a deeply interpersonal situation, in which the processes of introjection and projection are bidirectional. In Searles's writings he highlights how a fundamental phase of the analytical process is the symbiotic one, in which the patient experiences the clinician as a good mother with whom to fuse, an object from which he/she will then gradually differentiate him/herself, thus opening the way for a subsequent phase in which he/she will have feelings associated with the oedipal issue (correspondingly the therapist will experience countertransference feelings in which the patient is initially experienced as the object of oedipal love). It is in the above-mentioned symbiotic phase (in which the self-other boundaries are absent) that, according to Searles, the transference roots and reactions become submerged; what ensues is that the possibility for the therapist to arrive at an understanding of the inner world of the patient lies in the introjection process of the patient's projections (which are communications of what is happening deep within the analytical situation). Something similar also happens within the analyst, in which conscious and unconscious aspects of the experience merge; it is precisely beginning with the recognition of this continuity between the two dimensions of the experience that the clinician arrives at an understanding of what is happening within the transference-countertransference dynamic; at the same time the distinction between the unconscious experiences of the analyst and the patient begins to blur.

One must keep in mind that the symbiotic-fusion phase is primarily non-verbal, and therefore the interpretations play a role of minor importance, if they are not actually perceived by the patient as the clinician's defence against the serious pathology existing in the relationship. What is fundamental, according to Searles, is that in the different phases of the analytical process there is a connection between the patient's transference and the analyst's countertransference. The therapist is a person equipped to be able to access his/her own unconscious experiences, to fully experience the affective intensity of what is taking place in the here and now of the relationship: this entails an indispensable step towards putting oneself in a position that allows for an analytical use of countertransference feelings, conceptualising them and putting them into words. Considering that the patient's unconscious conflicts slide into (through the flow of the 'symbiotic transference') and resonate within the therapist's unconscious experiences, his/her work consists of experiencing these countertransference feelings (composed of the patient's conflicts, and the clinician's archaic conflicts reawakened by the patient), working through them on a conscious and unconscious intrapsychic level, and integrating them within his/her own ego. If all goes well, the patient, through the process of introjection, will reach a greater integration in ego functioning of those experiences, which previously he/she could not help but project. It becomes clear that for Searles the analytical situation develops as a deeply interpersonal situation in which the processes of introjection and projection are bidirectional, so much so that he highlighted the possibility, anything but remote or infrequent, that the patient could become the interpreter of some aspects of the functioning of the therapist's personality or of his (unconscious) countertransferential conflicts.

Now we have arrived at the beginning of the 1980s. This is the period characterised by Christopher Bollas's (1980–82) contribution on the subject. For this theoretician, a central role is played by the concept of the potential of the patient's true self, trapped by the defensive development of the false self. If the analyst wants to help the patient reappropriate his/her own authentic ways of being spontaneous, the analyst cannot help but resort to his/her true self, to authentic elements of his/her own personality and idiom. Bollas (1995) believes that the analyst's subjectivity makes his/her listening and reprocessing of what the patient has brought up unique; the clinician's mental content, a result of his/her own personal history, is transformed by the effect of the patient who thus helps shape anew the analyst's self. For Bollas (2003, quoted in Neri and Girelli, 2003), the analyst's focus of attention can be centred upon the transference-countertransference relationship, or on the passages through unconscious-preconscious-consciousness. In this way, in clinical work, it is essential that the analyst reflects in depth on his/her own dual experience of being the subject-object of his/her own observations and of being the object of the patient. If the analyst has the capacity to let him/herself be used by the patient, he/she will be able to understand how he/she is being used, thus being able to grasp aspects of the analysand's true self by means of such use of the object-analyst. Bollas maintains that countertransference (affective response for King, 1978) is necessary to reawaken in the patient, and in some way awaken in the analyst, a new experience of something already lived through but not yet thought, an experience that often passes through the soma: this should be indispensable to the analytical process, especially with seriously ill patients who need to pass on their own suffering to the analyst, in that this gives a representative importance to something that had been lived through without having being worked through. The countertransference can sometimes even represent a cure for the analyst, it being the bearer of unknown aspects of the self. According to Bollas (1980–82), "The most ordinary countertransference state is a not knowing yet an experiencing one" (p. 4). In order to describe the establishment of mental neutrality, which the analyst should have during the session, one must refer to the creation of an internal potential space (Winnicott, 1951) and to the frame (Milner, 1952a),[8] in that they allow a more complete and articulated expression of the transferences. Crucial here is the analyst's capacity to sustain the doubt and uncertainty of not knowing, a state which permits the patient to manipulate the clinician in the use of transference for reaching object identity. Bollas writes:

> By cultivating a freely roused emotional sensibility the analyst welcomes news from within himself that is reported through his own hunches, feeling states, passing images, fantasies, and imagined interpretive interventions. Interestingly, it is a feature of our present day understanding of the transference, that the Other source of the analysand's free association is the psychoanalyst's countertransference, so much so, that in order to find the patient we must look for him within ourself. This process inevitably points to the fact that there are two 'patients' within the session and therefore two complementary sources of free association.
>
> *(Bollas, 1980–82, p. 3)*

> Because the analyst is the Other patient, sustaining in himself some intersubjective discourse with the analysand, it is essential to find some way to put forward for analytic investigation that which is occurring in the analyst as a purely subjective and private experience. It is essential to do this because in many patients the truly free associative process takes place within the analyst, and the clinician must find some way to report his internal processes thereby linking the patient with something that he has lost in himself.
>
> *(ivi, p. 6)*

> The analyst must be prepared to be subjective in the presence of the patient in order for the patient to use his own nascent subjective states. . . . To some

> very considerable extent it is a question of the analyst's relation to his own feelings and thoughts.
>
> *(ivi, p. 7)*

> The gradual non traumatic use of my own subjectivity is an essential element in my work.
>
> *(ivi, p. 9)*

Bollas speaks also of 'direct use of the countertransference', referring to the rare occasions in which the analyst describes to the patient his/her own experience as object ('I sense that . . .'), occasions which, by making accessible representations of aspects split off from the self and the object, may prove of great value to the analyst's success. At the same time he underscores that such interventions must be used in a very limited and prudent way and that the revelation of subjective mental states is entirely different from a venting of affects ('You make me angry!'); the first demands intense mental work from the analyst so that he/she may be able to work through it. It should be pointed out that almost all British analysts did not believe and currently do not believe in the usefulness of direct disclosure of the counter-transference, not even in specific circumstances.

In treating problems of countertransference that are encountered with 'patients difficult to reach' by means of interpretations (a *medium* through which to offer them an authentic emotional understanding), or more precisely with those patients, often seemingly cooperative and involved, whose needs and anxieties prove difficult to uncover because of a splitting of the personality,[9] Betty Joseph (1975, 1983) – who was in analysis with Michael Balint and then with Heimann (for about four years), and in supervision with Segal, Klein and Heimann – suggested to focus one's attention on the patient's methods of communication (a form of 'acting out') rather than on the content or the symbolism of what they are recounting. The analytical process with these patients often seems to proceed well 'thanks' to the work of the pseudo-adult or pseudo-cooperative part of the patient, who in reality is opposed to the real emotional understanding that would emerge from the meeting between his/her truly needy part (the most infantile one) and the clinician, but – maintains Joseph – if one takes into consideration the countertransference, one would discover that it is all too easy and gratifying, and see that the conflicts, when present, get quickly dispelled. It is the total transference situation (Joseph, 1983) that offers the analyst the opportunity to see the different living, breathing parts of the patient's ego and their interaction at work – a type of acting out and projective identification; this is because, in transference, an actualisation of aspects of the patient's inner world takes place, just as they were forged back in the time of infantile object relations. But what is meant by transference as the 'total situation'?

> By definition it must include everything that the patient brings into the relationship. What he brings in can best be gauged by our focusing our attention on what is going on within the relationship, how he is using the analyst,

> alongside and beyond what he is saying. Much of our understanding of the transference comes through our understanding of how our patients act on us to feel things for many varied reasons; how they try to draw us into their defensive systems; how they unconsciously act out with us in the transference, trying to get us to act out with them; how they convey aspects of their inner world built up from infancy – elaborated in childhood and adulthood, experiences often beyond the use of words, which we can often only capture through the feelings aroused in us, through our countertransference, used in the broad sense of the word.
>
> *(Joseph, 1983, p. 157)*

It appears evident that for Joseph understanding the projective identification is fundamental to the therapist's understanding and awareness because it is precisely through projective identification and the pressure that it brings to bear upon the analyst that the needy part of the patient communicates the desire to be understood. According to Joseph (1984), projective identification (the putting of parts of the self into the object), in its varied aspects and irrespective of the motivations that trigger it, acts as a form of communication. This implies that the understanding (and the resulting communicability) of what happens in the analytical situation comes from the clinician's ability to be truly open to what happens in the session, from his/her ability to be in tune with the patient's projections, and from the awareness of his/her own experience. It is the immediate relationship between analyst and patient, with its verbal and non-verbal forms of expression, that is the central nucleus of interpretation (Malcolm, 1986), which must express the movement itself (life, experience, and change) of the transference.

A subsequent contribution to the subject comes from Irma Brenman Pick (1985): "the only paper I've written that really came out of a need to say something that wasn't being said" (Pick, 2015, p. 1). Brenman Pick wrote that article as a response to a paper – 'Slouching Towards Bethlehem' – given by Nina Coltart at the Psychoanalytical Society and in which "she talks about losing her temper with a patient, and in a way makes a virtue out of this" (Pick, 2015, p. 1). Starting from James Strachey's (1933) reflections on the fact that a full and deep transference experience disturbs the analyst to such a degree as to make him/her wish to avoid it, and on the (therapeutic) need to return an interpretation to the patient in a calm and relaxed way (a task that often is anything but easy, given the profound influence of the patient's projections on the analyst and his/her reactions; Money-Kyrle, 1955), Brenman Pick – heavily influenced by Bion, Rosenfeld and Joseph, with whom she was in supervision (she was also supervised by Heimann and Segal) – emphasised the fact that the clinician is faced with two problem areas: on the one hand, the area associated with the process of 'digestion' of the projections (viewed as the essence of analysis), through which the patient tries to provoke a response in line with his/her own needs and phantasies in the analyst (the clinician, for instance, will feel the urge to offer true maternal care to the patient); on the other, that which is relative to the process of assimilation of one's own responses, by being, like every other human being, eager to eliminate the discomfort. Both of these problem areas require investigation on the part of the clinician. What ensues is that, should the analyst be unable to acquire the awareness of his/her own conflicting responses produced by the analytic relationship, he/she runs the risk of acting instead of interpreting, a possible outcome that would mean confirming to the patient that what he/she has projected is really intolerable.

Brenman Pick underscored how the patient may be similar to a small child in terms of sensitivity, on the conscious and unconscious level, to the way in which the *caregiver*, in our case the analyst, functions (how he/she avoids or confronts specific feelings), and to how he/she interprets the internal dynamics. In other words, the patient evaluates in a more or less conscious way the clinician's ability to enter, stay, and work in the 'difficult' areas that inevitably are discovered within the clinician-patient relationship. The projective identifications of the patient, whose boundaries upon the intrusion are extremely labile, initiate a spontaneous emotional interaction with the internal world of the analyst; if the latter is not dominated by a defensive need to remain neutral ('neutrality' which in reality corresponds to a position of dishonesty and impenetrability in the face of the patient's shortcomings and neediness), he/she may be able to experience and tolerate the feelings elicited in him/her by the projective identifications[10] of the patient, or, in other words, he may be able to contain the projections and simultaneously work through his/her own feelings. The mental space granted to intense experiences, made up of tensions between conscious and unconscious urges and desires experienced in relation to the patient, ones which arise out of the analytic relationship, and which are due to the effort of working through them, constitutes the foundation of the help provided to the patient, a help which takes the form of a growing sensation that these feelings can be tolerated (a necessary condition for facing the problems relative to one's internal world). The process of working through is not a continuous process for either the patient or the psychoanalyst; the latter must therefore accept both the appearance of the desire to enact and the conflicts that such a desire create within him/her because only by allowing such an experience will he/she be able to provide the patient, once the experience is worked through, with an interpretation which the patient may find useful. It is interesting to point out that for Brenman Pick the 'depth' of an interpretation does not refer to the level it reaches within the patient, but it is the gauge of the level reached by the internal process of working through carried out by the clinician.

In the same year, Patrick Casement returned to the subject of countertransference twelve years after his first compelling article on the issue. Casement (1985) showed how he functioned in his clinical practice when, during a session or in the intervals between sessions, he found himself to be confused and not capable of understanding what was taking place in his relationship with the patient: in these types of circumstances, he used his own imagination in order to consciously identify with the patient in an attempt to sense how the latter heard the words of the analyst; we could say that he was trying to step into the shoes of the patient so that he could observe his/her own attitudes and behaviours. Casement's theory is based on the hypothesis that in therapeutic work it is necessary to acquire awareness of the dynamics of the clinician-patient interaction.

According to Casement, there exists a communication level resulting from the interaction between the members of the analytic duo, wherein lies the reason for which the clinician must be able to differentiate between the various ways with which he reacts to the patient (resonance), so that he will know if the response is due, for instance, to subjective countertransferential factors, or to the patient's unconscious communications; in other words, the clinician has to understand to whom the pathology belongs – a pathology emerging in that moment within the relationship between him/herself and the patient. Casement writes:

> [T]he first step must be to monitor one's feelings, in any therapeutic interaction, for personal countertransference. Even though this may be triggered by something about the patient, a therapist must first accept what belongs to himself. The next step is to determine whether a patient is prompting the therapist to feel or to respond in a given way.
>
> *(Casement, 1985, pp. 94–95)*

The clinician's emotional resonance to the patient's interactive pressures is the result of the joint action of elements specific to each of the participants in the therapeutic couple and is an indicator of the clinician's openness with regard to the patient's unconscious communications. Within the therapeutic process, the therapist must employ a sensitivity that is different than the one which leads to a cognitive understanding – a particular kind of sensitivity that is related to two personality traits of the therapist. The first of these is the extent or breadth of his/her unconscious resonance: it must be able to cover the widest possible emotional range, meaning that even when faced with experiences that are strange or alien to the therapist, he/she will not defensively limit him/herself to the adoption of his/her own way of being or feeling, but will be able to vibrate in an empathic way and experience within him/herself all the various emotions the patient has brought forward. It is the quality of the analyst's personal analysis that will allow him/her to 'reclaim' those personal unresolved or disregarded areas that inevitably cause deafness and blindness in the presence of specific stimuli. It is the experience of personal analysis that helps one to improve one's capacity for empathic resonance. The second personality trait of the therapist is his/her ability to open up to the 'otherness' of the one before him/her: it consists of a predisposition to experience whatever feeling is evoked during the interaction with the other person (it is something beyond the empathic identification with the patient, since the latter can only deal with familiar experiences, not those that are completely new, or unknown). It follows that "Therapists . . . have to develop an openness to, and respect for, feelings and experiences that are quite unlike their own. The greater freedom they have to resonate to the unfamiliar 'keys' or dissonant 'harmonics' of others, the more it will enhance their receptivity to these unconsciously interactive cues that are often central to an understanding of the patients" (p. 95).

Lastly, Casement highlights that in interactive communications the patients also employ modalities that are not mediated (for example, projective identification) in order to transmit to the clinician something that cannot be incorporated into words. The clinician might therefore find himself also experiencing very intense feelings, ones which are tolerated without being enacted or repressed. In situations where the clinician feels confused or blocked in his/her ability to think, the first thing that he/she should try to do, once he/she has sufficiently recovered mental lucidity, is to understand what kind of message is contained in the mood the patient has conveyed. As regards the use that the therapist can make of his/her own feelings as a source for formulating an interpretation, Casement clearly states that they must not be used in an immediate way. It is safer to be cautious and wait to understand how and whence such an affective reaction emerges; moreover, it is good if each interpretation is connected to some cue provided by the patient and that the patient may be able to recognise it when the therapist communicates it.

In 1987, a year after the death of its author, Herbert Rosenfeld, *Impasse and Interpretation* was published. It is a text in which it is possible to appreciate the great aptitude for empathic listening and semiotics of its author-analyst, who demonstrates that he is equally attentive to the sensibilities of very ill patients and to the blind spots of the clinician. Rosenfeld (1965, 1987) was convinced that with suitable therapeutic measures even the schizophrenic patient (who by nature sets traps for both the therapist and his/her technique, by applying concentrated unconscious pressures on the therapist, ones that lead him/her to abandon the analytic role) can develop transference. On the countertransference level, the dynamics can take on the form of intense boredom or overwhelming fatigue, psychophysical states that make it difficult, if not impossible, for the clinician to continue to pay attention to what is happening in the session. When the work with the patient allows the clinician to acquire a minimal ability for insight into his/her own psychic reality (including delirium, hallucinations, etc.), the immense pain that will come from it will bring about a violent negative therapeutic reaction, a reaction that will also impact his/her interpretations. This may prove discouraging for the clinician in his/her attempt to perceive and comprehend what is going on in the patient and in the analytic couple and may become a cause for discomfort and confusion. The ability to self-observe on the part of the clinician plays a key role.

Rosenfeld agreed with Paula Heimann (1975) in believing that if the analyst has many areas within his/her own inner world (usually having to do with unconscious childhood anxieties) labelled as 'private: no entry', the risk to the analytic couple is that of establishing an unconscious complicity with specific aspects of the patient's personality for excluding those areas from the analytic work, thus causing an *impasse* situation which could get unblocked only if the analyst knows how to diagnose the problem, be aware of the patient's communications, and examine those areas both within him/herself (feelings and behaviours) and within the patient. In these states the predominant anxiety is usually associated with the fear that one of the two participants in the dyad will make the other go insane (Searles, 1959); if the clinician does not undertake the above-mentioned work, the interpretations will communicate to the patient that the clinician is not in contact with the patient's internal world. Rosenfeld (1987) underlines "the importance of understanding the analyst's countertransference reaction as a central means of understanding a schizophrenic patient's communications expressed by way of powerful projective identification. . . . When the emotions are particularly violent the analyst may feel overwhelmed and be unable to function as a container" (p. 241). Confusional anxiety is a particularly important countertransference emotion, especially for those patients for whom access to their own normal thoughts and language filters through from the analyst's understanding. Therefore, "shifting away from some entangled state is enormously important to understand, because it implies that confusional anxieties, particularly if they are projected into the analyst and not clearly diagnosed by him, lead to a great need for the patient to find a way out. It is at that moment that delusions form" (ivi, p. 258). What must be transmitted to the patient is that the clinician will not be overcome and confused by the patient's anxieties, if not the patient's anxiety will be greatly intensified. Only if the clinician is secure enough in his/her own understanding of the patient's central issue (or rather, in what is essential to interpret), which comes across also from understanding the countertransference (which implies the need to endure the anxiety caused by the absence of clarity and uncertainties), will he/she be able to work through it via the dyadic relationship. In this way the verbal interpretations will be able to generate a sense of support within the patient to the extent that they convey the understanding arrived at by the analyst through intuitive empathy: "the analyst's capacity to function is mainly expressed by his ability to convey understanding through the way he gives interpretations and what he selects for interpretation" (ivi, p. 31).

From the beginning of the 1980s, the American Stephen Mitchell, who would become one of the principal exponents of the relational approach in psychoanalysis, began to develop his own personal vision of the analytic process, and more in general, of the nature of human experience. This is a vision in which American intersubjectivity enters into dialogue with British object relations. In fact, as Mitchell himself tells us,

> Having been trained at the White Institute between 1972 and 1977, I felt steeped in the interpersonal tradition. Yet, this was also the time during which British object relations theories were becoming more accessible. . . . The most exciting thing for me was that British-school object relations, in what I took to be its most essential features, was perfectly compatible with interpersonal psychoanalysis, as I understood and practiced it. Fairbairn, in particular, had provided an intrapsychic model of internal relationships that was a transformation of external, interpersonal relationships. So I regarded object relations theories as an extension of interpersonal psychoanalysis into a previously untheorized domain. . . .
>
> The term 'relational' was deliberately chosen to highlight the link between interpersonal relations and internal object *relations.*
>
> *(Mitchell, 1999, p. 356, emphasis in original)*

Starting from a relational perspective (Greenberg and Mitchell, 1983), which considers past and present relationships with others the basic element of mental life, Mitchell (1988) sets out to arrive at a selective integration of multiple psychoanalytic theories. The individual is born from and is incorporated into a matrix of relationships with other people – a reason why he/she is constantly in a struggle to both establish/maintain interpersonal links, as well as maintain some sort of differentiation from others and be able to express him/herself. The experiences, just like their psychological meanings, take shape within an interpersonal interactive field to which each of the two subjects involved greatly contribute. Such experiences are both intrapsychic and interpersonal, and thus the most useful way to view the patient's psychological realty is to operate from inside the relational matrix. It is the field of interaction between patient and analyst (in which disclosure takes place along with the transformation of relational configurations and their internal representations) that becomes the principal object of psychoanalytic investigation. More precisely, just as the analysand must first enter into the transference in order to be able to come out of it,

> the analyst must first *experience* the countertransference, or rather discover himself within it, before he can begin to find his way out of it. One cannot resist or master something one has not first been transformed by.
>
> The analyst discovers himself a coactor in a passionate drama involving love and hate, sexuality and murder, intrusion and abandonment, victims and executioners. Whichever path he chooses, he falls into one of the patient's predesigned categories and is experienced by the patient in that way. The struggle is toward a new way of experiencing both himself and the patient, a different way of being with the analysand, in which one is neither fused nor detached, seductive nor rejecting, victim nor executioner. The struggle is to find an authentic voice in which to speak to the analysand, a voice more fully one's own, less shaped by the configurations and limited options of the analysand's relational matrix, and, in so doing, offering the analysand a chance to broaden and expand that matrix.
>
> *(Mitchell, 1988, p. 295, emphasis in original)*

In this view of the analytic process, change is produced by the continuous struggle, in which each of the two participants engages, in order to overcome the difference between one's own experience and that of the other, a difference that makes it difficult to be able to reach the other person and, therefore, threatens the interpersonal bond. Inside the relational matrix of the analysis, the analyst, who is always in the middle of the transference-countertransference interactions, must let him/herself be moulded by the relational configurations of the analysand. Only by becoming the diverse figures of the analysand's internal world will the analyst be able to understand and reshape from inside the relational configurations delivered into the field by the analysand. The analysand will then be able to enjoy, within the psychoanalytic relationship, different and more intimate experiences and relationships, which will bring about a gradual transformation of his/her internal world, and by extension, lead to richer and more dialectic relationships with other people. It is clear that, according to Mitchell (1988), "the analytic process might be thought of as a broadening of the relational matrix to allow new experiences of self in relation to others" (p. 301). The analysand and analyst "grapple together with the transference and countertransference to yield an understanding of the way the patient experiences the analyst's interventions and to find a new way for both participants to speak to each other" (Mitchell, 1993, pp. 38–39). The analyst's and the analysand's participation in an interpersonal dialectic generated by the meeting of their subjectivities, and the analysis of the interaction between the two, represent the predominant aim of analytic work. In this work, the analyst's experience (which can contain essential information for the analysis, information that cannot be obtained in any other way), his/her ability to emerge from the transference-countertransference bottleneck, thanks to a continuous process of investigation and self-reflection, and his/her authenticity within the analytic relationship (both analyst and patient living in an authentic way and allowing their wishes and needs to coexist), play a central role in helping the analysand to create an authentic and personal subjectivity (Mitchell, 1993). A fundamental tool at the disposal of the analyst is the countertransference, by means of whose continuous deconstruction and analysis it is possible for the analyst to reach an understanding of the patient's experience and of his/her own internal dynamics.

To summarise, we can say that for Mitchell countertransference represents a compass that allows one to get oriented in an experience in which the contribution of each member of the analytic pair is – at least initially – confused with that of the other. The analysis of countertransference "is less like a storm from which one emerges periodically to regain one's perch and more like the weather itself" (1997, p. 182), which constantly changes but is always there. It resembles the way in "which the analyst attempts to reach the patient" (ivi, p. 146).

At the end of the 1980s, another important article of substantial clinical value was published. It dealt with how the clinician might draw clinical advantage from the intense feelings evoked in him by the patient during a session. The essay was written by Denis V. Carpy, a Scottish psychiatrist and psychoanalyst who unfortunately died prematurely. He especially focussed his attention on the work with those patients (such as borderline patients) who use projective identification in a massive way, divesting themselves completely of their own projection, which becomes completely estranged from the self and of which they retain no awareness. It is obvious that for these patients the analyst's interpretation, especially one which communicates that they are feeling something which they are simply not feeling – something that the analyst instead 'is feeling' in his own countertransference – is experienced as an attempt to forcibly throw them back into something that is intolerable, frightening, or crazy (a perception that reinforces the 'reality' of what is truthfully the phantasy of the projection). Interpretations of the above-mentioned type are, if all goes well, useless, but most probably, harmful to the therapeutic process and the patient. Carpy did not find Rosenfeld's (1971) interpretive technique useful either (however the latter referred to work with psychotics). Rosenfeld suggested interpreting both the defence (or rather, the projective identification) and the content of the projection, in that even in this type of case one verbalises something of which the patient is totally unaware. A question therefore arises: how can the clinician utilise the intense experiences of countertransference triggered in the analytic relationship for the purpose of producing the best therapeutic results? Carpy's (1989) response is the following:

> if the analyst is able to tolerate such feelings, then this by itself can help the patient, and produce psychic change. I shall explain what I mean by the word 'tolerate': . . . the ability to allow oneself to experience the patient's projections in their full force, and yet be able to avoid acting them out in a gross way. To do this, one must be able to avoid being taken over completely by the experience, but I believe it is *inevitable* that if the projections are fully experienced, then the countertransference will be acted out to some partial degree. . . .
>
> I think that this acting out can take many forms, including choice of the area of interpretation, the type of interpretation and its wording, and the tone of voice in which it is delivered.
>
> *(Carpy, 1989, p. 289, emphasis in original)*

In such a situation, the positive therapeutic value resides in the fact that "the analyst's partial acting out allows the patient to see, consciously or unconsciously, that she is affecting the analyst and inducing strong feelings in him, and it allows her to observe him attempting to deal with these feelings" (Carpy, 1989, p. 292).

> I believe it is through this process that the patient is able gradually to re-introject the previously-intolerable aspects of himself that are involved. He also is able to introject the capacity to tolerate them which he has observed in the analyst. . . .
>
> I think that in the interaction I have been describing, the analyst's tolerating the countertransference involves his making links in *his* mind, and it is this which allows the patient to do likewise.
>
> *(ivi, p. 293, emphasis in original).*

Carpy therefore is in disagreement with Winnicott (1947), according to whom

> An analyst has to display all the patience and tolerance and reliability of a mother devoted to her infant . . . and has to seem to want to give what is really only given because of the patient's needs. . . . There may be a long initial period in which the analyst's point of view cannot be (even unconsciously) appreciated by the patient. Acknowledgment cannot be expected because at the primitive root of the patient that is being looked for there is no capacity for identification with the analyst, and certainly the patient cannot

> see that the analyst's hate is often engendered by the very things the patient does in his crude way of loving.
>
> *(ivi, p. 74)*

This disagreement is connected to the fact that the British paediatrician sees the patient as incapable of reaching some sort of awareness of his/her analyst's emotional state. On the other hand, Carpy is in agreement, for instance with Brenman Pick (1985) who, as we have seen, emphasised the patient's sensitivity (on the conscious and unconscious level) to the way in which the analyst functions (he/she avoids or faces his/her feelings) and interprets the internal dynamics. It goes without saying that for Carpy the therapeutic factor of analytical work lies in the gradual process of introjection, and therefore it does not lie specifically in interpretation. The contents of the interpretation can acquire significance for the patient only as a consequence of the greater awareness of aspects of the self that arises from the process of introjection resulting from the non-verbal interaction which permeates the analytical situation. Only after such a process can the interpretation begin to contribute to the formation of a link between the preconscious and the conscious in the patient's mind. In this there are also points of contact with Bion's (1962) way of thinking.

In this same year, 1989, Ronald Britton, although not specifically dealing with countertransference, provided an important addition to the subject matter by introducing the concept of 'triangular space': a relational space which implies a 'third position' from which the object relationships can be observed, and from which "we can also envisage *being* observed. This provides us with a capacity for seeing ourselves in interaction with others and for entertaining another point of view whilst retaining our own, for reflecting on ourselves whilst being ourselves" (p. 87, emphasis in original). As a result, such an ability, namely the possibility of having a mental space for thinking and experiencing, if possessed by the analyst (and hopefully also by the patient), could represent the only potentially therapeutic way to work with some patients.

In terms of our present discussion on the concept of countertransference, we can point out that Britton did contribute to the subject more specifically when he talked not of the use the clinician makes of countertransference but of his/her vulnerability to it. Britton, who, as he himself says, had had the advantage of a training analysis with Ruth Malcolm, who linked his countertransference reactions with patients to his personal experience of transference in the analysis with her, and the good fortune of having Joseph, Rosenfeld, and Segal as supervisors, in reference to Racker's (1948) work, speaks about 'countertransference neurosis' to indicate

> something that is more than the transient, often recurrent, feelings and reactions that are part of psychoanalytic everyday life. I want to apply it to a state of mind that becomes endogenously active and persistent within the analyst though it is induced by the patient's transference. Once this is the case, it becomes a factor in the analysis and a source of resistance. I want to

> restrict the term 'countertransference neurosis' to denote a process in the analyst induced by the patient's transference and complementary to the particular patient whose transference has stimulated it. In other words, countertransference neurosis is a result of the analyst's encounter with a particular patient. If the analyst's aberrant state of mind is not a specific reaction to that patient's transference but is simply a reaction to all patients, or perhaps to people in general, we would do better to give it another name and to regard it as a different problem.
>
> *(Britton, 2003, p. 46)*

A further important contribution comes from another illustrious exponent of the Kleinian school, John Steiner, whose formative process overlaps considerably that of Britton. In fact Segal was his analyst, while Rosenfeld and Segal were his supervisors. Steiner (1993) maintains that the *impasse* situations that often occur in the analytic process are an expression of both the patient's resistance and the countertransference difficulties of the analyst. Thus, "the analyst can try to observe his own reactions to the patient and to the totality of the situation in the session and to use them to understand what the patient is projecting" (p. 140). It seems clear that for this particular author, countertransference, which includes the sum total of reactions evoked in the clinician by the relationship with the patient, is closely associated with projective identification and containment. Steiner however warns us that despite the fact that countertransference may potentially be a valuable source of information on the psychic state of the patient, there is no scarcity of problems that it creates in clinical practice. One need only think of the difficulties that the analyst's defensive needs may cause in the process of introspection by concealing many countertransferential reactions from awareness (reactions one often only becomes aware of after an *enactment*; Sandler, 1976, 1977; Joseph, 1981, 2003; Steiner, 2006a, 2006b). To these it is possible to add other difficulties, such as self-deceit and collusion with the patient, both of which render the countertransference rather unreliable, especially when the information that we draw from it is not supported by material coming from other sources (for example a colleague whom one consults and whose presence one interiorises; or the patient him/herself who, by means of his/her reactions to our interpretations, provides us with an important feedback). Without the back-up of a third point of view (Britton, 1989), which may help to identify possible blind spots and consolidate judgements, it is not possible to arrive at sufficient comprehension in terms of the interaction with the patient. This comprehension is possible only if the clinician resorts to all available tools: self-observation, observation of one's own (verbal and non-verbal) behaviour, of the patient's responses, and of the session's overall atmosphere.

> The frustration of having a stuck patient, who is at the same time out of reach, challenges the analyst, who as to avoid being driven either to give up in despair or to over-react and try to overcome opposition and resistance in too forceful a way. . . . The priority for the patient is to get rid of

> unwanted mental contents, which he projects into the analyst, and in these states he is able to take very little back into his mind. He does not have the time or the space to think, and he is afraid to examine his own mental processes. Words are used, not primarily to convey information, but as actions having an effect on the analyst, and the analyst's words are likewise felt as actions indicating something about the analyst's state of mind. . . . The formidable technical problems which arise from this situation are, in part, therefore, due to the uncomfortable counter-transference feelings which are evoked in the analyst.
>
> *(Steiner, 1993, pp. 131–132)*

Thus, according to Steiner, countertransference represents the tool that allows the clinician to contain and integrate the elements projected by the patient, and formulate, through the understanding he/she has attained, the interpretations[11] to pass on to the patient. Since the countertransference is often infused with a stress which the patient is not capable of facing, it is up to the analytic situation to function as container, and this function depends on the analyst's ability to recognise and confront the patient's projections (which are lodged inside the analyst's mind, where they acquire meaning) and his/her own countertransference reactions. If the clinician is able to bear this pressure, he will be able to achieve comprehension of the patient's psychic-emotional state, a comprehension necessary for formulating an interpretation which may create a feeling in the patient of being understood and contained (this fosters integration and further positive development, dependent on the achievement of *insight* and of the associated psychic pain; it is about moving from the paranoid-schizoid to the defensive position). On the other hand, if the analyst is not able to contain the patient's projections, closing him/herself off or counterprojecting, the patient will feel misunderstood and attacked, consequently resorting in an intensified way to primitive defence mechanisms. A basic task of the analyst is to recognise within the patient the presence of something terrible that cannot be contained, and accept the feelings that such a condition unleashes in him/her, avoiding reprojecting into the patient; he/she has to delude the phantasy of the patient who believes the analyst's psychic balance will be disturbed by these feelings that are so strong as to be impossible to face. In a more general sense, Steiner (2006b) maintains that within the patient-analyst interpersonal relationship, "His emotions have to be available and he has to be willing to observe and face uncomfortable truths about his patient, and also about himself. At the same time, my view is that the analyst has to keep his feelings under control; he must be involved and yet has also to stay separate; he has to fully engage in the relationship and also be able to observe and evaluate it" (p. 325). It is this observational work that allows a certain degree of control over the countertransferential reactions, and subsequently exercises a control over the interpretation and the enactment that accompanies it.

To conclude this historical reconstruction of the development of the concept of psychoanalysis, I would like to present the point of view of the American psychoanalyst Thomas Ogden. In his elaboration of previous contributions by Winnicott (1960), Bion (1962), and André Green (1975), Ogden (1994a) introduces the concept of the 'intersubjective analytic third' (or 'the analytic third'). Such a concept implies the idea that the analytic relationship is not only composed of the separate subjectivities of the analyst and the patient but also of the product of the unique dialectic generated by and between these subjectivities. The analytic third is therefore an unconscious intersubjective construction co-created by the analyst and analysand, who are created at the same time by the analytic third.

It must be said that the construction of the analytic third is asymmetrical, a characteristic caused by the nature of the analytic relationship and by the type of interaction structured by the very asymmetry of the role. Furthermore, the asymmetrical nature of the analytic relationship also implies that what is privileged is the exploration of the internal world, of the conscious and unconscious experience past and present of the analysand, both the subject of analytic inquiry and the subject in that analytic inquiry.

In terms of the analytic third's creation of the analyst and analysand, it is important to emphasise some consequences. Even though analyst and analysand may be individuals with their own life histories, personality structures, and mental functioning, in order to understand the experiences (emotions, phantasies, feelings, desires, thoughts, behaviours, etc.) that each one has of the analysis, these must be contextualised within the analytic third. These experiences are different (at least in the form they adopt) than the ones that the analyst and the analysand have or could have had outside of the specific and continuously changing intersubjectivity created and shared by that specific analyst-analysand pair. Moreover, despite the fact that the analytic third is co-created by the analyst and analysand (two subjects simultaneously inside and outside the intersubjectivity), the third "does not reflect each of its creators in the same way" (Ogden, 1994c, p. 5, emphasis in original). This means that the phenomena of transference and countertransference, although mutually reflected, are not mirror images, nor are they identical.

From what has been said so far, we may deduce that transference and countertransference are interconnected, inseparable elements, part and parcel of the same process. Ogden (1991, 1994c) speaks of the matrix of transference-countertransference. The experience of this matrix – as with every other human experience – is the product of the dialectic interaction of three modes of creating and generating experience: the autistic-contiguous mode (in which the experience of self is based upon the ordering of sensory experience), the paranoid-schizoid mode (in which the experience of self is mainly experienced as 'self as an object'), and the depressive mode (in which the experience of self is symbolically mediated; it allows for the creation of an historical, interpreting self). The dynamic interplay of these three modalities, connected to each other both diachronically and synchronically, determines the type of background state in which a person lives (or fails to bring to life) and creates (or fails to create) a personal psychological meaning in the here and now.

But what exactly does Ogden mean by the term *countertransference*?

> I believe the use of the term countertransference to refer to everything the analyst thinks and feels and experiences sensorially, obscures the simultaneity of the dialectic of oneness and twoness, of individual subjectivity and intersubjectivity that is the foundation of the psychoanalytic relationship. To say that everything the analyst experiences is countertransference is only to make the self-evident statement that we are each trapped in our own subjectivity. For the concept of countertransference to have more meaning than this, we must continually re-ground the concept in the dialectic of the analyst as a separate entity and the analyst as a creation of the analytic intersubjectivity. Neither of these 'poles' of the dialectic exists in pure form and our task is to make increasingly full statements about the specific nature of the relationship between the experience of subject and object, between countertransference and transference at any given moment.
>
> *(Ogden, 1994a, p. 8, footnote 3)*

It is from the experience in and of the analytic third that the analyst can ultimately understand and be able to describe the nature of the dialectic movement between individual subjectivity and the intersubjective field (which contains the psychic realities of the analyst and the analysand, and influences at the same time their perceptions and thought): "It is in part through [the] countertransference analysis . . . that the analyst gains access to the nature of the states of being comprising the matrix of the patient's internal world" (Ogden, 1991, p. 604). A basic tool at the disposal of the analyst for recognising and symbolising the unconscious meanings of the transference-countertransference experience are the clinician's experiences of rêverie, including ruminations, daydreams, fantasies, bodily sensations, images emerging from states of half-sleep, phrases that run through the mind, etc. (Ogden, 1997). Ogden specifies that rêveries "are not simply reflections of inattentiveness, narcissistic self-involvement, unresolved emotional conflict, and the like; rather, this psychological activity represents symbolic and proto-symbolic (sensation-based) forms given to the unarticulated (and often not yet felt) experience of the analysand as they are taking form in the intersubjectivity of the analytic pair (i.e. in the analytic third)" (1994a, p. 12). At the same time they are also personal psychological events of the analyst, and "intersubjective constructions generated by analyst and analysand" (Ogden, 1997, p. 567).

The use that the analyst will make of the understanding of the transference-countertransference matrix will depend upon the analysand's level of functioning in that given moment. And so, in the case of patients functioning at a clinical presymbolic level, the analyst will not be able to interpret by utilising (or only utilising) a verbally symbolic speech, but will have to resort to an activity, or rather to interpretations that predominantly arise from the clinician's actions instead of his/her words. In this regard, Ogden (1994b) speaks about 'interpretive action' (or 'interpretation-in-action'). Such interpretations acquire their specific symbolic meaning from the experiential context of the analytic third in which the transference-countertransference dynamic is generated. It is important to highlight that even if what is given to the patient is interpretation-in-action, the clinician must silently formulate the interpretations in words within him/herself.

Notes

1 Bion "puts a particular emphasis on mental understanding: mental understanding by the other, in his view, is what makes it possible for the individual to develop mental understanding in himself and thus to move towards having a mind of his own and an awareness of the minds of others. Further, he focuses attention not only on the effect of the container on the contained, but also of the contained on the container" (Spillius, 1994, pp. 343–344).

2 In 1956 Willi Hoffer distinguished between transference on the part of the analyst towards the patient and countertransference; he associated the first with the humanity of that specific analyst and his/her evaluation of the real needs of the patient, while he associated the second to the intrapsychic reactions of the analyst (including the limits in the process of understanding the material brought up by the patient).

3 As we will see, Betty Joseph also supported the belief that the clinician in the patient's phantasy is constantly being assigned a specific role. Recognising and analysing this allows the analyst to extract information on the defence system adopted by the patient, and on the type of object relations to which he/she usually resorts. In cases of enactment (Sandler, 1976; Joseph, 1981), to a certain degree inevitable, "The preservation of the analyst's reality sense is central if enactments are to be contained and used to provide information about mental mechanisms and object relationships. Like countertransference, enactment can be useful but, also like countertransference, it can be overvalued and misused. As with countertransference . . . its usefulness depends on a close observation of the interaction between analyst and patient as it takes place in the session" (p. 319).

4 This author was considered by Joseph Reppen (1985) to be one of the most important leading exponents of psychoanalysis at that time. Moreover, along with Otto Kernberg, Langs played a significant role in the diffusion of Klein's and Bion's ideas in a time when they were practically unknown in the United States; it must be pointed out that their work in spreading these ideas interested mainly the East Coast, while Bion was a West Coast spokesperson, in that he lived in Los Angeles from 1968 to 1979.

5 The ability of the analyst to perceive and contain the infantile parts of the patient depends on his/her own childhood experiences and on whether he/she has achieved enough ability to contain his/her own infantile parts, but it also depends on the capacity to maintain a certain distance from the emotional experience that characterises that specific analytical relationship.

6 In the preface to his *Collected Papers on Schizophrenia* (1965), Searles acknowledges a whole group of psychoanalysts from whom he drew his ideas; in this group the names of these analysts appear Balint, Bion, Brodey, Bowen, Cohen, Erikson, Heimann, Hill, Knight, Ruth and Theodore Lidz, Little, Milner, Rosenfeld, Sechehaye, Werner, Whitaker and Malone, Winnicott, Wynne, and many others. Searles does not cite Ferenczi (nor did he do so in his monograph on countertransference), despite the fact that the influence of this Hungarian's thinking seems obvious at times – for example the points of contact that exist between Searles's (1972) idea of the patient as therapist to his analyst and Ferenczi's (1932a) idea of mutual analysis.

7 The fate of this work, originally entitled 'Two suggested revisions of the concept of transference. comments regarding the usefulness of emotions arising during the analytic hour', is interesting: in 1949 it was rejected by both *Psychiatry* and *Psychoanalytic Quarterly*, probably because at the time the perspective of American analysts (with few exceptions, for example Harry Stack Sullivan and Frieda Fromm-Reichmann) viewed the clinician

as a scientific instrument and the patient as a scientific object, and it was published thirty years later after Langs, the then editor of the *International Journal of Psychoanalytic Psychotherapy*, became aware of its existence during an interview with Searles.

8 Winnicott and Milner believed that faith in the environment, necessary for allowing the child access to the potential space and to symbol formation, is born out of the experience of illusion (at the base of which these authors place the sensorial experience of object-self fusion). With the gradual diminishment of the mother's adapting to the needs of the child, what will take place is the progressive development of transitional phenomena and potential space. What materialises is mental space, the space for play, and space for the creation of symbols. Simply put, it is possible to define the frame about which Milner speaks as what is thought by the therapist about the patient. This frame can outline in space and time what passes on the part of the patient between the patient and the analyst. It is inside this frame that the transferences develop. The space-time reliability characteristic to the setting makes possible the development of a sense of continuity of both the patient's self and the relationship with the therapist, of the potential space essential to the ability to play, not sufficiently developed in the primary relationship.

9 These patients have been the subject of study of various authors, who referred to them using different names: 'as if' personality (Deutsch, 1942), false Self (Winnicott, 1960b), splitting-off of the dependent parts of the self in narcissistic patients (Rosenfeld, 1964), pseudo-normality (Meltzer, 1966), etc.

10 Brenman Pick highlighted a characteristic of the patient's projections, that of being directed towards particular aspects of the analyst; they penetrate the deep primitive anxieties associated with the need to be loved (protected and taken care of) and the terror that one's own defects will bring about catastrophic results.

11 According to Steiner (1993), the technical challenge which the analyst faces is to find an appropriate balance of patient-centred and analyst-centred interpretations: in the first (which are of the 'classical' kind), a thought, a desire, or an action of the patient gets interpreted, and often the relative motives and anxieties are also included within the interpretation; in the second what gets interpreted is the recognition that the patient's interest is more oriented towards what is happening in the analyst's mind rather than in the patient's own (for example: 'You experience me as . . .' or, 'You are afraid that I . . .').

10

SOME NON-CONCLUSIVE CONSIDERATIONS

As we have seen, the concepts of transference and countertransference share a similar fate, insofar as each went from being regarded first as an obstacle and later as an indispensable tool of analysis. It is therefore possible to state that in a certain sense the notion of countertransference is complementary to that of transference: countertransference as resistance/obstacle (Freud, 1910a) and as a therapeutic tool (Freud, 1912a). Using the term *countertransference* only five times, Freud places emphasis on the aspects that work against analysis and takes for granted that the analyst's subjectivity is fundamental to successful treatment (cf. Freud, 1937a), relegating to a grey area the monopersonal and interactive perceptions of the analytic situation. To the ambiguity surrounding these two perspectives, we can add the contradiction between Freud's praxis and his recommendations on technique. His recommendations are essentially of the negative variety, to the extent that in a letter in which he praised Ferenczi's work on elasticity of technique (a text which pointed out what is necessary to do: interaction, tact, empathy, humility, acknowledgement of one's own mistakes, etc.) Freud specified that: "I considered the most important thing to emphasize [was] what one should not do, to demonstrate the temptations that work against analysis" (Freud and Ferenczi, 1920–33, p. 332).

This is the basis upon which lies the development of the controversies surrounding countertransference, which only a schematic reading would classify in terms of 'countertransference as obstacle' (Freud, in his writings on technique; Abraham; Klein; Alexander, 1924; W. Reich; Heimann, 1959; and others) and 'countertransference as therapeutic tool' (Freud, in his clinical practice; Ferenczi, Rank, Balint, Reik, and Alexander, 1946; Heimann, 1949; Gitelson, 1949; Tower; Bion; Nacht; and others). The reality is much more complex and highly nuanced. Thus no clinician with any common sense would think of the analyst's subjectivity as exclusively hindering or exclusively helping the therapeutic work, even if obviously some analysts lean too far towards the first extremity while others too far towards the second. Furthermore, there is another fact that lends reality to its inherent complexity. It is one which psychoanalysts have become more and more aware of as psychoanalysis has gradually developed: there exists a gap between theory and clinical practice (Sandler, 1983; Stolorow, 1992; Fonagy, 2006) – a gap which over time has led to the formation of a multitude of psychoanalytic schools which at present characterises our discipline.

From a reading of the literature, cited in the first chapters, what emerges is that most of the issues that have engaged analysts over the last decades had already been confronted well before 1950 ('year zero' in the history of countertransference), when, in a more favourable climate, various scholars began to more systematically explore the theoretical aspects of countertransference as well as the technical aspects. This situation, which has come about not by means of a paradigm shift (Kuhn, 1962) but through a progressive accumulation of new discoveries, has promoted a freer and a fuller (both in quantitative and qualitative terms) debate on this particular feature of the analytic process, a debate out of which a gradual and widespread acceptance of countertransference has materialised, along with a more general recognition of the fact that the analyst's professional identity is inseparable from his/her being a person with feelings as well as thoughts. Nonetheless, despite the current overall acceptance of the concept of countertransference, it still retains its uncertain and contradictory aspect, forcing all of us, who wish to perform our therapeutic work in an appropriate manner, to undertake a thorough self-interrogation about who we are and how we function (Ferruta, 1998). This is so because accepting the existence of countertransference and the difficulties that can arise from it (something only potentially and partially enlightening) highlights the intrinsic complexity of the analytic situation and poses more questions than answers in our theoretical and clinical work (Turillazzi Manfredi, 1994).

Over the years, countertransference has undergone a continuous and profound redefining and reconceptualising process associated with the theoretical orientation, the type of patients in treatment, and the innate personological characteristics, etc., of every theorist who has focussed on it. In this diverse and variegated landscape, one point in common lies in seeing this phenomenon as the clinician's conscious or unconscious idiosyncratic response (broadly defined as sensory, affective, cognitive, and behavioural), triggered by the transference, by the patient's characteristics, and by various aspects of the therapeutic situation, but never by extra-therapeutic factors (Fauth, 2006). Even today analysts conceptualise countertransference in ways that can be extremely different – in a broad and comprehensive way by some, and in a more restricted way by others. Furthermore, analysts with similar theories differ in the way that they work with/on their countertransference. Vincenzo Bonaminio and Di Renzo (2003), basing their view on an independent matrix, write that "the analyst's countertransference 'work' [including the analyst's theories and unconscious interpretations and responses, but distinct from that private region composed of the analyst's person] consists of that part of personal emotions and thoughts [not representative of the whole self of the analyst] that is made progressively available from the preconscious to his/her awareness, and that also includes *something about the patient*, a something that alludes to that dissociated self of which the patient *knows nothing* (yet)" (p. 65, emphasis in original). Transference and countertransference, regulated by the setting, structure the therapeutic process, starting with the first analyst-patient[1] contact, and they represent the affective relationship of that pair, one in which "we all use, to a greater or lesser extent, countertransference as an indispensable guide, not only for what happens in the patient, but also for what happens within us" (Giannakoulas, 2010, p. 197), thus exploring who we are and how we function with that patient. This means that if the clinician does not bear the burden of his/her own countertransference, he/she will be led to scotomise both some areas of his/her own self and consequently some areas of the patient's existence. For example, the analyst could collude with some aspects of the patient's pathology, invert the flow of the patient's pathology, and/or invert the flow of the patient's projective identifications (Ferro, 1987). The analyst therefore finds that he/she has to accomplish a double analysis: one of the patient's psychic life ('objectified' in the transference) and the other of his/her own countertransference. Sometimes a third object of analysis is added to the first two: the analyst's transference onto the patient.

It is not the countertransference in and of itself that is the mechanism for understanding what happens in the relationship with the patient. It is rather the result of the profound and continuous concentration/reflection/investigation/self-analysis/processing that the clinician makes of his/her own countertransference. It is important to mention that countertransference is composed of both emotional and ideational elements, that the analyst must therefore be careful not to place excessive emphasis on one or the other aspect, but apply the method of free association to both, despite the fact that the application of such a method may be difficult for the analyst to tolerate (here a key role is played by the quality of the experience of the analyst's personal analysis), to such an extent that it is legitimate to ask ourselves "whether the excessive emphasis on affects might not also enable us to avoid expressing our own 'ideational' associations, which are inevitably *also* absolutely personal and bound up with our own history; just as [it is legitimate to ask] whether the over-emphasis on 'representations' might not be likely to have an analogous effect, but in this case displacing clinical exposition on to the theoretical level" (Semi, 2012, p. 51, emphasis in original).

What emerges from this is that countertransference is a 'potential' technical tool, whose utilisation is neither immediate nor easy (the countertransferential thoughts and feelings perceived by the analyst are not the thoughts and probably not the conscious or unconscious feelings of the patient either, but their underlying meaning could be). Furthermore we can deduce from this that countertransference may prove to be a misleading guide if the clinician is not adept at recognising and managing his/her own emotional and ideational response to the patient (managing it could mean allowing it to decant rather than removing it/acting on it), or if he/she is unsuccessful in the working-through process because of personal associative or representational difficulties. This intense work on countertransference must be done without neglecting the material brought up by the patient, material that remains of essential importance (in the case of an intensely negative countertransferential reaction or one of annoyance/indifference/boredom, such expended energy and work on countertransference could help the analyst to place greater attention on the patient and the therapeutic process).

It should be pointed out that some authors (cf. Eagle, 2000) believe that over time many theoreticians have created a more subtle version of the analyst as blank screen, a new unipersonal psychology in which attention is turned more towards the analyst than the analysand, effectively making the patient's search for self-intimacy difficult. This is certainly true in all of those cases in which the relational and intersubjective assumption goes beyond a certain limit. Besides this risk of usurping the patient and his/her individuality, Vincenzo Bonaminio (2001) sees a real threat to the privacy and idiom of the analyst who, going to extremes, could become totally engaged in tracking down the relational interweaving in the clinical material, and in localising within context the reciprocal movements of both participants, thus losing sight of him/herself, as well as the patient. André Green (1993) also points out the difficulty that the clinician encounters in the attempt to combine free-floating attention, in other words the listening to the patient, and the efforts of self-analysis, or rather the listening to one's own internal experiences. The risk, Green states, is a blockage in one's listening (to the patient) process, subsequently leading to the blocking of the process of formulating highly subjectivistic interpretations (of the kind rather distant from the generally accepted and practiced interpretations of the majority of analysts – in other words, those that lead to an interaction that takes place on the intrapsychic level between patient and analyst in the here and now of the session; O'Shaughnessy, 1983). I might add that it is easier to reach the patient with our interpretations if our countertransference draws on past personal experiences (as long as they are acknowledged and integrated): not so much for how it influences the interpretation's content or form, but more for how it affects the way in which we communicate our understanding of the dynamics, the conflicts, and the needs, etc. of the patient because for patients to feel welcome, understood, supported, and involved in the analytic work, what is important is not so much what we say to them, but how we are with them.

This could help us to "appreciate how often in analysis unconscious connections to our unique, but parallel, life experiences help fuel both our invaluable gut reactions – and our overreactions – to our patients" (Jacobs, 2007, p. 177). The countertransferential experience is therefore necessary to be able to walk in the shoes of the patient, to be able to enter into contact with his internal world. The analyst's concentration within the countertransference could also be

> the psychic state of the analyst who ends up abandoning him/herself to the surprise of being in contact with and of sharing in some of the modalities of the patient's psychic life, those communicated in the here and now of the transference and countertransference. This self-abandonment allows the therapist to refrain from asking the patient or him/herself the reason behind the thoughts. The therapist receives the feelings of transference in a kind of psycho-physical continuity that is relatively indeterminate and undifferentiated with respect to the patient. He/she operates by patiently working through this psycho-physical state. . . . The material the analyst works on is the form of what he/she feels: this form allows him/her to imagine that what he/she feels in the body is not a purely physical sensation.
>
> *(Bertolini, 2001)*

Nevertheless, such a concentration on countertransference by

> no means guarantees empathy (if one remains identified through countertransference, one limits oneself to repeating the same internal scene, without being able to understand or interpret it). However . . . going through, and especially working through the countertransference experience may develop empathy which is both deep and far-reaching, and which is not restricted to ego-syntonic concordance . . . the natural base-camp for the approach to and development of profound changes in the patient.
>
> *(Bolognini, 2002, pp. 84–85)*

This means that there exist archaic situations of bodily functioning and earlier times when the precariousness in the continuity of the self has been experienced, situations in which the analyst, in the transference, must (a) let him/herself be engulfed by the patient's functioning processes, (b) which he/she must recognise as the patient's functioning processes, and (c) around which he/she must be able to form thoughts. A lengthy coexistence with the patient and the slow and steadfast effort of working through that the clinician must undertake during the course of the therapeutic process are essential in order for him/her to be able to enter into contact with the patient's entire internal world, not only with certain aspects of it.

Countertransference is not only "the most personal of all professional tools" (Hinshelwood, 1999, p. 814), but it is, at the same time, also the most interpersonal of the professional tools at the clinician's disposal. It is an unconscious-preconscious phenomenon that at first can only be perceived at the preconscious level, with the result that whoever might wish to penetrate – to quote Dante – "the dark wood" of countertransference must accept that he/she will "wander off the straight path" before finding it again (cf. Green, 2012). To ensure that the countertransference experiences can enter the realm of recognition, it is necessary for the clinician to find inside him/herself the space to carry out the complex and often tiring process of working through the psychophysical sensations caused by the transference or by the communicating (by means of projective identification) of some undigested modalities of the patient's psychic life, ones which are often felt as discomfort or anxiety by the clinician (Di Chiara, 2012). The use of countertransference as a therapeutic tool becomes possible (but never certain!) only after such psychophysical effort is expended. The purpose of this work is to increase one's recognition of the dynamics at play in the here and now of the relationship. This implies that the countertransference experiences do not simply become acknowledged – certainly they are not to be rejected, repressed, or projected – but they must be tolerated and contained (Carpy, 1989) in order to be processed (this is so because in a case where they are connected to areas within the patient that have already been problematic for him/her, our denial would reinforce the phantasy that these areas of suffering cannot be dealt with at all; similarly, those areas that the patient could have perceived and dealt with could become contaminated by our inability to face them. Generally speaking, the danger for the clinician is that of an enactment,[2] with the subsequent risks to the patient: just think of the potential damage to the development of his/her freedom of thought). With John Steiner (2006a) we can say that "central to the analytic attitude is the capacity to receive the patient's communications in order that they be understood and in order to do this the analyst must make space for the patient in his own mind. First, he has to recognize his own reactions and values and to differentiate them from those of his patient. Only then can the patient develop and grow to discover his own potential and character in conditions where the influence of the analyst's values and preferences are kept to a minimum" (p. 317). This work of receiving and working through, just as the work of becoming aware of inevitable enactments, means that the clinician must not lower the curtain (Heimann, 1978b) on the material brought up by the patient (including the reactions to our interjections or silences, reactions which can provide us with information on how the patient is experiencing us in that moment), and must continuously engage in the activity of self-analysis.

Psychoanalysis is the talking cure *par excellence*. The question, however, whether it heals by means of words (the interpretation) or by means of the experience of affective states (that also pass through words) brought on by and worked through within the analytical relationship, or to what extent and in what way it does so through both of these components, remains an open question of fundamental importance. In a perspective that takes into account the multiple modes of therapeutic action in psychoanalysis (Gabbard and Westen, 2003), whose conceptualisation is closely dependent on the clinician's theory of reference, a more comprehensive comparison between analysts of different theoretical orientation, between analysts for adults and those for children, and between psychoanalysis in general and the other sciences of the mind (infant research, neuroscience, cognitive science, psychotherapies of different types of theoretical orientations, etc.) could prove not just advantageous but also crucial for the further development of psychoanalysis in its entirety. It is equally desirable and essential that we explore more completely all aspects of non-verbal communication, the channels through which the emotions that permeate the analyst-patient relationship travel, and the modalities of that communication between unconsciouses already theorised at the outset of psychoanalysis but never fully researched.

Notes

1 Donald Winnicott (1971a) said he was surprised at "the frequency with which the children had dreamed of me the night before attending" (p. 4, emphasis in original), having placed him in the role of subjective object, that is within the area of his own omnipotence.
2 Graham Wallas (1926), British political sociologist and scholar asked, "How can I know what I think till I see what I say?" (p. 106).

BIBLIOGRAPHY

Abraham K. (1911). Notes on the psycho-analytical investigation and treatment of manic-depressive insanity and allied conditions. In: Abraham K., editor, *Selected Papers on Psychoanalysis*. London: Hogarth Press, pp. 137–156.

Abraham K. (1924). A short study of the development of the libido. In: Abraham K., editor, *Selected Papers on Psychoanalysis*. London: Hogarth Press, pp. 418–501.

Abraham K. (1927). *Selected Papers on Psychoanalysis*. London: Hogarth Press.

Albarella C. and Donadio M., editors (1986a). *Il controtransfert: Saggi psicoanalitici*. Naples: Liguori.

Albarella C. and Donadio M. (1986b). Introduzione al controtransfert. In: Albarella C. and Donadio M., editors, *Il controtransfert: Saggi psicoanalitici*. Naples: Liguori, pp. 3–24.

Alexander F. (1924). A metapsychological description of the process of cure. *International Journal of Psychoanalysis*, 1925, 6: 13–34.

Alexander F., French T.M., et al. (1946). *Psychoanalytic Therapy: Principles and Applications*. New York: Ronald Press.

Appignanesi L. and Forrester J. (1992). *Freud's Women*. London: Weidenfeld & Nicholson.

Balint A. (1936). Handhabung der Übertragung auf Grund der Ferenczischen Versuche. *Internationale Zeitschrift für Psychoanalyse*, 22: 47–58.

Balint A. and Balint M. (1939). On transference and counter-transference. *International Journal of Psychoanalysis*, 20: 223–230.

Balint E. (1954). Three phases of a transference neurosis. In: *Before I Was I: Psychoanalysis and the Imagination*. London: Free Association Books, 1993.

Balint M. (1933). On transference of emotions. In: *Primary Love and Psycho-Analytic Technique*. London: Tavistock, 1965.

Balint M. (1949). Changing therapeutical aims and techniques in psycho-analysis. *International Journal of Psychoanalysis*, 1950, 31: 117–124.

Balint M. (1965). *Primary Love and Psychoanalytic Technique* (2nd rev. edition). London: Tavistock.

Balint M. and Balint E. (1968). *The Basic Fault: Therapeutic Aspects of Regression*. London: Tavistock.

Baranger M. and Baranger W. (1961–62). The analytic situation as a dynamic field. *International Journal of Psychoanalysis*, 2008, 89: 795–826.

Berman L. (1949). Countertransference and attitudes of the analyst in the therapeutic process. *Psychiatry*, 12: 159–166.

Bertolini M. (2001). Sulla concentrazione e sugli scopi della psicoanalisi. Paper read at a meeting of the Associazione Italiana di Psicoanalisi (AIPsi), Rome, December 16.

Bettelheim B. (1983). Scandal in the family. *The New York Review of Books*, 30, 11, 30 June, pp. 39–44.

Bick E. (1961). Symposium on child analysis. *International Journal of Psychoanalysis*, 1962, 43: 328–332.

Bick E. (1968). The experience of the skin in early object-relations. *The International Journal of Psychoanalysis*, 49: 484–486.

Bick E. (1975). Further considerations on the function of the skin in early object-relations, findings from infant observation integrated into child and adult analysis. *British Journal of Psychotherapy*, 1986, 2: 292–299.

Binswanger L. (1956). *Sigmund Freud: Reminiscence of a Friendship*. New York/London: Grune & Stratton, 1957.

Bion W.R. (1953). Notes on the theory of schizophrenia. *International Journal of Psychoanalysis*, 1954, 35: 113–118.

Bion W.R. (1957). Attacks on linking. *International Journal of Psychoanalysis*, 1959, 40: 308–315.

Bion W.R. (1959–78). *Cogitation*. London: Karnac Books, 1992.

Bion W.R. (1961a). *Experiences in Groups and other Papers*. London: Tavistock.

Bion W.R. (1961b). A theory of thinking. *International Journal of Psychoanalysis*, 1962, 43: 306–310.

Bion W.R. (1962). *Learning from Experience*. London: Heinemann.

Bion W.R. (1963). *Elements of Psychoanalysis*. London: Heinemann.

Bion W.R. (1965). *Transformations: Change from Learning to Growth*. London: Heinemann.

Bion W.R. (1967a). Notes on memory and desire. *Psychoanalytic Forum*, 2: 272–273, 279–280.

Bion W.R. (1967b). *Second Thoughts*. London: Heinemann.

Bion W.R. (1975–78). *Clinicals Seminars and Four Papers*. Abingdon: The Fleetwood Press, 1987.

Bion W.R. (1978–80). *Bion in New York and São Paulo*. Perthshire: Clunie Press.

Blanton S. (1971). *Diary of My Analysis with Sigmund Freud*. New York: Hawthorne.

Bleuler E. (1896). Dr. Jos. Breuer und Dr. Sigm. Freud: Studien über Hysterie. *Munchener medizinische Wochenschrift*, 43: 524–525.

Bleuler E. (1909). Vortrag über Ambivalenz. *Zentralblatt für Psychoanalyse*, 1910, 1: 266.

Bleuler E. (1911). *Dementia Praecox, oder Gruppe der Schizophrenien*. Leipzig: Deuticke.

Bokanowski T. (1996). Freud and Ferenczi: Trauma and transference depression. *International Journal of Psychoanalysis*, 77: 519–536.

Bolko M. and Merini A. (1991). Osservazioni sulla identificazione proiettiva: Through the looking glass. *Psicoterapia e Scienze Umane*, 25, 4: 19–34.

Bollas C. (1980–82). Expressive uses of the countertransference: Notes to the patient from oneself. *Contemporary Psychoanalysis*, 1983, 19: 1–33.

Bollas C. (1987). *The Shadow of the Object*. London: Free Association Books.

Bollas C. (1995). *Cracking Up*. London: Routledge.

Bolognini S. (2002). *Psychoanalytic Empathy*. London: Free Association Books, 2004.

Bonaminio V. (1991). D.W. Winnicott and the position of the analyst and the analysand in the psychoanalytic situation. *Rivista di Psicoanalisi*, 37: 626–666.

Bonaminio V. (2001). The person of the analyst. *Bulletin of the British Psychoanalytic Society*, 37: 28–42. Reprinted in expanded edition In: Borgogno F., Luchetti A. and Marino Coe L., editors, *Reading Italian Psychoanalysis*. London: Routledge, 2016.

Bonaminio V. and Di Renzo M. (2003). L'imprescindibilità dell'altro: Un percorso nel pensiero clinico di Winnicott sul Sé e l'altro, e il lavoro di controtransfert dell'analista nella situazione psicoanalitica. *Interazioni*, 20, 2: 62–73.

Borgogno F. (1992). The development of psychoanalytic technique: A tribute to Paula Heimann. In: Borgogno F., editor, *Psychoanalysis as a Journey*. London: Open Gate Press, pp. 57–84.

Borgogno F. (1999a). *Psychoanalysis as a Journey*. London: Open Gate Press, 2007.

Borgogno F. (1999b). Sándor Ferenczi's first paper considered as a 'Calling Card'. *International Forum of Psychoanalysis*, 8, 3–4: 249–256.

Borgogno F. (2005). Ferenczi's clinical and theoretical conception of trauma: A brief introductory map. *American Journal of Psychoanalysis*, 2007, 67: 141–149.

Borgogno F. (2007). Ferenczi's clinical and theoretical conception of trauma: A brief introductory map. *American Journal of Psychoanalysis*, 67: 141–149.

Borgogno F. (2010). Sándor Ferenczi, the 'introjective psychoanalyst'. *American Imago*, 2011, 68: 155–172.

Bowlby J. (1944). Forty-four juvenile thieves: Their characters and home-life. *International Journal of Psychoanalysis*, 25: 19–53, 107–128.

Bowlby J. (1951). *Maternal Care and Mental Health*. London: World Health Organization.

Breuer J. and Freud S. (1892–95). Studies on Hysteria. *SE*, 2.

Brierley M. (1945). Further notes on the implications of psychoanalysis: Metapsychology and personology. *International Journal of Psychoanalysis*, 26: 89–114.

Brierley M. (1947). Notes on psycho-analysis and integrative living. *International Journal of Psychoanalysis*, 28: 57–105.

Britton R. (1989). The missing link: Parental sexuality in the Oedipus complex. In: Steiner J., editor, *The Oedipus Complex Today: Clinical Implications*. London: Karnac Books, pp. 83–101.

Britton R. (1998). *Belief and Imagination*. London: Routledge.

Britton R. (2003). *Sex, Death and the Superego*. London: Karnac Books.

Brome V. (1982). *Ernest Jones: Freud's Alter Ego*. London: Caliban Books.

Carotenuto A. (1982). *A Secret Symmetry: Sabina Spielrein between Jung and Freud*. New York: Pantheon Books.

Carpy D.V. (1989). Tolerating the countertransference: A mutative process. *International Journal of Psychoanalysis*, 70: 287–294.

Casement P. (1973). The supervisory viewpoint. In: Finn W.F., editor, *Family Therapy in Social Work: Conference Papers*. London: Family Welfare Association.

Casement P. (1985). *On Learning from the Patient*. London: Tavistock.

Cassullo G. (2010). Back to the roots: The influence of Ian D. Suttie on British psychoanalysis. *American Imago*, 67, 1: 5–22.

Cassullo G. (2014). Charles Rycroft and the making of an independent psychoanalyst. *Contemporary Psychoanalysis*, 50, 3: 332–370.

Cassullo G. (2015). *L'uomo dietro al lettino: Charles Rycroft e la psicoanalisi indipendente britannica*. Lecce: Freenis Zero.

Cohen M.B. (1952). Countertransference an anxiety. *Psychiatry*, 15: 231–243.

Cremerius J. (1984). Die psychoanalytische Abstinenzregel: Vom regelhaften zum operationalen Gebrauch. *Psyche*, 38: 769–800.

Cremerius J. (1986). Preface. In: Carotenuto A., editor, *Kant's Dove: The History of Transference in Psychoanalysis*. Wilmette: Chiron, 1989, pp. 9–16.

de Bernardi B.D. (2000). The countertransference: A Latin American view. *International Journal of Psychoanalysis*, 81: 331–351.

de Urtubey L. (1995). Countertransference effects of absence. *International Journal of Psychoanalysis*, 76: 683–694.

Deutsch H. (1926). Occult processes occurring during psychoanalysis. In: *The Therapeutic Process, the Self, and Female Psychology: Collected Psychoanalytic Papers.* New Brunswick, NJ: Transaction Publishers, 1992, pp. 223–238.

Deutsch H. (1942). Some forms of emotional disturbance and their relationship to schizophrenia. *Psychoanalytic Quarterly*, 11: 301–321.

Di Chiara G. (1992). L'incontro, il racconto, il commiato: Tre fattori dell'esperienza psicoanalitica. In: Nissim L.M. and Robutti A., editors, *L'esperienza condivisa: Saggi sulla relazione psicoanalitica.* Milan: Raffaello Cortina, pp. 43–61.

Di Chiara G. (2012). La identificazione proiettiva normale e patologica (una rilettura della 'Fiaba della mano verde' vent'anni dopo). Paper read at a meeting of the Centro milanese di psicoanalisi 'Cesare Musatti', Milan, May 12.

Dupont J. (1985). Introduction. In: Ferenczi S., editor, *The Clinical Diary of Sándor Ferenczi.* Cambridge, MA: Harvard University Press, pp. 11–27.

Dupont J. (1989). La relation Freud-Ferenczi ä la lumière de leur correspondance. *Revue Internationale d'Histoire de la Psychanalyse*, 2: 181–201.

Dupont J. (2009). Alice Balint: una vita breve ma fruttuosa. In: Borgogno F. and Vigna-Taglianti M., editors, Identificazione e trasmissione psichica fra gli adulti e il bambino / 1. *Quaderni di Psicoterapia Infantile*, 56: 15–21.

Eagle M.N. (2000). A critical evaluation of current concepts of transference and countertransference. *Psychoanalytic Psychology*, 17, 1: 24–37.

Eitingon M. (1923). Report of the Berlin Psychoanalytical Polyclinic. *Bulletin of the International Psychoanalytical Association*, 4: 254.

Ellenberger H.F. (1970). *The Discovery of the Unconscious.* New York: Basic Books.

English O.S. and Pearson H.J. (1937). *Common Neuroses of Children and Adults.* New York: W.W. Norton.

Epstein L. and Feiner A.H., editors (1979). *Countertransference: The Therapist's Contribution to the Therapeutic Situation.* New York: Jason Aronson.

Etchegoyen R.H. (1986). *The Fundamentals of Psychoanalytic Technique.* London: Karnac Books, 1999.

Etchegoyen R.H. (2014). Introduction to the life and work of Heinrich Racker (1910–1961). In: Lisman-Pieczanski N. and Pieczanski A., editors, *The Pioneers of Psychoanalysis in South America: An Essential Guide.* New York: Routledge, pp. 87–91.

Fabozzi P., editor (2003). *Forme dell'interpretare.* Milan: FrancoAngeli.

Fairbairn W.R.D. (1941). A revised psychopathology of the psychoses and psychoneuroses. *International Journal of Psychoanalysis*, 22: 250–270.

Fairbairn W.R.D. (1944). Endopsychic structure considered in terms of object-relationships. *International Journal of Psychoanalysis*, 25: 70–93.

Fairbairn W.R.D. (1946). Object relationships and dynamic structure. *International Journal of Psychoanalysis*, 27: 30–37.

Fairbairn W.R.D. (1952). *Psychoanalytic Studies of the Personality.* London: Tavistock.

Fairbairn W.R.D. (1957). Fairbairn's reply to the comments of Balint, Foulkes, and Sutherland. *British Journal for the Philosophy of Science*, 7, 28: 333–338.

Fairbairn W.R.D. (1958). On the nature and aims of psycho-analytical treatment. *International Journal of Psychoanalysis*, 39: 374–385.

Falzeder E. (1994). The threads of psychoanalytic filiations or psychoanalysis taking effect. In: Haynal A. and Falzeder E., editors, *100 Years of Psychoanalysis: Contributions to the History of Psychoanalysis.* Geneva: Cahiers Psychiatriques Genevois, Special Issue, pp. 169–194.

Fauth J. (2006). Toward more (and better) countertransference research. *Psychotherapy: Theory, Research, Practice, Training*, 43: 16–31.

Feldman M. (1993). The dynamics of reassurance. *International Journal of Psychoanalysis*, 74: 275–285.

Feldman M. (1995). Projective identification: The analyst's involvement. *International Journal of Psychoanalysis*, 1997, 78: 227–241.

Fenichel O. (1935). Concerning the theory of psychoanalytic technique. In: *The Collected Papers of Otto Fenichel*. New York: W.W. Norton, 1953, pp. 363–374.

Fenichel O. (1936). *Problems of Psychoanalytic Technique*. New York: The Psychoanalytic Quarterly Press, 1941.

Ferenczi S. (1908). The effect on women of premature ejaculation in men. In: Ferenczi S., editor, *Further Contributions to the Theory and Technique of Psychoanalysis*. London: Hogarth Press, pp. 291–294.

Ferenczi S. (1909). Introjection and transference. In: Ferenczi S., editor, *First Contributions to Psycho-Analysis*. London: Hogarth Press, pp. 35–93.

Ferenczi S. (1913). Stages in the development of the sense of reality. In: Jones E., editor, *Sex in Psychoanalysis*. New York: Basic Books, 1950, pp. 213–219.

Ferenczi S. (1915). Psychogenic anomalies of voice production. In: Ferenczi S., editor, *First Contributions to Psycho-Analysis*. London: Hogarth Press, pp. 105–109.

Ferenczi S. (1918). On the technique of psychoanalysis. In: Ferenczi S., editor, *Further Contributions to the Theory and Technique of Psychoanalysis*. London: Hogarth Press, pp. 177–189.

Ferenczi S. (1919). Technical difficulties in an analysis of hysteria. In: *Further Contributions to the Theory and Technique of Psycho-Analysis*. London: Hogarth Press, pp. 189–197.

Ferenczi S. (1920). The further development of the active therapy in psycho-analysis. In: *Further Contributions to the Theory and Technique of Psychoanalysis*. London: Hogarth Press, pp. 198–216.

Ferenczi S. (1923). A pszichoanalízis a gyakorló orvos szolgálatában. *Gyógyászat*, 23: 332–333 and 24: 350–351.

Ferenczi S. (1927). The problem of the termination of the analysis. In: Ferenczi S., editor, *Further Contributions to the Theory and Technique of Psychoanalysis*. London: Hogarth Press, pp. 77–86.

Ferenczi S. (1927–28). The elasticity of psychoanalytic technique. In: Ferenczi S., editor, *Further Contributions to the Theory and Technique of Psychoanalysis*. London: Hogarth Press, pp. 87–101.

Ferenczi S. (1932a). *The Clinical Diary of Sándor Ferenczi*. Cambridge, MA: Harvard University Press, 1988.

Ferenczi S. (1932b). Confusion of tongues between adults and the child – the language of tenderness and of passion. *International Journal of Psychoanalysis*, 1949, 30: 225–230.

Ferenczi S. (1952). *First Contributions to Psycho-Analysis*. London: Hogarth Press.

Ferenczi S. (1955). *Further Contributions to the Theory and Technique of Psychoanalysis*. London: Hogarth Press.

Ferenczi S. and Rank O. (1923). *The Development of Psychoanalysis*. New York/Washington: Nervous & Mental Disease Publishing Co., 1925.

Ferro A. (1987). Il mondo alla rovescia. L'inversione di flusso delle identificazioni proiettive. *Rivista di Psicoanalisi*, 33: 59–77.

Ferruta A. (1998). Tra Corinto e Tebe: Il controtransfert all'incrocio tra riconoscimento e accecamento. *Rivista di Psicoanalisi*, 44: 295–308.

Fliess R. (1953). Countertransference and counteridentification. *Journal of the American Psychoanalytic Association*, 1: 268–284.

Fonagy P. (2006). The failure of practice to inform theory and the role of implicit theory in bridging the transmission gap. In: Canestri J., editor, *Psychoanalysis: From Practice to Theory*. West Sussex: Whurr Publications, pp. 69–86.

Fonagy P. and Target M. (2003). *Psychoanalytic Theories: Perspectives from Developmental Psychopathology*. London: Whurr Publications.

Fordham M. (1957). Notes on the transference. In: *New Developments in Analytical Psychology*. London: Routledge, pp. 60–103.

Fordham M. (1959). Countertransference. *British Journal of Medical Psychology*, 1960, 33: 1–8.

Fordham M. (1970). Reply to Plaut's 'Comment'. *Journal of Analytical Psychology*, 15: 177–181.

Fordham M. (1979). Analytical psychology and countertransference. *Contemporary Psychoanalysis*, 15: 630–646.

Fordham M., Gordon R., Hubback J. and Lambert K., editors (1974). *Technique in Jungian Analysis*. London: Karnac Books.

Freud A. (1926). Four lectures on child analysis. In: *The Writings of Anna Freud, 1*. New York: International Universities Press, 1974, pp. 3–62.

Freud A. (1936). *The Ego and the Mechanisms of Defence*. London: Hogarth Press and Institute of Psycho-Analysis, 1937.

Freud S. (1895). Extracts from the Fliess papers. *SE*, 1.

Freud S. (1899 [1900]). The interpretation of dreams. *SE*, 4–5.

Freud S. (1901 [1905]). A fragment of a case of hysteria. *SE*, 7.

Freud S. (1908 [1909]). Notes upon a case of obsessional neurosis. *SE*, 10.

Freud S. (1910a). The future prospects of psychoanalytic therapy. *SE*, 11.

Freud S. (1910b). Psycho-analytic notes on an autobiographical account of a case of paranoia (dementia paranoides). *SE*, 12.

Freud S. (1912a). The dynamics of transference. *SE*, 12.

Freud S. (1912b). Recommendations to physicians practising psycho-analysis. *SE*, 12.

Freud S. (1913a). Introduction to Pfister's the psychoanalytic method. *SE*, 12.

Freud S. (1913b). On beginning the treatment. *SE*, 12.

Freud S. (1914a). Remembering, repeating and working-through. *SE*, 12.

Freud S. (1914b [1915]). Observations on transference-love. *SE*, 12.

Freud S. (1914b [1918]). From the history of an infantile neurosis ('Wolf Man'). *SE*, 17.

Freud S. (1915a). The unconscious. *SE*, 14.

Freud S. (1915b [1917]). Mourning and melancholia. *SE*, 14.

Freud S. (1915c). Thoughts for the times on war and death. *SE*, 14.

Freud S. (1915–17 [1916–17]). Introductory lectures on psychoanalysis. *SE*, 15–16.

Freud S. (1918 [1919]). Lines of advance in psychoanalytic therapy. *SE*, 17.

Freud S. (1920). Beyond the pleasure principle. *SE*, 18.

Freud S. (1921). Group psychology and the analysis of the ego. *SE*, 18.

Freud S. (1922 [1923]). The ego and the id. *SE*, 19.

Freud S. (1937a). Analysis terminable and interminable. *SE*, 23.

Freud S. (1937b). Constructions in analysis. *SE*, 23.

Freud S. (1938 [1940]). An outline of psychoanalysis. *SE*, 23.

Freud S. and Abraham K. (1907–25). *The Complete Correspondence of Sigmund Freud and Karl Abraham*. London: Karnac Books, 2002.

Freud S. and Andreas-Salomé L. (1912–36). *Letters*. London: Hogarth Press, 1985.

Freud S. and Ferenczi S. (1908–14). *The Correspondence of Sigmund Freud and Sándor Ferenczi. Volume 1*. Cambridge, MA: Harvard University Press.

Freud S. and Ferenczi S. (1914–19). *The Correspondence of Sigmund Freud and Sándor Ferenczi. Volume 2*. Cambridge, MA: Harvard University Press.

Freud S. and Ferenczi S. (1920–33). *The Correspondence of Sigmund Freud and Sándor Ferenczi. Volume 3*. Cambridge, MA: The Belknap Press of Harvard University Press.

Freud S. and Jones E. (1908–20). *The Complete Correspondence of Sigmund Freud and Ernest Jones 1908–1939*. Cambridge, MA: Harvard University Press, 1993.

Freud S. and Jung C.G. (1906–13). *The Freud/Jung Letters: The Correspondence between Sigmund Freud and C.G. Jung*. London: Hogarth Press with Routledge & Kegan Paul, 1974.
Freud S. and Pfister O. (1909–39). *Psychoanalysis and Faith: The Letters of Sigmund Freud and Oskar Pfister*. London: Hogarth Press, 1963.
Fromm-Reichmann F. (1950). *Principles of Intensive Psychotherapy*. Chicago: University of Chicago Press.
Gabbard G.O. (1995). Countertransference: The emerging common ground. *International Journal of Psychoanalysis*, 76: 475–485.
Gabbard G.O. and Westen D. (2003). On therapeutic action. *International Journal of Psychoanalysis*, 84: 823–841.
Gammill J. (1989). Some personal reflections on Melanie Klein. *Melanie Klein and Object Relations*, 7: 1–15.
Giannakoulas A. (2010). *La tradizione psicoanalitica britannica indipendente*. Rome: Borla.
Giannakoulas A. and Fizzarotti Selvaggi S. (2006). *Il counselling psicodinamico*. Rome: Borla.
Gill M.M. (1994). *Psychoanalysis in Transition: A Personal View*. Hillsdale, NJ: The Analytic Press.
Gitelson M. (1949). The emotional position of the analyst in the psycho-analytic situation. *International Journal of Psychoanalysis*, 1952, 33: 1–10.
Glenn J. (1986). Freud, Dora, and the maid: A study of countertransference. *Journal of the American Psychoanalytic Association*, 34: 591–606.
Glover E. (1927). Lectures on technique in psycho-analysis. *International Journal of Psychoanalysis*. 8: 311–338, 486–520.
Glover E. (1955). *The Technique of Psychoanalysis*. London: Baillière, Tindall & Cassell.
Glover E. and Brierley M. (1940). *An Investigation of the Technique of Psychoanalysis*. London: Baillie`re, Tindall & Cox.
Green A. (1975). The analyst, symbolization and absence in the analytic setting (On changes in analytic practice and analytic experience)—In memory of D. W. Winnicott. *International Journal of Psychoanalysis*, 56: 1–22.
Green A. (1990). *On Private Madness*. London: Karnac Books, 1997.
Green A. (1993). Two discussions of 'The inner experiences of the analyst' and a response from Theodore Jacobs. *International Journal of Psychoanalysis*, 74: 1131–1136.
Green A. (2012). *La Clinique psychanalytique contemporaine*. Paris: Editions d'Ithaque.
Greenberg J. and Mitchell S. (1983). *Object Relations in Psychoanalytic Theory*. Cambridge, MA: Harvard University Press.
Grinberg L. (1956). Aspectos mágicos en la transferencia y la contratransferencia: sus implicaciones técnicas. Identificación y contraidentificación proyectiva. *Revista de Psicoanálisis*, 1958, 15: 347–368.
Grinberg L. (1962). On a specific aspect of countertransference due to the patient's projective identification. *International Journal of Psychoanalysis*, 43: 436–440.
Grinberg L. (1963). Psicopatologìa de la identificatión y controidentificatión proyectivas y de la controtransferencia. *Revista de Psicoanálisis*, 20: 113–123.
Grinberg L. (1979). Countertransference and projective counteridentification. *Contemporary Psychoanalysis*, 15: 226–247.
Grosskurth P. (1986). *Melanie Klein: Her World and Her Work*. New York: Knopf.
Grotstein J.S. (1981). *Splitting and Projective Identification*. New York, Jason Aronson.
Grotstein J.S. (2005). 'Projective transidentification': An extension of the concept of projective identification. *International Journal of Psychoanalysis*, 86: 1051–1069.
Grotstein J.S. (2007). *A Beam of Intense Darkness*. London: Karnac Books.
Guntrip H. (1961). *Personality Structure and Human Interaction: The Developing Synthesis of Psychodynamic Theory*. New York: International Universities Press.

Hann-Kende F. (1933). On the role of transference and counter-transference in psychoanalysis. In: Devereux G., editor, *Psychoanalysis and the Occult.* New York: International Universities Press, 1970, pp. 158–167.

Harris M. and Bick E. (2011). *The Tavistock Model: Papers on Child Development and Psychoanalytic Training.* London: Karnac Books.

Haynal A. (1987). *La technique en question: Controverses en psychanalyse.* Paris: Payot.

Healy W., Bronner A.F. and Bowers A.M. (1930). *The Structure and Meaning of Psychoanalysis as Related to Personality and Behavior.* New York: Knopf.

Heimann P. (1949). On countertransference. *International Journal of Psychoanalysis,* 1950, 31: 81–84.

Heimann P. (1959). Counter-transference. *British Journal of Medical Psychology,* 1960, 33: 9–15.

Heimann P. (1975). Obituary, Lois Munro, 1907–1973. *International Journal of Psychoanalysis,* 56: 99–100.

Heimann P. (1978a). On the necessity for the analyst to be natural with his patients. In: *About Children and Children-No-Longer.* London: Institute of Psycho-Analysis, 1989, pp. 238–247.

Heimann P. (1978b). La sfida di Freud al coraggio e alla creatività dell'individuo. *Neuropsichiatria infantile,* 1981, 242: 707–720.

Heimann P. (1980). L'importanza del transfert e controtransfert nel rapporto medico paziente. *Neuropsichiatria infantile,* 1981, 235–236, 117–128.

Heuer G. (2001). Jung's twin brother: Otto Gross and Carl Gustav Jung. *Journal of Analytical Psychology,* 46: 655–688.

Hinshelwood R.D. (1989). *A Dictionary of Kleinian Thought.* London: Free Association Books.

Hinshelwood R.D. (1999). Countertransference. *International Journal of Psychoanalysis,* 80: 797–818.

Hoffer W. (1956). Transference and transference neurosis. *International Journal of Psychoanalysis,* 37: 377–379.

Hoffman I.Z. (1983). The patient as interpreter of the analyst's experience. *Contemporary Psychoanalysis,* 19: 389–422.

Hoffman I.Z. (1998). *Ritual and Spontaneity in the Psychoanalytic Process: A Dialectical-Constructivist View.* Hillsdale, NJ: The Analytic Press.

Hollós I. (1933). Psychopathologie alltäglicher telepathischer Erscheinungen. *Imago,* 19: 529–546.

Horney K. (1939). *New Ways in Psychoanalysis.* New York: W.W. Norton.

Imbasciati A. (2007). *Fondamenti psicoanalitici della psicologia clinica: Nuova edizione.* Turin: Utet.

Jacobs T.J. (1999). Countertransference past and present: A review of the concept. *International Journal of Psychoanalysis,* 80: 575–594.

Jacobs T.J. (2007). Listening, dreaming, sharing: On the use of the analyst's inner experiences. In: *The Possible Profession: The Analytic Process of Change.* London: Routledge, 2013, pp. 166–178.

Jones E. (1953). *The Life and Work of Sigmund Freud* (3 volumes). New York: Basic Books.

Joseph B. (1975). The patient who is difficult to reach. In: Giovacchini P.L., editor, *Tactics and Techniques in Psychoanalytic Therapy, Volume II: Countertransference.* New York: Jason Aronson, pp. 205–216.

Joseph B. (1981). Defence mechanisms and phantasy in the psycho-analytic process. *Psycho-Analytical Federation,* 17: 11–24.

Joseph B. (1983). Transference: The total situation. *International Journal of Psychoanalysis,* 1985, 66: 447–454.

Joseph B. (1984). Projective identification: Clinical aspects. In: Sandler J., editor, *Projection, Identification, Projective Identification.* New York: International Universities Press, 1987.

Joseph B. (2003). Ethics and enactment. *Bulletin of the European Psycho-Analytical Federation*, 57: 147–153.

Jung C.G. (1911–52). Symbols of transformation. *Collected Works*, 5.

Jung C.G. (1921–28). The therapeutic value of abreaction. *Collected Works*, 16.

Jung C.G. (1929). Problems of modern psychotherapy. *Collected Works*, 16.

Jung C.G. (1951). Fundamental questions of psychotherapy. *Collected Works*, 16.

Jung C.G. (1957). Schizophrenia. *Collected Works*, 3.

Jung C.G. (1961). *Memories, Dreams, Reflections.* New York: Vintage Books, 1989.

Kernberg O. (1963). Notes on countertransference. *Journal of the American Psychoanalytic Association*, 1965, 13: 38–56.

Kierkegaard S. (1841). *Concept of Irony*. New York: Harper & Row, 1965.

King P. (1951). Change: The psychoanalysis of a four-year-old boy and its follow-up. In: *Time Present and Time Past.* London: Karnac Books, 2005, pp. 15–40.

King P. (1978). Affective response of the analyst to the patient's communications. *International Journal of Psychoanalysis*, 59: 329–34.

King P. and Steiner R., editors (1991). *The Freud-Klein Controversies 1941–45*. London: Routledge.

Khan M.M.R. (1963). The concept of cumulative trauma. *Psychoanalytic Study of the Child*, 18: 286–306.

Khan M.M.R. (1969a). Vicissitudes of being, knowing and experiencing in the therapeutic situation. In: *The Privacy of the Self.* London: Hogarth Press, 1974.

Khan M.M.R. (1969b). On the clinical provision of frustrations, recognitions, and failures in the analytic situation: An essay on Dr Michael Bálint's researches on the theory of psychoanalytic technique. *International Journal of Psychoanalysis*, 50: 237–248.

Klein M. (1921–58). *The Writings of Melanie Klein* (4 volumes). London: Hogarth Press, 1975.

Klein M. (1927). Symposium on child analysis. *International Journal of Psycho-Analysis*, 8: 339–370.

Klein M. (1929). Personification in the play of children. *International Journal of Psychoanalysis*, 10: 193–204.

Klein M. (1932). *The Psychoanalysis of Children.* London: International Psychoanalytical Library, 1932.

Klein M. (1934). A contribution to the psychogenesis of manic-depressive states. *International Journal of Psychoanalysis*, 1935, 16: 145–174.

Klein M. (1938). Mourning and its relation to manic-depressive states. *International Journal of Psychoanalysis*, 1940, 21: 125–153.

Klein M. (1946). Notes on some schizoid mechanisms. *International Journal of Psychoanalysis*, 27: 99–110.

Klein M. (1951). The origins of transference. *International Journal of Psychoanalysis*, 1952, 33: 433–438.

Klein M. (1952a). On observing the behaviour of young infants In: Klein M., Heimann P., Isaacs S. and Rivière J., editors, *Developments in Psycho-Analysis.* London: Hogarth Press, 1952, pp. 237–270.

Klein M. (1955). On identification. In: Klein M., Heimann P. and Money-Kyrle R., editors, *New Directions in Psycho-Analysis: The Significance of Infant Conflict in the Pattern of Adult Behaviour.* London: Tavistock Publications, pp. 309–345.

Klein M. (1957). *Envy and Gratitude.* London: Tavistock.

Klein M., Heimann P. and Money-Kyrle R., editors (1955). *New Directions in Psycho-Analysis: The Significance of Infant Conflict in the Pattern of Adult Behaviour.* London: Tavistock Publications.

Kuhn T.S. (1962). *The Structure of Scientific Revolutions.* Chicago: University of Chicago Press.

Langs R. (1976). *The Bipersonal Field.* New York: Jason Aronson.

Langs R. (1978a). The adaptational-intraactional dimension of countertransference. *Contemporary Psychoanalysis*, 14: 502–533.

Langs R. (1978b). A model of supervision: The patient as unconscious supervisor. In: *Technique in Transition.* New York: Aronson, 1978, pp. 587–625.

Langs R. (1980). *Interactions: The Realm of Transference and Countertransference.* New York: Aronson.

Langs R. (1986). Diventare uno psicoanalista comunicativo. *Psicoterapia e Scienze Umane*, 1986, 20, 3: 273–277.

Langs R. (1987). *A Primer of Psychotherapy.* New York: Gardner Press.

Laplanche J. and Pontalis J.B. (1967). *The Language of Psychoanalysis.* London: The Hogarth Press and the Institute of Psycho-Analysis, 1973.

Letley E. (2013). *Marion Milner: The Life.* London: Routledge.

Limentani A. (1977). Affects and the psychoanalytic situation. *International Journal of Psychoanalysis*, 58: 171–182.

Limentani A. (1985). Variations on some Freudian themes. *International Journal of Psychoanalysis*, 67: 235–243.

Lipton S.D. (1977). The advantages of Freud's technique as shown in his analysis of the Rat Man. *International Journal of Psychoanalysis*, 58: 255–274.

Little M. (1950). Counter-transference and the patient's response to it. *International Journal of Psychoanalysis*, 1951, 32: 32–40.

Little M. (1956). 'R' – the analyst's total response to his patient's needs. *International Journal of Psychoanalysis*, 1957, 38: 240–254.

Little M. (1959). Countertransference. *British Journal of Medical Psychology*, 1960, 33: 29–31.

Little M. (1986). *Transference Neurosis and Transference Psychosis: Toward a Basic Unity.* London: Free Association.

Little M. (1990). *Psychotic Anxieties and Containment: A Personal Record of an Analysis with Winnicott.* Northvale, NJ: Jason Aronson.

Low B. (1935). The psychological compensations of the analyst. *International Journal of Psychoanalysis*, 16: 1–8.

Makari G.J. (1997). Dora's hysteria and the maturation of Sigmund Freud's transference theory: A new historical interpretation. *Journal of the American Psychoanalytic Association*, 45: 1061–1096.

Malcolm R.R. (1985). Interpretation: The past in the present. *International Review of Psychoanalysis*, 1986, 13: 433–443.

Malin A. and Grotstein J.S. (1966). Projective identification in the therapeutic process. *International Journal of Psychoanalysis*, 47: 26–31.

Massidda G.B. (1999). Shall we ever know the whole truth about projective identification? *International Journal of Psychoanalysis*, 80: 365–367.

Massidda G.B. (2009). *Identificazione proiettiva.* Milan: Lampi di Stampa.

Meltzer D. (1966). The relation of anal masturbation to projective identification. *International Journal of Psychoanalysis*, 47: 335–342.

Meltzer D. (1974). Adhesive identification. *Contemporary Psychoanalysis*, 11: 289–310.

Meneguz G. (2011). *Il mondo degli psicoanalisti.* Naples: Liguori.

Migone P. (1988). La identificazione proiettiva. In: *Terapia psicoanalitica. Seminari.* Nuova edizione. Milan: FrancoAngeli, 2010, pp. 119–133.

Migone P. (2013). Personal communication.

Milner M. (1952a). The framed gap. In: Milner M., editor, *The Suppressed Madness of Sane Men.* London: Institute of Psycho-Analysis, pp. 79–82.

Milner M. (1952b). Aspects of symbolism in comprehension of the not-self. *International Journal of Psychoanalysis*, 33: 181–195.

Milner M. (1956). The sense in nonsense. In: Milner M., editor, *The Suppressed Madness of Sane Men*. London: Institute of Psycho-Analysis, pp. 168–191.

Milner M. (1960). The concentration of the body. In: Milner M., editor, *The Suppressed Madness of Sane Men*. London: Institute of Psycho-Analysis, pp. 234–240.

Milner M. (1969). *The Hands of the Living God*. London: Hogarth Press.

Milner M. (1987). *The Suppressed Madness of Sane Men*. London: Institute of Psycho-Analysis.

Mitchell S.A. (1988). *Relational Concepts in Psychoanalysis: An Integration*. Cambridge, MA: Harvard University Press.

Mitchell S.A. (1993). *Hope and Dread in Psychoanalysis*. New York: Basic Books.

Mitchell S.A. (1997). *Influence and Autonomy in Psychoanalysis*. Hillsdale, NJ: The Analytic Press.

Mitchell S.A. (1999). Are interpersonal and relational psychoanalysis the same?: Commentary. *Contemporary Psychoanalysis*, 35: 355–359.

Money-Kyrle R. (1955). Normal counter-transference and some of its deviations. *International Journal of Psychoanalysis*, 1956, 37: 360–366.

Moody R. (1955). On the function of the countertransference. *Journal of Analytical Psychology*, 1: 49–58.

Natterson J.M. (1966). Theodor Reik: Masochism in modern man. In: Alexander F., Eisensten S. and Grotjahn M., editors, *Psychoanalytic Pioneers*. New York/London: Basic Books, pp. 249–264.

Neri C. and Girelli R. (2003). Note sull'interpretazione. In: Fabozzi P., editor, *Forme dell'interpretare*. Milan: FrancoAngeli, pp. 183–189.

O'Shaughnessy E. (1983). Words and working through. *International Journal of Psychoanalysis*, 64: 281–289.

O'Shaughnessy E. (1992). Enclaves and excursions. *International Journal of Psychoanalysis*, 73: 603–611.

O'Shaughnessy E. (2012). The views of contemporary Freudians and independents about the concept of projective identification. In: Spillius E. and O'Shaughnessy E., editors, *Projective Identification: The Fate of a Concept*. London: Routledge, pp. 150–166.

Ogden T.H. (1979). On projective identifications. *International Journal of Psychoanalysis*, 60: 357–373.

Ogden T.H. (1982). *Projective Identification and Psychotherapeutic Technique*. New York: Jason Aronson.

Ogden T.H. (1991). Analysing the matrix of transference. *International Journal of Psychoanalysis*, 72: 593–605.

Ogden T.H. (1994a). The analytic third: Working with intersubjective clinical facts. *International Journal of Psychoanalysis*, 75: 3–19.

Ogden T.H. (1994b). The concept of interpretive action. *Psychoanalytic Quarterly*, 63: 219–245.

Ogden T.H. (1994c). *Subjects of Analysis*. Northvale, NJ/London: Aronson.

Ogden T.H. (1997). Rêverie and interpretation. *Psychoanalytic Quarterly*, 66: 567–595.

Ogden T.H. (2004). The analytic third: Implications for psychoanalytic theory and technique. *Psychoanalytic Quarterly*, 73: 167–195.

Pick I.B. (1985). Working through in the countertransference. *International Journal of Psychoanalysis*, 66: 157–166.

Pick I.B. (2015). Irma Brenman Pick on 'Working through in the Countertransference' (IJP, 1985). *PEP/UCL Top Authors Project*, 1: 1.

Plaut A. (1956). The transference in analytical psychology. *British Journal of Medical Psychology*, 29: 15–19.

Racker H. (1948). A contribution to the problem of counter-transference. *International Journal of Psychoanalysis*, 1953, 34: 313–324.

Racker H. (1953). The meanings and uses of countertransference. *Psychoanalytic Quarterly*, 1957, 26: 303–357.

Racker H. (1958). Classical and present technique in psychoanalysis. In: *Transference and Countertransference*. London: The Hogarth Press and the Institute of Psycho-Analysis, 1988, pp. 23–71.

Rank O. (1924). *The Trauma of Birth*. New York: Dover Publications, 1929.

Rayner E. (1991). *The Independent Mind in British Psychoanalysis*. London: Free Association.

Reich W. (1926). On the technique of interpretation and of resistence analysis. In: Reich W., editor, *Character Analysis*. New York: Orgone Institute Press, pp. 20–38.

Reich W. (1933). *Character Analysis*. New York: Orgone Institute Press, 1949.

Reich A. (1949). On counter-transference. *International Journal of Psychoanalysis*, 1951, 32: 25–31.

Reich W. (1967). *Reich Speaks of Freud*. New York: Noonday Press.

Reik T. (1915). Some remarks on the study of resistances. *International Journal of Psychoanalysis*, 1924, 5: 141–154.

Reik T. (1932). New ways in psycho-analytic technique. *International Journal of Psychoanalysis*, 1933, 14: 321–334.

Reik T. (1935). *Surprise and the Psycho-Analyst: On the Conjecture and Comprehension of Unconscious Process*. London: Kegan Paul, Trench, Trubner & Co., 1936.

Reik T. (1948). *Listening with the Third Ear: The Inner Experience of a Psychoanalyst*. New York: Farrar, Straus & Co.

Reppen J., editor (1985). *Beyond Freud: A Study of Modern Psychoanalytic Theorists*. Hillsdale, NJ: The Analytic Press.

Rosenfeld H. (1947). Analysis of a schizophrenic state of depersonalization. *International Journal of Psychoanalysis*, 28: 130–139.

Rosenfeld H. (1950). Notes on the psychopathology of confusional states in chronic schizophrenia. *International Journal of Psychoanalysis*, 31: 132–137.

Rosenfeld H. (1952). Notes on the psychoanalysis of the superego conflict in an acute schizophrenic patient. *International Journal of Psychoanalysis*, 33: 111–131.

Rosenfeld H. (1963). On the psychopathology of narcissism a clinical approach. *International Journal of Psychoanalysis*, 1964, 45: 332–337.

Rosenfeld H. (1965). *Psychotic States*. London: Hogarth Press.

Rosenfeld H. (1971). Contribution to the psychopathology of psychotic states: The importance of projective identification in the ego structure and the object relations of the psychotic patient. In: Doucet P. and Laurin C., editors, *Problems of Psychosis*. Amsterdam: Excerpta Medica, pp. 115–128.

Rosenfeld H. (1983). Primitive object relations and mechanisms. *International Journal of Psychoanalysis*, 64: 261–267.

Rosenfeld H. (1987). *Impasse and Interpretation*. London: Tavistock.

Rycroft C. (1957). An enquiry into the function of words in the psychoanalytic situation. *International Journal of Psychoanalysis*, 39: 408–415.

Rycroft C. (1965–73). On ablation of the parental images, or the illusion of having created oneself. In: Rycroft, C., editor, *Psychoanalysis and Beyond*. London: Chatto & Windus, pp. 214–232.

Rycroft C. (1968). *A Critical Dictionary of Psychoanalysis*. London: Thomas Nelson and Sons Ltd.

Rycroft C. (1984). Where I Came from. In: Rycroft, C., editor, *Psychoanalysis and Beyond*. London: Chatto & Windus, pp. 198–206.

Rycroft C. (1985). *Psychoanalysis and Beyond*. London: Chatto & Windus.

Sacchi D. (2010). *Theodor Reik e il 'terzo orecchio'*. Milan: Centro Scientifico Editore.

Sandler J. (1976). Countertransference and role-responsiveness. *International Review of Psychoanalysis*, 3: 43–47.

Sandler J. (1977). Actualization and object relationships. *Journal of Philadelphia Association of Psychoanalysis*, 50: 79–90.

Sandler J. (1983). Reflections on some relations between psychoanalytic concepts and psychoanalytic practice. *International Journal of Psychoanalysis*, 64: 35–45.

Sandler J. (1984). The concept of projective identification. *Bulletin of the Anna Freud Centre*, 1987, 10: 33–49.

Sandler J., editor (1987). *Projection, Identification, Projective Identification*. Madison: International Universities Press.

Sandler J. (1988). On internal object relations. *Journal of the American Psychoanalytic Association*, 38: 859–879.

Sandler J. (1993). On communication from patient to analyst: Not everything is projective identification. *International Journal of Psychoanalysis*, 1993, 74: 1097–1107.

Sandler J. and Sandler A.M. (1978). On the development of object relationships and affects. *International Journal of Psychoanalysis*, 59: 285–296.

Sandler J. and Sandler A. (1987). The past unconscious, the present unconscious and the vicissitudes of guilt. *International Journal of Psychoanalysis*, 68: 331–341.

Schröter M. (2002). Max Eitingon and the struggle to establish an International Standard for Psychoanalytic Training (1925–1929). *International Journal of Psychoanalysis*, 83: 875–893.

Searles H.F. (1947–48). Concerning transference and countertransference. *International Journal of Psychoanalytic Psychotherapy*, 1979, 7: 165–188.

Searles H.F. (1957). Oedipal love in the countertransference. *International Journal of Psychoanalysis*, 1959, 40: 180–190.

Searles H.F. (1959). The effort to drive the other person crazy: An element in the aetiology and psychotherapy of schizophrenia. *British Journal of Medical Psychology*, 32: 1–18.

Searles H.F. (1965). *Collected Papers on Schizophrenia and Related Subjects*. London: Hogarth Press and the Institute of Psycho-Analysis.

Searles H.F. (1975). The patient as therapist to his analyst. In: Giovacchini P.L., editor, *Tactics and Techniques in Psychoanalytic Therapy, Volume II: Countertransference*. New York: Aronson, pp. 94–151.

Searles H.F. (1979). *Countertransference and Related Subjects*. New York: International Universities Press.

Searles H.F. (1986). *My Work with Borderline Patients*. New York: Aronson.

Sedgwick D. (1994). *The Wounded Healer: Countertransference from a Jungian Perspective*. London: Routledge.

Segal H. (1950). Some aspects of the analysis of a schizophrenic. *International Journal of Psychoanalysis*, 31: 268–278.

Segal H. (1955). Notes on symbol formation. *International Journal of Psychoanalysis*, 1957, 38: 391–397.

Segal H. (1977). Countertransference. *International Journal of Psychoanalytic Psychotherapy*, 6: 31–37.

Segal H. (1979). *Klein*. London: Fontana.

Segal H. (1981). *The Work of Hanna Segal*. New York: Jason Aronson, 1981.

Segal H. (1982). 'Mrs Klein as I knew her'. Paper read at a meeting of the Tavistock Clinic.

Semi A.A. (1998). Il controtransfert nell'ottica freudiana: una nota. *Rivista di Psicoanalisi*, 44: 319–328.

Semi A.A. (2012). The psychoanalytic method and the countertransference. *Italian Psychoanalytic Annual*, 2013, 7: 39–56.
Sharpe E.F. (1927). Contribution to symposium on child analysis. *International Journal of Psychoanalysis*, 8: 380–384.
Sharpe E.F. (1947). The psycho-analyst. *International Journal of Psychoanalysis*, 28: 1–6.
Sharpe E.F. (1950). *Collected Papers in Psycho-Analysis*. London: Hogarth Press.
Sodré I. (2004). Who's who? Notes on pathological identifications. In: Hargreaves E. and Varchevker A., editors, *In Pursuit of Psychic Change: The Betty Joseph Workshop*. London: Routledge, pp. 53–68.
Sohn L. (1985). Narcissistic organization, projective identification, and the formation of the identificate. *International Journal of Psychoanalysis*, 66: 201–213.
Speziale-Bagliacca R. (1994). Introduzione. In: Ogden T.H. (1991). *La identificazione proiettiva e la tecnica psicoterapeutica*. Roma: Astrolabio, pp. 7–14.
Spillius E.B. (1983). Some developments from the work of Melanie Klein. *International Journal of Psychoanalysis*, 64: 321–332.
Spillius E.B., editor (1988a). *Melanie Klein Today: Development in Theory and Practice, Volume I: Mainly Theory*. London: Routledge.
Spillius E.B., editor (1988b). *Melanie Klein Today: Development in Theory and Practice, Volume II: Mainly Practice*. London: Routledge.
Spillius E.B. (1992). Clinical experience of projective identification. In: Anderson R., editor, *Clinical Lectures on Klein and Bion*. London: Routledge, pp. 59–73.
Spillius E.B. (1994). Development in Kleinian thought: Overview and personal view. *Psychoanalytic Inquiry*, 14: 324–364.
Spillius E.B. (2007). *Encounters with Melanie Klein*. London: Routledge.
Spillius E.B. (2012a). The emergence of Klein's idea of projective identification in her published and unpublished work. In: Spillius E. and O'Shaughnessy E, editors, *Projective Identification: The Fate of a Concept*. London: Routledge, pp. 3–18.
Spillius E.B. (2012b). Developments by British Kleinian analysts. In: Spillius E. and O'Shaughnessy E., editors, *Projective Identification: The Fate of a Concept*. London: Routledge, pp. 49–60.
Spillius E.B. and O'Shaughnessy E., editors (2012). *Projective Identification: The Fate of a Concept*. London: Routledge.
Spillius E.B., Milton J., Garvey P., Couve C. and Steiner D. (2011). *The New Dictionary of Kleinian Thought*. London: Routledge.
Spitz R.A. (1956). Countertransference: Comments on its varying role in the analytic situation. *Journal of the American Psychoanalytic Association*, 4: 256–265.
Stefana A. (2011). Introduzione al pensiero di Marion Milner. *Psicoterapia e Scienze Umane*, 45, 3: 355–374.
Stefana A. (2013). Marion Milner, il ruolo dell'esperienza estetica nella creazione artistica. *Gli argonauti*, 139, 4: 337–356.
Stefana A. (2014). Marion Milner e il passaggio dall'oggetto primario all'oggetto secondario. *Richard e Piggle*, 22, 3: 288–301.
Stefana A. (2015). Adolph Stern, father of term 'borderline personality'. *Minerva Psichiatrica*, 56, 2: 95.
Stefana A. (2016). Carl Gustav Jung e le radici umane del suo pionieristico contributo alla psichiatria. *Rivista Sperimentale di Freniatria*, 140, 2: 151–172.
Steiner J. (1993). *Psychic Retreats*. London: Routledge.
Steiner J. (2006a). Interpretative enactments and the analytic setting. *International Journal of Psychoanalysis*, 87: 315–320.

Steiner J. (2006b). Reply to Dr Levenson. *International Journal of Psychoanalysis*, 87: 325–328.

Steiner R. (1999). Who influenced whom? and how?: A brief series of notes on E. Weiss, M. Klein (and I. Svevo) and the so-called 'origins' of 'projective and introjective identification'. *International Journal of Psychoanalysis*, 80: 367–375.

Stekel W. (1911). Die verschiedenen Formen der Übertragung. *Zentralblatt für Psychoanalyse*, 2, 2: 27.

Sterba R. (1932). The fate of the ego in analytic therapy. *International Journal of Psychoanalysis*, 1934, 15: 117–126.

Sterba R. (1982). *Reminiscences of a Viennese Psychoanalyst.* Detroit: Wayne State University Press.

Stern A. (1923). On the counter-transference in psychoanalysis. *Psychoanalytic Review*, 1924, 11: 166–174.

Stern A. (1938). Psychoanalytic investigations and therapy in the borderline group of neuroses. *Psychoanalytic Quarterly*, 7: 467–489.

Stolorow R. (1992). Closing the gap between theory and practice with better psychoanalytic theory. *Psychotherapy: Theory, Research, Practice, Training*, 29, 2: 159–166.

Strachey J. (1933). The nature of the therapeutic action of psycho-analysis. *International Journal of Psychoanalysis*, 1934, 15: 127–159.

Strachey J. (1958). Editor's introduction to 'Papers on technique'. In: *The Standard Edition of the Complete Psychological Works of Sigmund Freud, 12*. London: The Hogarth Press and the Institute of Psycho-Analysis, pp. 85–88.

Sullivan H.S. (1953). *The Interpersonal Theory of Psychiatry.* New York: Norton.

Suttie I.D. (1935). *The Origins of Love and Hate.* London: Kegan Paul, Trench, Trubner & Co.

Tauber E.S. (1954). Exploring the therapeutic use of countertransference data. *Psychiatry*, 17: 331–336.

Thomä H. and Kächele H. (1985). *Lehrbuch der psychoanalytischen Therapie 1: Grundlagen.* Berlin: Springer.

Tower L.E. (1955). Counter-transference. *Journal of the American Psychoanalytic Association*, 1956, 4: 224–255.

Turillazzi Manfredi S. (1994). *Le certezze perdute della psicoanalisi clinica.* Milan: Raffaello Cortina.

Trombi G. (1987). La teoria della tecnica di Robert Langs: l'approccio 'comunicativo'. *Psicoterapia e Scienze Umane*, 21, 3: 55–93.

Vitolo A. (1987). Freud, Gross, Spielrein alle origini del tema paterno in Jung. *Rivista di Psicologia Analitica*, 34: 188–205.

Wallas G. (1926). *The Art of Thought.* New York, Harcourt, Brace and Co.

Wallerstein R.S. (1988). One psychoanalysis or more? *International Journal of Psychoanalysis*, 69: 5–21.

Wallerstein R.S. (1990). Psychoanalysis: The common ground. *International Journal of Psychoanalysis*, 71: 3–20.

Weiss E. (1924). Über eine noch nicht beschriebene Phase der Entwicklung zur heterosexuellen Liebe. *Internationale Zeitschrift für (ärztliche) Psychoanalyse*, 1925, 11: 429–443.

Winnicott D.W. (1931–56). *Collected Papers: Through Pediatrics to Psychoanalysis.* New York: Basic Books, 1958.

Winnicott D.W. (1945). Primitive emotional development. *International Journal of Psychoanalysis*, 26: 137–143.

Winnicott D.W. (1947). Hate in countertransference. *International Journal of Psychoanalysis*, 1949, 30: 69–74.

Winnicott D.W. (1950–55). Aggression in relation to emotional development. In: Winnicott D.W., editor, *Collected Papers: Through Pediatrics to Psychoanalysis.* New York: Basic Books, pp. 204–218.

Winnicott D.W. (1951). Transitional objects and transitional phenomena. *International Journal of Psychoanalysis*, 1953, 34: 89–97.

Winnicott D.W. (1956). Primary maternal preoccupation. In: Winnicott, D.W., editor, *Collected Papers: Through Pediatrics to Psychoanalysis.* New York: Basic Books, pp. 300–305.

Winnicott D.W. (1959). Counter-transference. *British Journal of Medical Psychology*, 1960, 33, 1: 17–21.

Winnicott D.W. (1960a). The theory of the parent-infant relationship. *International Journal of Psychoanalysis*, 41: 585–595.

Winnicott D.W. (1960b). Ego distortions in terms of true or false self. In: *The Maturational Processes and the Facilitating Environment.* London: Hogarth Press, 1965, pp. 140–152.

Winnicott D.W. (1968). The use of an object. *International Journal of Psychoanalysis*, 1969, 50: 711–716.

Winnicott D.W. (1971a). *Therapeutic Consultation in Child Psychiatry.* London: Hogarth Press.

Winnicott D.W. (1971b). *Playing and Reality.* London: Hogarth Press.

Winnicott D.W. (1987). *The Spontaneous Gesture: Selected Letters of D.W. Winnicott.* London: Karnac Books.

Young R.M. (1995). The vicissitudes of transference and countertransference: The work of Harold Searles. *Free Associations*, 5: 171–195.

INDEX